CANADIAN COURAGE

CANADIAN COURAGE

True Stories of Canada's Everyday Heroes

Linda Pruessen

Collins

HarperCollins books may be purchased for educational, business or sales promotional use through our Special Markets Department.

HarperCollins Publishers Ltd
Bay Adelaide Centre, East Tower
22 Adelaide Street West, 41st Floor
Toronto, Ontario, Canada
M5H 4E3

www.harpercollins.ca

Library and Archives Canada Cataloguing in Publication

Title: Canadian courage : true stories of Canada's everyday heroes / Linda Pruessen.
Other titles: True stories of Canada's everyday heroes
Names: Pruessen, Linda, author.
Description: First edition. | Includes bibliographical references.
Identifiers: Canadiana (print) 20210185600 | Canadiana (ebook) 20210185724 |
ISBN 9781443459563 (softcover) | ISBN 9781443459570 (ebook)
Subjects: LCSH: Heroes—Canada—Biography. | LCSH: Courage—Canada. | LCSH: Canada—Biography. | LCGFT: Biographies.

Classification: LCC FC25 .P78 2021 | DDC 920.071—dc23

Printed and bound in the United States of America
LSC/C 9 8 7 6 5 4 3 2 1

CONTENTS

Part 3: Courage in the Face of Injustice

CANADIAN COURAGE

INTRODUCTION

The Many Faces of Courage

YOU DON'T HAVE TO LOOK far to find examples of Canadian courage; they are all around us, although not always in the places you'd expect them to be.

When we think about courage, certain obvious images come to mind: members of the military charging into battle, law enforcement personnel helping civilians in danger; firefighters racing into a burning building. We think about the men and women who are willing to put their lives on the line for their country, or for others; about those remarkable folk who run toward danger instead of away.

This kind of courage is probably the easiest to call in mind. It's celebrated in war movies like *1917*, or *Passchendaele*. It's addressed in the shelves upon shelves of true crime books in shops and libraries. And it's recognized in newspapers and online, as the exploits of those who serve and protect in various ways are covered on a daily basis.

But you don't have to wear a uniform to be courageous, or have undergone training in emergency protocols or crisis management. Each of us is presented with opportunities to be courageous in our everyday lives. You can exhibit courage during a workday, when you risk getting swept down a mountain by an avalanche to save a co-worker who disappeared under a wall of snow and debris—as Trevor Smith did near Mayo, Yukon. You can show it in the dead of night, like Winnipeg native Les Lehmann, who stood up to an intruder to protect a group of students staying at his Dominican Republic resort. Or like off-duty lifeguard Rebecka Blackburn, from Leduc, Alberta, you can demonstrate courage when you brave the rushing waters of a river to save a drowning man. And take note: fully grown men and women don't have a corner on courage: Nova Scotia's six-year-old Sophia LeBlanc had it in spades when she escaped an upside-down and partially submerged minivan and climbed a steep embankment to get help for her family in the aftermath of an accident. We can't forget our animal friends, either. Horses, dogs, even pigeons can get the job done. Just consider Sergeant Gander, the dog whose statue stands in Newfoundland and Labrador's Gander Heritage Memorial Park in recognition of the sacrifice he made when he saved the lives of several Canadian soldiers in Hong Kong during the Second World War.

As it turns out, we can also exhibit courage without putting ourselves in harm's way. Courage is demonstrated when we choose to fight injustice instead of turning a blind eye. This is exactly what Vishal Vijay did when, following a trip to India, he decided to work within his community of Oakville, Ontario—and then beyond—to help children who weren't as fortunate as him and his brothers. It's also what McGill student Tomas Jirousek did when he chose to stand for and with other Indigenous students to push for a change to the institution's troublesome name for its athletic teams.

And, finally, we can exhibit courage by overcoming adversity. Just ask Terry Fox, who pushed through—and far, far past—a cancer diagnosis to raise awareness and money and inspire a nation. Or Toronto's Timea Nagy, whose own experience as a survivor of human trafficking compelled her to become an advocate for others and a voice for change.

When we read stories about people who have acted courageously—whether in the face of danger, injustice, or adversity—we're captivated. We may also find ourselves engaging in a bit of introspection. We wonder what it really takes to be courageous, and whether we have that secret ingredient somewhere in our own DNA. Faced with a similar situation, we ask ourselves, what might we do? Would we have the courage to run toward the danger and not away? Would we have the courage to stand up and fight injustice, instead of choosing not to see and not to act? Would we have the courage to overcome adversity and inspire others?

The remarkable Canadians you will meet here have exactly this kind of courage. Their stories are moving, thrilling, and, most of all, inspiring. In addition to having the secret "courage" ingredient in their DNA, they also have a superpower: the ability to make us want to be the very best version of ourselves.

PART 1
Courage in the Face of Adversity

RYAN STRASCHNITZKI

Keeping the Dream Alive

"When one door closes, another one opens."

GROWING UP IN AIRDRIE, ALBERTA, Ryan Straschnitzki had lots of dreams—many of which revolved around hockey. Playing pond hockey with his friends and siblings, he imagined countless "he shoots, he scores" scenarios. He dreamed about working his way up through the ranks of the game he loved—playing junior hockey, and then maybe making it to the NHL. He dreamed of donning Team Canada's iconic red-and-white jersey and lacing up his skates in the Olympics. He dreamed of bringing home a Stanley Cup, or a gold medal, or both.

In April 2018, as an eighteen-year-old playing for Saskatchewan's Humboldt Broncos, Ryan was on the path to making those dreams come true. And then, in an instant, everything changed. Or almost everything. Some dreams, it turns out, can survive even in the toughest of circumstances.

7

....

RYAN HAS CLEAR MEMORIES OF the horrific crash that took the life of sixteen people and seriously injured thirteen others. It was late afternoon on April 6, 2018, and the Humboldt Broncos were on the team bus, making their way to Nipawin to face the Hawks in a semi-final playoff game. He remembers where he was sitting—left side, near the middle—and the chatter of the guys around him as everyone tried to get into the right mindset for a win-or-go-home playoff game. He remembers texting his girlfriend, and the scream from the front of the bus that caught his attention just before everything went black. And he remembers waking up on the highway, his back against the body of the semi-trailer truck that had blown through a stop sign and slammed into the bus. He remembers a ringing in his ears, debris on the road, and his teammates all around him. "My first instinct was to get up and try and help, but I couldn't move my body," he recalls. "It was terrible."

By the time his parents arrived at Royal University Hospital in Saskatoon, Ryan was two hours in to a seven-hour surgery on his back. His injuries were catastrophic: four broken ribs, a broken shoulder blade, a punctured lung, bleeding on the brain, and spinal cord damage so severe it would leave him paralyzed from the chest down. After the surgery, Michelle and Tom sat by their son's bed, waiting for him to wake up and trying to come to terms with everything that had happened and what it meant for Ryan's future. They were reeling, but their son, apparently, had already sorted a few things out. Eyes open, but still groggy, Ryan looked at his parents and apologized for not being able to move. Then he asked what seemed like a strange question. The PyeongChang Winter Olympics had wrapped up a little more than a month ago. Had Team Canada, he asked, won at sledge hockey? They hadn't, Tom told him; the gold had gone to the United States.

Tom has a crystal-clear memory of what came next: "And then he looks and he goes, 'I'm going to try out for sledge hockey,'" he says, noting that his son also planned to bring the gold medal home for Canada. "Michelle and I, our eyes bugged out and went, 'Where did he come up with that?'"

Sledge hockey dreams or not, the days just after the crash weren't easy. Ryan struggled to recalibrate, to adjust the expectations he'd had for himself. The pain—physical, emotional—was intense. There were plenty of bleak moments, plenty of times he allowed himself to ask the "why me" and "how come us" questions that are so common in the wake of a personal tragedy. But he tried hard not to let himself sink into a dark place. The visitors helped. The week he spent in the ICU is foggy, but he does remember Justin Trudeau stopping in, and Don Cherry and Ron MacLean, and Sheldon Kennedy and Connor McDavid. Others came as well, and they all brought the same message: they were pulling for him; they believed in him and his teammates. He quickly came to realize just how much support he had from family, friends, and the community at large. The crash had captured the attention of the entire country. Across Canada, people were placing hockey sticks beside their front doors as a tribute to the players. A GoFundMe campaign raised $15.2 million in less than two weeks; a tribute concert raised another $428,000. The number of his father's Twitter followers ballooned as the family used the social media platform to post updates about Ryan's progress.

People were invested in him, and he decided early on that he wasn't going to let them—or the teammates he'd lost—down.

Ryan's friends and family have always known he's a determined guy, someone willing to put in the work it takes to achieve goals. They'd seen this determination in action throughout his hockey career, and on April 25, 2018, the whole of Canada got to see it too. Just three weeks after the crash, Ryan wheeled himself into the lobby at Calgary's Foothills Medical Centre and answered questions from the media. His parents—shocked at the size of the crowd of reporters and photographers—asked if he wanted to cancel the press conference. The sudden attention was a bit overwhelming, to be sure, but he never considered turning around and heading back to his room. He provided details about the accident when asked, shared his dream of playing sledge hockey for the Paralympic team, and gave an update on his physiotherapy. It was tough, he acknowledged, but he wasn't about to give up. "I'm just hoping one day I'll get to that point where I'll be able to walk again," he said. "Some people have said that I won't be able to, but I kind of want to prove them wrong. . . . If you're negative, I don't think anything can be done. If you're positive, you can set those challenges for yourself."

He also talked about the bond—stronger than ever now— that he shared with his teammates. "I'm just trying to push through and get better for those guys that didn't make it."

"PUSHING THROUGH" IS AN APT way to describe what Ryan has accomplished in the years since that press conference in the Foothills lobby.

He's pushed through every step of the long and gruelling rehabilitation process—at Foothills, and at Calgary's Synaptic Spinal Cord Injury and Neuro Rehabilitation Centre; and in Philadelphia, where he spent a month undergoing intensive and specialized spinal treatment at the Shriners Hospitals for Children. He's mastered the use of a wheelchair, learned to take care of most of his own daily needs, and is able to drive a car designed specifically for him. It took more than a year for his family to get back to their own home—which needed extensive renovations to become wheelchair accessible—but these days, he lives in his own basement "bachelor pad," complete with a kitchenette, barrier-free bathroom, and an elevator that allows him easy access to the main floor.

He's also pushed the limits of his own recovery. In November 2019, Ryan and his father travelled to Thailand so Ryan could undergo a spinal surgery not available in Canada. First, an epidural stimulator was implanted in his spine; and then, a week later, stem cells were injected above and below the injury site. The hope was that the stem cells might reverse some of the damage, while the stimulator would send electrical currents through the spinal cord in an attempt to activate nerves. Ultimately, the goal was to regain core strength and potentially allow Ryan to move his legs. It worked. On November 20, with the help of a wheeled walker and physiotherapists supporting his knees and ankles, he took his first steps in nearly nineteen months. The extra core strength, he figures, is a bonus when it comes to those sledge hockey ambitions he shared with his parents and the media in the aftermath of the crash.

....

GETTING BACK OUT ON THE ice was a driving factor in the early days of Ryan's recovery. On July 20, 2018—just three and a half months after the accident—he strapped into a sled and tried sledge hockey for the first time. Former Team Canada player Chris Cederstrand, who lost his leg in a 2004 construction accident, was on the ice with him that day, as was NHL player Corban Knight. Cederstrand had gotten in touch with Ryan early in his recovery and offered to help, but no one had expected Ryan to get out there quite as quickly as he did. And yet there he was, tackling a whole new skill set with the same grit and determination he'd always brought to his game.

"It was good," he said at the time, "just the smell of the ice and it was lots of fun. Obviously, it's a different sport I have to practice a lot but it was really enjoyable."

Ice time was quickly factored into his weekly routine. The learning curve was steep—mastering turns was a challenge, not to mention shooting from an entirely different angle—but being back on the ice again made it all worthwhile. And not for the first time in his life, the hard work and positive attitude paid off. Adidas reached out with an endorsement deal and produced a sixty-second inspirational ad that showed Ryan taping his stick and donning a Team Canada jersey before pushing off in his sled. "As a kid I always dreamed of playing for Team Canada," Ryan says in the spot, "and I still do." Canada's Sports Hall of Fame nominated him for its first People's Choice award.

But the best news came in December 2019, when he learned that he'd cracked the Alberta sledge hockey team roster.

"When one door closes, another one opens," he says. "Obviously, I can't play stand-up hockey anymore. But now there's another door open and that's sledge hockey."

AND SO, WITH THE THIRD anniversary of the accident now behind him, Ryan Straschnitzki is still pursuing those hockey dreams he had as a kid. Before the COVID-19 pandemic threw a wrench into his plans, he was looking forward to the 2020 sledge hockey nationals, which were set to take place in Leduc, Alberta, just a few hours north of home. To prepare, he'd been spending four or five days a week on the ice with his sled. The pandemic changed his routine, forcing him to work out at home rather than at physio or on the ice, but he stuck with it. That red-and-white Team Canada jersey, and the Winter Olympics, remain high on his list of goals.

There's something else that drives him to keep returning to the ice, to keep pushing through each challenge he faces. Every time he's at the rink—or grinding through a challenging physio session, or just having a tough day—his teammates are, in a sense, with him. Like so many of the Broncos who survived the crash, Ryan got a tattoo to honour those who did not survive. It runs the length of his right arm: an angel's wing, cross, and dove, along with pucks bearing the initials or jersey numbers of his teammates. Pulling it all together are the words head coach Darcy Haugan used to say before his team hit the ice: "It's a great day to be a Bronco, gentlemen."

If Ryan's attitude toward his own recovery and post-accident life have become an inspiration to so many, it may be in part because his team and his coach's words are such an inspiration to him. "It's what gets me up and gets me going every day," he says, "doing stuff that they aren't able to do now. I do it for them. I do it for them because they can't be here doing it for themselves.

"Obviously, they're watching over us."

TIMEA NAGY
One Girl at a Time

"There's nothing you can do to change the past.
But you can do everything to change the future."

IT WASN'T SO LONG AGO that the sound of the phone ringing in the middle of the night was an experience both terrifying and hopeful for Timea Nagy. The terrifying part is easy enough to explain: good news is rarely delivered at three o'clock in the morning, and calls about young women who have fallen prey to human trafficking operations are certainly no exception to that rule. For Timea, these calls—often from police officers looking for help or advice when dealing with victims—came with a built-in ability to send her hurtling into her own past, back to a time when she herself was one of those girls. Every ring that shattered the quiet of her bedroom brought with it a host of memories: of confusion and fear, of sexual abuse and assault, of utter helplessness and hopelessness. And yet, as difficult as it was to pick up the receiver and immerse herself, once again, in that world, the fact that she was getting the call at all meant that something was going right. It meant that the steps she'd taken to turn her life around, and to help others do the same, had been worth it. It meant that for hundreds of young women, there was a light in the dark. It meant there was hope.

HOPE IS SOMETHING TWENTY-YEAR-OLD Timea Nagy had in spades back in 1998, when she answered a classified ad in Budapest, looking to earn a bit of extra money for her family. Life was difficult in post-communist Hungary. Jobs were scarce, and those that could be found didn't pay very well. Her father was out of the picture; her mother was sick and in the hospital; and she and her brother, who was in debt and couldn't find a job, were largely left to fend for themselves. She'd been making a bit of money producing music videos for a local company, but it wasn't enough, not by a long shot, and she'd racked up a considerable debt of her own. So when she saw the ad in the paper—"Young females needed to work in Canada. No English Necessary"—it seemed like a dream come true, a lifeline. She applied, was granted an interview, and learned that there were several types of positions available: nightclub dancer, house-keeper, or nanny. "Nanny" sounded perfect: she liked kids and had always been good with them; plus, the exposure to a new culture would be an adventure. She'd have to pay the agency back for her plane ticket, but there would be more than enough money for that, with some left over to send home. And know-ing she was doing something good for her family would offset any feelings of homesickness she might have. Two weeks later, she was on a plane, headed for Toronto.

The trouble started as soon as she landed. She'd been told to report to immigration, show her papers, and wait for someone from "the agency" to pick her up. It sounded simple enough, but unbeknownst to Timea, her visa application indicated that she would be working as an exotic dancer. Figuring it was an error, she insisted she was in the country to babysit—a discrepancy that earned her a return ticket to Budapest for attempting to enter the country under false pretenses. With no flight home until the next day, she was released into the agency's hands for the evening.

Once with her handlers—who were furious at the turn of events—she learned that there had been no error, and that it was simply easier for exotic dancers to get fast-track work visas. If she'd just kept her mouth shut, they told her, she could have been through immigration without a hitch and on her way to her new job. Instead, she'd created a huge mess. Now, an unexpected return flight home was necessary, and they'd have to get her a fake passport so she could come back and fulfil her contract. She was going to need money to pay for all of that—a lot of it—so she might as well start working. They took her to a strip club, put her in front of a rack of clothes and a pile of shoes, and told her to find something that fit. When she presented herself to the manager for approval, he sexually assaulted her on his desk.

In the space of twenty-four hours, the dream of a good job in Canada had turned into a nightmare.

Soon enough, it became clear that there had never been a babysitting job, that exotic dancing and work at a massage parlour was the only employment on offer, and these jobs were the only way she could earn enough to pay off her existing and mounting debts. Installed at a cheap hotel with several other girls, under the watchful eyes of two men from the agency, she learned the lay of the land. In addition to the money she owed for the plane tickets, work visa, and fake passport, there was a dizzying array of fees for everything under the sun: towels at the hotel were $10 apiece; the agency fee was $140 a day, and sometimes more; weekly oil changes for the car that shuttled them to and from the strip clubs and massage parlours were an astonishing $350; and at the club, the DJs had to be paid between $40 and $70 a day to cue up and play each girl's songs. Even if a girl managed to make good money—up to $1,000 a day if she was willing to work the VIP room, and do whatever it took to keep those special customers happy—she still ended up handing 90 percent of what she made over to the agency in one way or another.

"We were fed one meal a day," Timea says, explaining that at one point her weight dropped to an alarming eighty-nine pounds. "We were tortured emotionally and physically. We were raped more times than I can count."

Two and a half months in, a confrontation with one of her handlers revealed a hard truth: she was still heavily in debt, no closer to being able to send money home to her family, no closer to escape. Every day, she was told what would happen to her, and to her family, if she tried to get away.

"When you don't speak English in a country that you don't know and the only voice in your head is these people telling you in your language what's going to happen if you leave, what's going to happen if you talk to others, it takes you a long time to figure out what's a lie and what's real," she says.

In a sense, Timea was lucky. During her time at the strip club, she'd made friends, men and women who were willing to put themselves on the line to help her escape. And eventually—after secretly squirrelling away clothes and money, and an ongoing and dangerous search for her passport that finally bore fruit—she managed to get out, and to hide in a friend's place for a few days before making her way back to Budapest. She was, she thought, finally free.

BUT HOME WASN'T THE REPRIEVE Timea had imagined it would be. Law enforcement officials weren't inclined to help a young woman who admitted to travelling under a fake passport and working as an exotic dancer, and the agency she'd just escaped knew exactly where she was, and that she'd spoken to the police. With no one to turn to in Budapest, she decided to go back to Canada, back to the friends who'd offered to help in any way they could.

Working under the table—first as a dancer, then as a waitress and bartender, and eventually as a hairdresser—she put the pieces of her life back together. She stayed with friends who knew of her past and worked to protect her. She learned English, saved a bit of money. Eventually, through a chance encounter, she spoke with an investigator working on Project Almonzo—a police and immigration effort to find and assist underage and illegal workers. He introduced her to Detective Mike Josifovic, who listened to her story and eventually charged the men who had worked as her pimps. For Timea, it was a turning point.

"I thought that that was enough justice for me," she says. "One person believed me. I'm not crazy. He believed me and he believed in me."

In 2009—after years of working to heal herself and helping the police, informally, with other trafficking victims—Timea decided to take that gift and pay it forward in a more deliberate manner, to help others in the same way she'd been helped when she needed it the most. "There's nothing you can do to change the past," she says. "But you can do everything to change the future."

She founded Walk With Me Canada Victim Services, a non-profit organization dedicated to combating human trafficking in Canada. Walk With Me supported Canada's first safe house for those who have escaped human trafficking, and also operated a 24/7 mobile crisis victim care unit—the source of many of those phone calls that used to wake Timea in the wee hours of the night. With the help of several "angels," Timea ran Walk With Me until 2015, when a funding crisis forced her to turn her attention to a more sustainable business model. That turned out to be Timea's Cause, a social enterprise committed to advocating for change and creating second chances for victims of what their website calls "modern day slavery." In addition to supporting survivors through a number of ventures—including employment opportunities, education, and reintegration services—the initiative offers seminars to law enforcement, the financial and healthcare sectors, hospitality services, and any other group that might be in a position to spot and assist victims. In recognition of her work on behalf of victims, Timea has received the Queen Elizabeth II Diamond Jubilee medal, the Prime Minister's Award, and a Meritorious Service Medal, among other honours.

The work isn't always easy, and effecting change is almost never fast, but progress is being made. Although Timea's own trafficker was found not guilty, others haven't fared as well. In 2012, Ferenc Domotor—leader of what was believed to be the largest human trafficking ring in Canada at the time—was sentenced to nine years in prison. And in 2019, the Canadian government released its National Strategy to Combat Human Trafficking, a five-year plan that proposed a "whole of government" approach that will allow the problem to be tackled from a number of different angels.

"When I started, I was just really wanting to be there for the girls, one girl at a time," Timea says. "And I still do. But I realized that we need to find a root cause, and we need to attack the root cause as well. So, now, human trafficking to me means something a lot more than just one victim."

Wanting to reach as wide an audience as possible with her message, Timea released a memoir in 2019. *Out of the Shadows*, co-written with Shannon Moroney, became a national bestseller.

"I can't hide it anymore, which is why I stepped out," Timea says of her past. "It's part of the whole self-love. Love yourself for who you are, not for what you think people want to love you for. So, I accepted myself as I am, with my past. If that's what I'm known for, then that's what I'm known for."

Today, Timea says, she feels strong. She knows who she is and she values herself for it. Her past—as difficult as it was—is part of what made her who she is, and a big part of what's led her to fight for those who find themselves in the same position she was once in.

"There are so many things going wrong with the world, we're so bombarded with bad things," she says. "I want to spread the light. The light is the love that I got from Canadian people."

LUCA "LAZYLEGZ" PATUELLI

No Excuses, No Limits

> *"There's always a way to take the negative and turn it into a positive."*

LUCA "LAZYLEGZ" PATUELLI STOOD IN a darkened BC Place Stadium on the night of March 12, 2010, doing his best to keep his nerves, and his exhaustion, in check. The days leading up to the opening ceremonies of the 2010 Paralympic Winter Games had been hectic. As a co-director and headline performer, the twenty-five-year-old Montreal native had been working tirelessly to get everything just right. And now, at last, it was time to put the pieces together.

As the music started and a single spotlight shone down, Luca took a deep breath, leaned on his crutches, and made his way toward the glowing blue circle at centre stage. Moving with the heartbeat rhythm that echoed through the stadium, he slid effortlessly into some of his signature breakdancing moves. He was joined first by a small crew of dancers, and then by a bigger group. Within moments, the stage was a riot of colour and

sound and movement, with Luca and the other dancers leap-
ing, lifting, spinning, balancing, and striking poses, bringing the
crowd of sixty thousand to its feet in the process.

"You know in movies when you have that opening scene
where you can hear the crowd roaring for a rock star?" he says.
"That was the emotion that I got."

And then it was over, ending in the same way as it had
begun: in the dark, with Luca alone in a spotlight. This time,
though, he held one of his crutches high, raised to the rafters in
a victory salute.

LUCA PATUELLI NEVER PLANNED to be a b-boy. Breakin'
(breakdancing) wasn't his thing, at least not at first. As a kid
growing up in Bethesda, Maryland, Luca was all about skate-
boarding. He dreamed about becoming the next Tony Hawk—
and he wasn't about to let arthrogryposis get in his way. Born
with the rare neuromuscular disorder that affects muscle growth
and causes joints to contract, Luca couldn't walk in an upright
position. His legs were bent stiff at the knees, and from the age
of three he relied on crutches to get around. It didn't matter.
Luca wasn't raised to think about what he couldn't do. If he
wanted to try something, his parents or his older brother helped
to make it happen.

"My father would take me to the hills and pull me while I
skied on my butt," Luca recalls. "I think we started a trend. We
always found a way."

When Luca was eight, his parents bought him a skateboard,
and he taught himself to use it from a kneeling position. His

goal was to eventually go pro, but a diagnosis of scoliosis, a curvature of the spine, set him on a different course. By the time he reached his mid-teens, he'd had sixteen operations—some to straighten his spine by inserting a titanium rod and fusing vertebrae, others to correct the angle of his legs. When he finally got back on his skateboard after an operation on his knees, he realized his Tony Hawk dreams were over.

"After the operations, I couldn't skateboard anymore because the vibrations of the board were bothering my scar," he says.

In an effort to help lift Luca's spirits, a group of his high-school buddies introduced him to breakin' as an alternative activity. He took to it like a duck to water. For the first time in his life, he found that his underdeveloped, or "lazy," legs, along with the extreme upper-body strength he'd developed after years of using crutches, were an advantage. "For me to lift myself up, technically, it's easier than the average person," he says. "My moves are based on strength."

For as long as he could remember, he'd been doing push-ups while holding his legs off the ground. Now, he incorporated that move into his breakdancing routines, while also using his crutches as an extension of his arms. He learned to balance and twist, to contort his body like an acrobat, to walk across the stage on his hands. Audiences were captivated, and Luca himself felt the magic in what he was able to achieve.

"Dance gave me an opportunity to accept my difference and embrace myself," he says, "to use my difference as my strength and not look at it as a weakness. I've got crutches, but I've got gold crutches. I don't look at it like a crutch. I look at them like an extension of my arms, like dancing shoes. It's not a limitation, it's something I use to empower myself."

A broken leg in his first breakdance competition was a setback, but not for long. When the Patuellis moved back home to Montreal in 2002, following Luca's high-school graduation, the young man who was missing his friends returned to dance as a way to make connections. Soon, he was travelling to competitions in the United States and elsewhere in Canada, and in 2004 he joined the Illmatic Styles—"ill" being slang for "cool." Two years later, the crew appeared on *America's Got Talent*. In 2006, Luca made a YouTube video of himself breakdancing in locations around Montreal. People watched it, and shared it, and before long, the b-boy with the unique style was attracting attention. The *Today Show* reached out, as did CBC's *The Hour*.

In 2007, Luca decided to build on the success and recognition coming his way. "I wanted to start a crew with some of the best dancers in the world. . . . These dancers motivate me on a daily basis, and so [I thought], rather than compete [against] them, let's join them," he says. He reached out to some of his fellow competitors with an idea: "Let's compete, let's do performances, let's show the world what we're all capable of doing; let's make an impact [and] let's make a movement."

Those conversations led to the formation of ILL-Abilities, a crew of seven dancers from around the world, all of whom are differently abled. Their motto—derived from the words Luca uses to inspire himself—is "No Excuses, No Limits."

"When I say 'no excuses, no limits,' I want to clarify," he explains. "Yes, there are physical limitations. There are financial limitations, psychological limitations, emotional limitations, but it's the minute that you create that excuse, saying 'I can't' without giving it a try first that the limitation really gets in the way. It's about getting out of your own way!"

Luca's message resonated. As ILL-Abilities competed and toured, word spread. The Paralympics called, and so did Ellen DeGeneres. (The night before his appearance on her show, he didn't sleep. "I told Ellen it was like Christmas and my birthday and final exams all wrapped up into one because I was excited, but I was also nervous—like for a final exam—because of the pressure to perform," he says.) He competed and made it to finals week on *So You Think You Can Dance Canada*. He travelled to Paris to dance a lead role in the Théâtre National de Chaillot's production of *Orphée*. He served as Canada's dance ambassador in 2015 and 2016. And along with his wife, Melissa Emblin-Patuelli, a dancer and occupational therapist, and teacher, dancer, and choreographer Marie-Élaine Patenaude, he launched Projet RAD—an inclusive urban-dance program for youth with disabilities.

"It's about making dance inclusive and making dance studios physically accessible—like having bars installed in the bathrooms," Luca says. "What impresses me is to see the change in the dance students, how their confidence and levels of independence increases. They start to make friends. And because they are in a dance studio, they come in contact with professional dancers and those professional dancers, in turn, are inspired by what they see."

In 2015, Luca and his partners received the Meritorious Service Medal from Governor General David Johnston in recognition of their commitment to creating a more inclusive society for people with disabilities. Perhaps most remarkably, in 2018, Les Grands Ballets Canadiens de Montréal announced that Luca and Melissa would be joining the team of adapted-dance teachers at its National Centre for Dance Therapy.

For Luca, this last achievement is a particular source of pride. "Hip-hop . . . was never welcome [at Les Grand Ballets]," he explained at the time. "And to know that they're opening their doors to hip-hop, and they're allowing us to do that, that's history in the making. It's a turning point in my personal career, for ILL-Abilities, as well as for the Montreal dance community."

LUCA STILL LIVES BY HIS original "no excuses, no limits" motto. In the midst of building his dance career, he completed a marketing degree at Montreal's Concordia University, got married and had two children, and trained for and completed a 2.5-kilometre walk without crutches or leg braces for the Defi Je Peux in Montreal. He also launched a secondary career as a motivational performer and speaker (he can deliver his remarks in English, French, Italian, or Spanish). He's busy, sometimes too busy—"I remember taking thirty-six airplanes in one month," he says—but he continues to find joy in his work.

During his talks, he stresses the importance of adapting, staying positive, and learning to do things your own way. In front of a group of three hundred children at the 2018 Abilities Arts Festival in Toronto—many of whom use crutches, just like him—Luca opens with a rousing performance featuring the moves that have made him such a popular and inspirational performer. After a call-and-answer session—"No excuses," he yells; "No limits," comes the reply—he speaks candidly to his audience about the message he wants them to take away.

There will be people in your life, he says, who jump to a conclusion, who say that there's no way you can do this or that. But how can you really know if you don't try?

"One of the things I want you guys to know is it's about taking the bad and making it good," he says. "In life, no matter what situation you're in, there's always a way to take the negative and turn it into a positive."

There are days when the crutches don't seem so golden: during snowy Montreal winters when slush and ice make getting around a challenge, or when he finds himself in a building that hasn't quite embraced accessibility. But even when life gets hard, there's always dance.

"Dance has allowed me to accept myself. When I'm moving to the music and having fun . . . I feel great. That's what dance does."

TERRY FOX

Inspiring a Nation to Fight for a Cure

*"Even if I don't finish, we need others to continue.
It's got to keep going without me."*

THERE AREN'T TOO MANY PEOPLE swimming in St. John's Harbour, Newfoundland and Labrador, in April. The weather can be nasty—snow and wind are typical, and the water is barely above the freezing mark. And so, if you'd happened by the harbour on the morning of April 12, 1980, you might have stopped for a second look at the young man standing ankle deep in the Atlantic Ocean. Strange as it might have seemed, he appeared to be filling jugs with water—though the task was proving somewhat difficult. It was a windy day, with temperatures hovering near zero, and the waves battering the shore carried one of the jugs out to sea. Undeterred, the curly-haired young man stripped down to a pair of grey athletic shorts and a white T-shirt, dipped a leg into the water, and then made his way up the steep hill to the road. As a few people applauded and a van followed close behind, he began to run.

31

You might have shaken your head, wondered a bit about his odd gait, and then carried on with your business. In all likelihood, you wouldn't have realized that the young man hop-stepping his way up Water Street was twenty-one-year-old Terry Fox, that he was planning to run across Canada to raise money for cancer research, and that he was doing so despite having had his right leg amputated above the knee as a result of his own battle with the disease. Without knowing it, you would've witnessed the first steps of the Marathon of Hope—a journey that began as one man's dream and ended up captivating an entire nation.

ALTHOUGH THE FIRST STEPS OF Terry Fox's Marathon of Hope were taken on that windy morning in Newfoundland and Labrador, the dream of doing something big to raise money for cancer research began years earlier. In November 1976, eighteen-year-old Terry rear-ended a truck in his hometown of Port Coquitlam, British Columbia. His car was wrecked, but Terry—a promising young basketball player in his first year at Simon Fraser University—was more or less okay. It was in the aftermath of the crash, however, that Terry's right knee began to bother him. He wasn't overly concerned: the basketball season always took a toll on his body, and with the accident added to the mix, a bit of soreness was to be expected. He waited until the end of the season to go and get it checked out, and was prescribed painkillers to help with the lingering ache. And that, he hoped, would be the end of it.

But in early March 1977, during a routine training run,

things took a turn for the worse. Returning home in so much pain that he could barely move, he made an appointment with his family doctor for the following day. He was quickly referred to an orthopedic surgeon at Royal Columbian Hospital in New Westminster, where an X-ray and a bone scan confirmed a grim diagnosis: osteogenic sarcoma, a particularly aggressive type of bone cancer. The doctor's advice? Amputate Terry's right leg fifteen centimetres above the knee to stop the spread.

On March 8, 1977, the night before the amputation surgery, Terry's high-school basketball coach, Terri Fleming, visited his former player in his hospital room. No doubt looking to inspire and encourage the young athlete, Fleming passed along an article from *Runner's World* magazine—a feature on Dick Traum, who in 1976 had become the first known amputee to complete the New York City Marathon. The next morning, when the nurse came in to prepare Terry for surgery, he showed her the article. "Someday, I'm going to do something like that," he said.

Although the days and weeks following Terry's surgery were challenging, he kept that article in his mind. He thought about it as he struggled to learn to walk, and then run, with a prosthetic leg. He thought about it as he worked to embrace athletics in a new way, training as hard for the wheelchair basketball team he joined in the summer of 1977 as he'd trained for his university and high-school teams. And he thought about it, especially, during a sixteen-month course of chemotherapy treatments, when he saw so many others around him who were suffering from one form of cancer or another. As he listened to screams of pain, and to doctors telling patients of all ages that they had virtually no chance of survival, Terry decided that something had to be done to stop this disease—and that maybe he should be the one to do it.

With Dick Traum's achievement in mind, Terry dreamed up a plan: he would run across Canada—starting at the Atlantic Ocean and ending at the Pacific—to raise awareness of and funds for cancer research. In the letters he wrote to governments and companies asking for support and sponsorship, he explained that on the day he'd walked out of his last chemo appointment, he'd done so with a new feeling of responsibility for the patients still undergoing treatment. "I could not leave knowing these faces and feelings would still exist even though I would be set free from mine," he wrote. "Somewhere, the hurting must stop . . . and I was determined to take myself to the limit for those causes."

TERRY TRAINED HARD, ENSURING THAT his body and mind were prepared for the rigours of the run he was planning—a journey he'd named the Marathon of Hope. In mid-February 1979, he was able to run just less than a kilometre around a track before the pain, bone bruising, and blisters forced him to stop. Modifications to his prosthesis were made, and training continued. That summer, he completed a twenty-seven-kilometre marathon in Prince George, British Columbia. He finished last—but only ten minutes behind the final two-legged runner to cross the line. The results were encouraging, and they inspired him to finally share his plans with his parents. Both were supportive, although his mother thought the plan was a bit extreme. His father simply wanted to know when he planned to start.

For more than a year, Terry kept training. He logged kilometre after kilometre—more than five thousand in all—in good weather and bad, on days when he felt fine, and on those when he had to count telephone poles to keep pushing himself forward. By the time he arrived in St. John's in April 1980, he was ready. The Ford Motor Company had donated a van, which his best friend, Doug Alward, would drive. Imperial Oil covered the gas. Other companies pitched in with shoes, food, and clothing. Finally, it was time to run.

So it was that Terry Fox came to be standing in the Atlantic Ocean on the morning of April 12, 1980, scooping water into jugs. The plan was to pour one into the Pacific at the end of the run, and to keep the other as a souvenir (Terry's parents still have it). But the waves carried one jug away, and Terry set off without it. For the next 143 days, he ran: through Newfoundland and Labrador, through Nova Scotia, through Prince Edward Island and New Brunswick, and on into Quebec and Ontario. He averaged an astonishing forty-one kilometres a day. Sometimes the pain was intense, and it was all he could do to keep going. But as one day became two, and two became a week, and a week became a month, word of his mission got out, and the crowds began to grow. By the time he reached Ontario, supporters were lining the streets as he passed through towns, and television crews were turning out, cameras in tow. Along the running route, people handed donations through the van window, while in cities and towns, receptions and rallies were held. He shook hands with politicians and journalists, celebrities and sports stars. At a rally in Toronto's Nathan Phillips Square, Maple Leafs captain Darryl Sittler presented his All-Star jersey to Terry.

It was gruelling, but it was working. The run was attracting more and more attention, and with it, donations were pouring in. Terry knew he was making a difference, and that kept him going, even when it hurt—and it almost always hurt. But on September 1, just outside of Thunder Bay, Ontario, something changed. As people along the road called out their support, Terry started coughing and felt a pain in his chest. He knew something was wrong. He asked his brother Darrell—who had joined Doug Alward in the van in New Brunswick—to take him to the doctor. And just like that, after 5,373 kilometres, the Marathon of Hope came to a screeching halt.

Later that day, sitting upright on a stretcher outside of the hospital, Terry spoke to the reporters who had gathered, eager for an update. "Well, you know, I had primary cancer in my knee three and a half years ago," he said, the emotion clear on his face and in his voice, "and now the cancer is in my lung and I have to go home."

The Marathon of Hope was clearly over, but Terry wasn't about to quit. "When I started this run, I said that if we all gave one dollar, we'd have $22 million for cancer research," he said, "and I don't care man, there's no reason that isn't possible. No reason. I'd like to see everybody go kind of wild, inspired with the fund-raising."

The country, it would seem, was listening. As Terry battled the cancer that cut short his run, Canadians kept the dream alive. A national television network organized and broadcast a five-hour telethon, featuring some of the biggest stars of the day. Plans were made for a foundation and an annual fund-raising run that would bear Terry's name. People continued to donate in ways big and small. And on February 1, 1981, Terry's goal of raising one dollar for each Canadian was realized: the country's population reached 24.1 million, and the Terry Fox Marathon of Hope—an improbable dream that had inspired a nation—announced a fundraising total of $24.17 million.

TERRY FOX DIED ON JUNE 28, 1981, at the age of twenty-two. Decades later, though, his legacy lives on. The young man born in Winnipeg and raised in Port Coquitlam would likely be surprised to learn that fourteen schools across Canada now bear his name, along with thirty-two roads or streets, a mountain peak in British Columbia, a Coast Guard ship, nine hiking trails, several buildings, and a stretch of the Trans-Canada Highway. He might be slightly embarrassed by the sight of his face on a Canadian stamp or a one-dollar coin, or the life-size statues that stand in various cities around the country. But he'd be beyond proud to learn that, as he'd wished, the work he started with the Marathon of Hope has continued.

In the years since Terry's death, the Terry Fox Run has become an annual event in Canada and around the world, with more than 5.2 million people joining in. Each fall, Canadians from coast to coast remember and honour Terry and his dream by participating in runs and walks; in dance-a-thons and skate-a-thons and treadmill marathons; in head-shaving challenges and birthday party fundraisers. In October 2019, seven-year-old Ethan Smallwood from Clarke's Beach, Newfoundland and Labrador, dressed up as his hero on Halloween—complete with a white Marathon of Hope T-shirt, grey shorts, and a

curly-haired wig—and collected donations instead of choco-
late and candy. Through his trick-or-treating efforts and online
donations, he raised $25,000. He's off to a good start, but he has
a long way to go before he catches up to n Will Dwyer. The Second World War veteran from Barrie, Ontario, has been raising
money for the Terry Fox Foundation for thirty-nine years; in
2019, the ninety-four-year-old crossed the $1 million mark—
and he has no intention of quitting, even though he's in the
midst of treatment for prostate cancer.

Ethan and Will are joined in their efforts by people around
the world: Terry Fox fundraising events regularly take place in
India, Vietnam, Spain, Argentina, Abu Dhabi, and beyond. To
date, the annual Terry Fox Runs have raised more than $750
million to support cancer research.

It's safe to assume that Terry would be thrilled. In July 1980,
about two-thirds of the way through his Marathon of Hope run,
Terry was in the Toronto area, doing events to raise awareness.
During a speech to a crowd of thousands at the Scarborough
Civic Centre, he stressed the need for the work he'd started to
be bigger than him, to continue beyond his own efforts, even if
he couldn't complete the run. "Even if I don't finish," he said,
"we need others to continue. It's got to keep going without me."

Mission accomplished.

JOHN CAIRNS
Making Every Step Count

"You don't park it. You keep moving."

REACHING GILMAN'S POINT IS NOT an easy task. Tanzania's Mount Kilimanjaro ranks as the world's highest free-standing mountain, and its snow-capped tip is 19,341 feet above sea level. It's a challenging climb, even for experienced trekkers. Work on your stamina, they are told. Break in your hiking books to avoid blisters that will stop your climb in its tracks. And please do see a doctor to ensure that your body can handle the rigours of the elevation. Slow and steady wins the race here, and a minimum six-day climb is recommended to help avoid altitude sickness—the leading cause of failed summits. It goes without saying that not everyone who sets out will make it. But John Cairns did.

On August 7, 2016, at 6:30 in the morning, the man who'd nearly died in a workplace accident twenty-four years earlier—and who'd lost his right arm above the elbow and right leg above the knee in the process—stood at the point and took in the spectacular view: the sun rising in the biggest sky he'd ever seen, the Serengeti spread out below, the grins on the faces of those who'd climbed with him. There was a time he'd felt as if the weight of the world was sitting squarely on top of him. But now? "Now I'm standing on top of the world at 19,000 feet," he recalls. "I'll never forget that."

THE DAY JOHN CAIRNS'S LIFE changed completely, irrevocably, started out just like so many others. The twenty-six-year old woke up "assuming that life will be much as it was the day before." He got up and got dressed, grabbed breakfast, and kissed his wife goodbye, telling her he'd see her at three o'clock—the time he usually got home from his job with CN Rail.

On that particular day—crisp, windy, and cold, he remembers—John was working as a foreman at the MacMillan railyard in Vaughan, a suburb just north of Toronto. At about 11:30 a.m., he was in the midst of a process called shunting, in which single rail cars are moved from one position in the yard to another. As John looked on, a sixty-eight-ton unmanned car was slowly gathering speed as it headed toward a work crew farther down the tracks. He didn't hesitate. "I boarded the car and put the brake system on and successfully stopped the car," he says.

And then, things went horribly wrong. With no idea that another car was right behind his, John wasn't braced for the impact that followed. He lost his balance and, seconds later, found himself lying on the tracks in the path of the oncoming car.

"I remember thinking to myself, I am lined up with the wheels and wherever the wheels touch, if it doesn't break it and it doesn't sprain it, it will remove it. I could be decapitated, cut in half, and in that instant I knew I had zero control and surrendered to fate."

He must have blacked out, because the next thing he remembers is looking up at the blue sky and realizing that he was alive. He had no idea that he'd been run over—no idea that his right arm and leg had both been crushed, that he was essentially bleeding to death on the ground.

Much of what John now knows about the hours and weeks that followed has been pieced together since, with the help of those who were on the scene both at the railyard and in the hospital. But he does remember the fourteen minutes he spent on the tarmac, waiting for the paramedics to arrive. "That, my friends, is an eternity," he says. He knew he was losing blood at an alarming rate and could feel himself slipping out of consciousness. Gazing up at the blue sky, he contemplated if this was what it was like to die. When the paramedics arrived, they put him in a pressure bag to slow the bleeding. Briefly, he wondered whether he'd actually died and was now being zipped into a body bag. As the EMTs scrambled to whisk his near-lifeless body into an ambulance, two questions echoed in his brain, loud enough to drown out what seemed like "a thousand medical voices" chattering around him: *Why me? What did I do to deserve this?*

John would ask himself those questions over and over again during the gruelling months that followed. His prognosis was bleak. After arriving at a local hospital in a state of multiple organ failure, he was loaded into a helicopter and airlifted to the trauma centre at Toronto's Sunnybrook Health Sciences

Centre. He spent a week on life support in the intensive care unit. So touch and go was the situation that the doctors didn't even amputate right away, choosing to wait until they were more confident that he would pull through. He lost his total body volume of blood four times over and needed ninety-six units of blood and nine surgeries just to stabilize.

And that was just the beginning. After two weeks in the ICU, he was moved to the rehabilitation unit. The doctors were brutally honest about the road ahead. "I was told I would never walk unassisted," he recalls. "I was told I would not be much of a productive member of society. I was told I should get used to this idea. I went from a life of total independence to a state of total dependence, and into an abyss of helplessness and hopelessness."

Rehabilitation wasn't easy—not physically, and certainly not emotionally. He spent four months in Sunnybrook in acute trauma recovery, a time he remembers as a "roller coaster of anger, guilt, disappointment, rejection, confusion, isolation, and relentless fear." He was, he knows now, in mourning: for the life he'd once led, for his sense of identity and self-worth, for the hopes and dreams he'd had for his future. His marriage fell apart; he attempted suicide three times. He wanted to "simply give up and die."

Somehow, though, he kept waking up in the morning, kept making the incremental progress that led to his discharge from Sunnybrook in April 1993. His next stop was Downsview Rehabilitation Centre, where he would start down the long road to rebuilding his life. The reality of his new situation quickly sank in: there were no nurses here at the press of a button, no one to do for him what he needed to begin doing for himself. Challenging though it was, things slowly started to come together. He remastered activities he'd once taken for granted—how to walk, eat, dress, and bathe. He adjusted to life as a leftie and learned to use both a prosthetic arm and leg. He spent countless hours in the gym, getting used to his new physicality. It took three months of therapy before he could walk fifteen feet. "It was," he says, "as if I'd been reborn as someone else."

Physically, he was healing. It was a long, slow process, but he could see the improvements, and they kept him moving forward. Emotionally, it was an entirely different story. "Mentally, psychologically, and spiritually, I was bleeding to death," he says. Eventually, his psychologists and other team members helped him realize he was "stuck in the muck and mire" of post-traumatic stress disorder. "Physically, I had a face, but emotionally, I had no face, no identity, no cause, no purpose, no reason to be alive. I felt like a hollow shell of a human."

It wasn't easy to deal with that, or to find a new way to think about his life and what he might have to offer the world, now that he was so different from the way he'd been before. But after countless sessions with his support team, and a great deal of help from friends and family, he came to see that his survival was nothing short of a miracle. The odds had been against him from the moment he lost his footing and fell to the tracks. And yet, here he was—walking, talking, *living*. He'd been granted a rebirth, and he realized that what he would make of it was entirely up to him. Would he be a victim, he asked himself, or a victor?

••••

THESE DAYS, JOHN CAIRNS CALLS Belleville, Ontario, home. It's the base from which the fifty-three-year-old operates his Wheelchair of Hope non-profit organization, founded in 2014 to raise awareness of the needs and abilities of people with physical disabilities, and to deliver wheelchairs—and the gift of mobility—to those who might otherwise not have resources of their own, or access to funding, for wheelchairs. And it was here, in 2016, where he learned he would receive Canada's Walk of Fame Unsung Hero Honour, a recognition he calls humbling. At the ceremony, he spoke with emotion about the twists and turns his own life have taken, and how they've inspired him to give back. "I do what I do from my heart, without measure," he said, "just because I know that I was given a miracle after my accident and my life is about sharing that miracle."

John has come a long way since those days in the mid-1990s when he wanted nothing more than to go to sleep and not wake up. When he finally walked out of rehab, two and a half years after being wheeled in, he did so with a mission to "aspire to inspire." It's a mission he's not only embraced but made his life's work. He's completed several Terry Fox Runs—the first was a goal he set for himself while still in rehab—to demonstrate that physical challenges can be overcome. He's backflipped into the nearby Bay of Quinte on more than one occasion, and his foundation has donated two wheelchair-accessible Mobi-Mats to make sure others can enjoy the water as well. And he's hopped on his bike to complete the 136-mile bike ride along the Highway of Heroes from Belleville to Toronto, raising funds to support the injured or ill Armed Forces members, veterans, first responders, and other heroes for whom this stretch of road is named.

And of course, there's Mount Kilimanjaro. These days, when John Cairns thinks back on that first Kilimanjaro climb—oh yes, there was another, as well as a trek to Everest's base camp— what strikes him most is the epiphany he had as he looked out over the plains of the Serengeti. The summit, he recalls thinking, was *a* goal but not *the* goal. "The ultimate goal was I'm here, and while I might fail, and fail many times, I will get up again."

For Cairns, that means constantly pushing himself out of his comfort zone, and always looking for new ways to contribute: earning a degree in social work from the University of Waterloo; learning to scuba dive, sky dive, and snowboard; and embracing his work as a motivational speaker, both with the general public and specifically for the military, which made him an honorary colonel of the 2 Air Movements Squadron at 8 Wing Canadian Forces Base Trenton. His goal, he says, is to empower and inspire, to take people on a journey. And on days when life might get a bit tough, the tattoo on his left forearm reminds him of the philosophy that's brought him this far: *It's not what happens to you in life, it's how you choose to respond that will make the difference.*

"You don't park it," he says, "you keep moving."

Onward and upward.

JOHN WESTHAVER
Turning Tragedy into Purpose

"One life lost in a car crash is one life too many."

ON ANY GIVEN DAY DURING the academic year, there's a good chance that John Westhaver will be standing in a front of a group of students. Depending on the size of the school, he could be behind a podium up on stage, although he's just as likely to be on the floor of the gym, with the kids he's come to address crammed onto the bleachers lining the wall. John loves this work, loves speaking to young adults on the cusp of bright and promising futures, but it comes with a cost. In order to make a difference, to really drive home the message he's here to deliver, he needs to relive the worst day of his life. More than twenty-five years on, that's still not easy. But he's willing to do it—over and over again, as often as it takes—if it means that just one kid, one family, one community will be spared the pain he experienced the day his life changed forever.

····

THE DATE THAT DIVIDES John Westhaver's life into "before" and "after" is April 29, 1994. In the "before" time, John says, "[I was] a regular teenage guy who thought I was invincible." A member of the high-school wrestling team, he enjoyed the new alternative bands coming out of Seattle, Washington, and spent hours in front of the mirror before going out, getting his hair just right. Friday nights were party nights in St. Stephen, New Brunswick. At eighteen years old, he and his buddies were too young to buy their own alcohol, but they always managed to find some. They'd head off in someone's car, find a place to drink, and just listen to music and hang out. They weren't stupid about it, though; their parents had hammered the "designated driver" message into their heads, and it stuck. The person behind the wheel was always sober.

That particular Friday night was no different than so many others. With six weeks to go before graduation, the world was full of possibilities. The four friends decided to make a forty-five-minute drive to a nearby community to check out a pool hall that had been getting good buzz. When it was time to head home, they piled into the car, cranked the tunes, and hit the road. "We thought we were safe because we had a designated driver," John says.

That night, it didn't matter. Whether due to speed, driver inexperience, or a combination of factors, the car lost control around a hairpin turn, hit a telephone pole, rolled several times into a ditch, and burst into flames. The driver, seventeen-year-old James Zografos, was ejected from the vehicle and killed. In the back seat, Jason McKeeman and John Aaron Williams burned to death. John, riding shotgun, managed to escape—not that he remembers.

"The next moment I wake up in a hospital room," he says. "I look around and don't recognize the room, and I look down at my body and I'm covered in bandages. I'm scared. I have no idea what happened or what went wrong, why I'm here."

That "next moment" was actually a month later. For thirty days, John had been in a coma, medically induced by his doctors to give him a fighting chance to survive. Barely alive when he arrived at the hospital following the crash, he had third-degree burns over 75 percent of his body, as well as a broken arm. His heart stopped multiple times as his vital systems tried to shut down. His parents were advised to say their goodbyes.

But even unconscious, John had other ideas. He survived one night, and then the next. Once his condition stabilized, his medical team got started on what would be a long string of surgeries—some to reduce the risk of infection, some for skin grafts and reconstruction, and some to restore movement in his badly burned neck and hands. Over the course of the next eighteen years, John would undergo thirty-five surgeries in all.

When the doctors woke him up, they told him the worst was over. It wasn't. No one would tell him what had happened to his friends, regardless of how often he asked. He wasn't allowed to look in a mirror, which told him pretty much everything he needed to know about the shape he was in. And the twice daily dressing changes he endured were pure agony, leaving him with the feeling of being peeled alive. Eventually, he found out that his friends were gone, killed in the crash that he'd somehow survived. And eventually, someone handed over the mirror he'd been demanding.

"I wanted to crawl in a hole and die," he says, remembering that first glance at his new face.

He spent two and a half months in the Saint John Regional Hospital Burns Unit before being sent home, with a schedule of regular nurse visits to deal with the bandages that still covered his body and a series of planned surgeries marking the years ahead. But even that, he says, wasn't the worst of it.

"Surviving the burns was the easy part. Surviving life, the surgeries was the easy part," he says. "The hard part was losing my friends. Losing three teenage guys, one of whom was my best friend, was one of the hardest things I went through. I struggled for twenty-three years with the blame and the guilt that overcame me every time I thought about it."

John wasn't in this alone. The community rallied around him, trying to help one of its own, and his family—he is one of eight siblings—was a constant source of support. But it hardly mattered. The grief, the guilt, and the anger were overwhelming. He was angry at the driver, angry at the doctors who hadn't been able to do more to repair the damage, and angry at fate, which had put him in the car that night and then allowed him to survive when the others didn't.

"I was just angry and I hated everything," he says. "I hated life."

Not surprisingly, given the physical trauma he'd endured and the emotional scars that marked him as surely as the scars the fire had left across his body, the once outgoing and friendly teenager withdrew into a world of his own. Figuring no one could love him looking the way he did, he convinced himself that he would live his life alone.

For a time, his family let him be, giving him the space he needed to grieve and come to terms with the changes in his life. But only for a time. Eventually, his dad sat him down for a talk, and some tough love. He told John that he had a choice between anger and forgiveness.

"[My dad told me] you can sit around and sulk and be angry with the world, but it's not going to help you out," he recalls. "And he really had me get the forgiveness piece, because I was able to forgive Jimmy and everyone in the car. I was able to let go of the anger."

Slowly, things began to improve. His body continued to heal, and this time, his mental health kept pace. His sister encouraged him to get back out into the community, and he listened. He enrolled in college, became a computer repair technician, and in 2000, took a cross-country bus trip to visit his brother, who was stationed at a Canadian Forces base in Victoria, British Columbia. He quickly fell in love with the city and decided to make it his home.

In so many ways, the move to Victoria represented a fresh start. It was in this West Coast city that John joined a support group for burn survivors, finding comfort in being around others who were struggling with the same challenges he faced each day. He soon became a volunteer with the same organization and got involved with the local Firefighters' Burn Fund as well. It was in Victoria, too, that a physical therapist suggested he might get some satisfaction out of helping others by sharing his story. He joined Toastmasters and, in 2002, gave his first public presentation. These days, he manages his talks through his own website (www.johnwesthaver.com), and keeps busy as an established and powerful motivational speaker on issues ranging from overcoming adversity to personal accountability to workplace and car safety.

The last topic, in particular, is near and dear to his heart—and the subject of many of the presentations he gives to high-school students across Canada and the United States. When someone dies in a car accident, he explains, the grief and trauma don't stop with the immediate family. The St. Stephen community of roughly five thousand suffered greatly in the wake of the accident that changed his life and killed his three friends.

"Everyone that cares and loves you is impacted when you are involved in a crash like this," he says.

He tries hard not to lecture the young men and women he speaks to, knowing full well that telling teenagers what to do is often bound to have the opposite effect of the one intended. Instead, he lets the scars on his face speak for themselves. And he offers what he calls a "heads-up" about the things that can go wrong even when you think you're being safe, underlining the importance of making the right choices when you get behind the wheel or even into a car with a group of friends.

"It's simple to make the right choice," he says, "but not always easy. But it's a lot easier to speak up than to go through all the trauma and pain I've been through."

Some days, the presentations are smoother than others: the vibe is right, he's feeling good, and he knows he's on a roll. Other days, it's harder to relive the past, to grapple with the memories that talking about the accident brings up. But he keeps at it, knowing it's his purpose, and that it's making a difference. "If I can save one person my effort is worth it," he says. "One life lost in a car crash is one life too many."

IF SOMEONE HAD HANDED eighteen-year-old John Westhaver a crystal ball and asked him to look ahead a quarter century or so, he would've been shocked on several fronts. The John from the "before" time would clearly have had a lot to take in. There's the new look, of course, along with a new home and an unexpected career. He might be surprised to find out that he's the recipient of a Queen Elizabeth II Diamond Jubilee Medal, awarded in 2012 for his work with the community and public speaking, not to mention the 2017 Coast Mental Health Courage to Come Back Award. That one's given to British Columbians who have overcome tremendous challenges and yet still reach out to help others.

But even the "after" John would have had some catching up to do. The angry, guilty, lonely young man who decided he was destined to live life alone would be stunned to see the gold band adorning the ring finger of his left hand, and the pictures of his wife, Brianna, and daughter, Abigail, on the phone he carries in his pocket. Looking back now, though, John wonders whether there was a clue about his future just waiting to be discovered in those dark days following the accident.

"My hands were badly burnt," he says. "But the only finger on my hands that wasn't burnt was my ring finger. As so here I am, there's one finger that's not damaged, so that must mean something. And that's what I held on to."

Even the darkest stories, it seems, can have happy endings.

EVERYDAY HEROES
Conquering COVID-19

"A small action can go a long way in difficult times."

FOR MANY CANADIANS, IT WAS in early March 2020 that the world turned upside down. There had been rumblings of a novel coronavirus outbreak for a few months, with cases identified in Asia as early as December. In some ways, it was a slow build: Asia first, then Europe—with Italy hit the hardest—then the western provinces and states, and then, in alarming fashion, New York. But even as the case counts and death tolls mounted and emergency rooms were overwhelmed, there was still the hope that this would be "no worse than the flu," or perhaps "just like SARS." That all changed on March 11, when the World Health Organization declared a pandemic. COVID-19—so named because the first cases had appeared in China at the end of 2019—wasn't like the flu, or SARS, or anything else we'd seen in quite some time.

In the space of a week, much of the world was in lockdown, or preparing for it. Airplanes were grounded and borders closed. Sports leagues hit the Pause button. Concerts and live theatre were cancelled. Restaurants and coffee shops and malls shut their doors. Schools sent students home, and workers at all but essential businesses soon joined them. The world, in many ways, went quiet.

Except it didn't. While countless Canadians were hunkered down in their homes, learning how to cope with virtual meetings, online grocery orders (not to mention toilet paper shortages), and a whole new vocabulary ("physical distancing," "flattening the curve," "super-spreader events"), many others were doing the difficult work of managing the crisis. Across all levels of government, public health officials became trusted voices for information and advice. In every city, town, and village, front-line healthcare workers looked after the sick and vulnerable while trying to stay safe themselves. Grocery store clerks, fast-food employees, and public transit operators kept us fed and moving. Soon enough, it became clear that our most "essential" workers are those who are often overlooked, those who don't ask for recognition for just "doing their job." All around us, people pitched in in ways big and small, helping where help was needed. Their stories were a bright light in a dark time. Here are just a few.

Keeping the Doors Open

The Damascus Food Market isn't a big store, but there's no shortage of supplies on its shelves. The speciality here is Middle Eastern fare—the canned goods, spices, fruits and vegetables, and meats that were favourites back in Syria, where Marwa

Ataya, Mohamad Salem Ajah, and their four children lived before immigrating to Canada as refugees in 2016.

It wasn't an easy move. Everything, says Salem Ajah, was different. But the people in Victoria, British Columbia—the family's new home—made all the difference. "People helped us a lot," he says. "People supported us."

After a few years, the couple was settled enough to open the market. Like the move that brought them to a country halfway around the world from home, the new venture wasn't easy to get off the ground.

"It was very difficult to start," Salem Ajah says. "Different language, and different area, and different business." Marwa Ataya recalls how much there was to learn: the language, to be sure, but also how to run a business in this new country.

When the pandemic hit in early 2020, the couple was faced with a decision. Should they close the store and protect themselves and their family, or stay open and support the community that had supported them when they arrived?

They decided to keep the doors open. "We want to feel part of the community and help the community," says Marwa Ataya, adding that many people seemed to feel safer in small stores like theirs as opposed to large grocery stores, which were typically more crowded.

Even at the height of the pandemic, visitors to the store often found eleven-year-old Mohamad—one of the couple's children—at the checkout. He was happy to be working with his mother and father, and for the chance to repay a kindness.

"Lots of Canadian people, they helped us a lot when we came here," he says. "So we wanted to help them also."

For Salem Ajah, keeping the store open was about more than doing a good deed. He'd smile whenever someone thanked him for staying open. It felt good, knowing that he was helping out; it made him feel "like I am Canadian."

Marwa Ataya adds, "Canada, to me, is my home."

Pitching In Where It's Needed Most

Across Canada, long-term care (LTC) facilities were particularly hard hit by COVID-19. The combination of an elderly population in precarious health and a communal living setting allowed the virus to take hold, with devastating results. By June 2020, it was estimated that upward of 80 percent of the deaths Canada attributed to COVID-19 came from long-term care homes.

As a nursing instructor at Montreal's Vanier College, Else Leon was familiar with the challenges healthcare practitioners were facing on the front lines. With her classes moved online, and the Quebec government desperate for volunteers to help in LTC homes, she answered the call.

"I decided that I just couldn't help myself," she says. "I had to get out there and do what I could."

With a husband and two young children at home, Else took every precaution she could. She set up a bedroom for herself in the basement, followed all the public health protocols, and headed off to work at CHSLD Denis-Benjamin-Viger—a West Island facility with confirmed cases of COVID-19.

At first the work was overwhelming. There were new and numerous safety procedures to follow, and so many sick patients to care for. And shortly after she started, the military was called in to help manage the crisis. Her brother Gat was so impressed by the work she was doing that he, too, volunteered. Before long, they were working shifts together. Slowly, the staff settled into a rhythm and improvements were made. At that point, Else says, "I became more of a coach/leader, voicing my appreciation for the work being done and helping staff prioritize what needed to be done."

And then she got sick.

It started with a cough during her shift, and by the time she got home, her head was pounding. "The next morning, I was sneezing and coughing," she says. "The symptoms weren't typical. I didn't have a fever."

Less than twenty-four hours after she was tested, the results came back positive.

"I was devastated," Else says. "Being worried about spreading it to my husband and kids was nerve-wracking."

Else's story has a happy ending: none of her family members got sick, and she herself made a full recovery. She's looking forward to returning to teaching and to passing along what she learned in the LTC to her students. And despite her own brush with the virus that has led to so much sickness and death, she doesn't regret a moment of the time she spent at Denis-Benjamin-Viger.

"It's the most rewarding thing I've ever done," she says, adding, "I was just so happy that I could get in there and lend a helping hand."

A Mission to Help

Situated as far north as it is, and with the second-smallest population in the country, the Yukon escaped the worst of

COVID-19's ravages—just sixty cases and one death, as of December 24, 2020. Which isn't to say that the pandemic wasn't felt here, or that people's lives weren't affected.

Springtime in the territory typically sees the return of winter travellers and the arrival of miners eager to see what their gold claims might have to offer. In the early days of the pandemic, those travellers were encouraged to get home as quickly as possible and were advised—along with anyone coming in from other provinces and territories—to quarantine for fourteen days once they landed. Add to those numbers a bunch of people choosing to self-isolate and you've got a challenge on your hands.

Thankfully, this is a place where folks know how to help each other out.

Elaine Corden is one of the organizers of Dawson City's Helping Hands program. Within twenty-four hours of putting out a call on Facebook for volunteers to pick up groceries or prescriptions, make runs to the dump, sew masks, shovel driveways, prepare tax returns, or help out with employment insurance applications, sixty volunteers had raised their virtual hands. Shortly after, they were paired with twenty individuals.

"I'm sure this is going on in every little community across Canada and North America and all over the world," Elaine said. "But as always with Dawson, this town never fails to knock my socks off with its generosity and its team spirit."

Roughly five hundred kilometres to the southeast, in Whitehorse, Steve Berger-Huffon and Sandra Jost saw the same issues playing out and also decided to help. The couple, who own and operate the Caribou RV Park, opened early to welcome returning travellers who needed a place to isolate. They cut capacity to allow each guest to have their own washroom, lowered their rates to cover operating costs only, followed provincial health guidelines, and hung out the welcome sign.

"We want to help out," said Steve, "especially Yukoners not finding places to stay, so we thought it was our mission to help."

Celebrating in a Different Way

If anyone had asked Cooper Waisberg, in early 2020, about his plans for his eighteenth birthday, he would have mentioned go-karting. That was the idea—at least until COVID-19 threw a wrench into those works, along with his plans for prom, grad, and so much else that makes the final year of high school a pivotal moment in a young person's life.

Rather than let it get him down, Cooper decided to turn a bad situation into something good. The Toronto student had been volunteering as a sighted guide with the Alliance for Equality of Blind Canadians. As his birthday approached, he thought of the men and women he'd worked with and realized the pandemic would present a unique set of challenges for them.

"Those who are blind, it's already challenging for them to go out and about, [and] they can't even meet virtually like the rest of us are doing," he said.

Cooper gathered up the $150 of spending money he'd received, asked to borrow his mother's car, and convinced his brother Ethan—home from university—to tag along. Then he went grocery shopping. A few hours later, the car was stuffed with canned goods, bottled water, toilet paper, and cleaning supplies. The Alliance passed along the names of three people in need, and over the next two days, Cooper and Ethan made their deliveries.

"It just felt like the right thing to do," Cooper says. "It was definitely different than going go-karting. It was my day, but they were the present, in a way, and I was blown away by how grateful they were."

Seventy-three-year-old Josie Mullins was one of the people Cooper and Ethan helped. She was so thankful that she wanted to pay them. When they refused, she offered to knit them scarves instead.

"I just wanted to make them feel comfortable, brighten their day a little bit. A small action can go a long way in difficult times," Cooper says.

"I still want to go go-karting," he adds. "But I've been thinking, for next year, it would be nice to do something even on a bigger scale to help the blind, so, really, I think this was just the start for me."

PART 2
Courage in the Face of Danger

DAVID SILVERBERG

On the Wrong Track

"I just knew what had to be done."

THE VIDEO IS GRAINY AND a bit jumpy, a typical closed-circuit recording of the type that cops review in television shows when they're trying to identify a perp. The scene is a subway platform, one that runs down the centre of a station, with tracks on either side. There are only a few people sitting on benches, waiting for the train—it's definitely not rush hour—and if you're not focused on the top of screen, you could almost miss what's about to happen. A person in a wheelchair rolls slowly toward the edge of the platform. You're waiting for them to stop, because of course they're going to stop. But they don't. They just roll—gently, it seems, without the benefit of sound—right onto the tracks.

There's a split second where no one moves, and then commuters are on their feet, racing toward the spot where the person and the chair went over and are now lying on the tracks.

A small crowd gathers. Someone rushes off, beyond camera range, presumably to get help. Someone else peers down the tracks toward the tunnel as if watching for an oncoming train. And then there's the man in the dark jacket. He's been walking along the platform the entire time, carrying what appears to be both a suitcase and a shoulder bag. At first, he doesn't seem to notice what's happening. But as the crowd forms he strides quickly toward it. He puts his suitcase down on the platform and shrugs his shoulder bag off beside it. And then—carefully, deliberately—he does what no one else present has done: he jumps down onto the tracks to help.

DAVID SILVERBERG IS A HUMBLE man. Ask him about the events of April 22, 2015, and he's likely to say that he happened to be in the right place at the right time, that he "just knew what had to be done." Or he might tell you about his brother, Ronny, who passed away one month to the day before the incident on the tracks and once rescued a woman whose car had flipped over and was partially submerged in a pond. There was no video of Ronny's rescue to "go viral," David says, and it makes him feel a bit guilty about all the attention he's gotten. "A true hero," he says, "is someone who goes about his or her business unnoticed."

Maybe doing good deeds runs in the Silverberg family. And maybe a video of Ronny's rescue would have gone viral, too, if one existed. But security cameras are much more common on subway platforms in Washington, DC, than they are on the back roads of Prince Edward Island. And it was David's rescue, not Ronny's, that was captured for the world to see.

David Silverberg's presence on that subway platform was the result of a series of decisions that, made differently, could have put him far from the scene. The sixty-six-year-old neurologist from Charlottetown, PEI, was in the US capital for the annual meeting of the American Academy of Neurology, a gathering he'd been attending since the latter half of the 1970s, when he was a resident studying in Ottawa. The day had started typically enough, with some conference events followed by a lunch with a few colleagues. If David was a different sort of person, he might have gone straight back to the Marriott, where he'd spent the first few nights of the conference. But he'd paid for that stay with "pinky points," earned on some loyalty card or another, and since he generally prefers not to "shell out great wads of cash on hotel rooms," he decided to decamp for a bed-and-breakfast in a different part of the city.

Not wanting to get into the inevitable tussle over who was paying for a shared cab, he bid his lunchmates farewell and headed off on his own. He'd called the B & B ahead of time and asked for directions, making sure to inquire as to the closest metro stop. After years of attending conferences in Washington, he'd learned the importance of that word—*metro*. If you omitted it, and asked a local for directions to the nearest subway, you'd all too soon find yourself at the popular fast-food shop that serves foot-long sandwiches. He doesn't remember the name of the station, save for the fact that it either had a "U" in it or started with a "U," but he does recall getting off the train and taking a moment to sort out which street exit he should use. He figured the one at the far end of the platform would be closer to his destination, so instead of climbing the flight of stairs that was right in front of him, he decided to walk along the platform to the far exit.

And that is when David Silverberg—the man with the small suitcase and the shoulder bag—quite literally enters the picture.

DAVID WAS ABOUT HALFWAY DOWN the platform when he heard a woman shouting on the opposite side. He crossed over to see what the commotion was about.

"Lying right in the middle of the tracks was an unconscious man who had no legs," he recalls. "His heavy electric wheelchair was just over the side, lying on its side."

David had no idea what had happened, or how the man had ended up on the track, but one thing was perfectly clear: "There was no way that this poor fellow was going to be able to get himself out of there."

Although the video shows no hesitation between David's arrival on the scene and his jump down onto the tracks to help the man, a complex inner monologue played out as he assessed the scene. He was familiar enough with public transit in Washington to know that the trains have bright lights, clearly visible from the tunnel as the trains approach. He peered down the tunnel: no lights. That was the good news; it meant there was at least some time to act. The bad news? Subway tracks can be dangerous, with high-voltage wires running through one of the rails. And of course, there was no telling when a train might come rolling into the station . . .

But what if?

What if he waited for a minute and no train came? He knew he'd be kicking himself for not doing something. And then what if *another* minute passed and still no train? And what if the train eventually did come and he had to stand there and watch the demise of a precious human being he could have helped? Well, then he'd have the rest of his life to regret it. That was not something he wanted to contemplate.

There are benefits to having been a physician for decades—one of which is a certain comfort level in urgent situations. David lowered himself onto the tracks, careful not to touch anything in the process, and tried to sort out his next steps. The man lying on the tracks probably weighed about 150 pounds, but he had no legs, which meant he couldn't be cradled in anyone's arms and lifted off the tracks. With no other course of action available, David grabbed him under his shoulders and dragged him toward the edge of the track. He remembers feeling relief at the discovery that the tracks were not electrified, but then realizing that getting the man onto the platform was going to be another challenge. He was trying to figure out how to manage the lifting that would be required when another good Samaritan jumped down and joined him on the track. David took the man's upper half, and the new helper took the lower, and together they managed to get him onto the platform. Next up was the wheelchair—another challenge, given its weight. David was close to abandoning it when other commuters pitched in and helped.

All told, less than a minute had passed between the man's fall and his return to the safety of the platform.

With the immediate danger over, David hauled himself up onto the platform and turned his attention back to the man.

He had started to come around and was moaning, obviously in some pain. The man was a bit bloodied and shaken up, David concluded, but he seemed alert; he even managed to call his daughter on his cellphone to let her know what had happened.

"I spent a few minutes with him on the deck," David says. The man said several times that he couldn't remember what had happened and that he must have passed out somehow. His hip was sore, he told David, and his face was bleeding. "I tried to clean him up a bit and reassure him that this would all be an amusing story within a few days. By this time there was a small gathering around and we were assured that an ambulance was coming. I stayed with him for a few minutes until I was sure he was in good hands, and then I left."

On his way out of the station, David noticed that his shirt—new, and purchased specifically for the conference—was ruined.

"It was covered in black [grease] and blood, but that was okay," he told reporters a few days later, when news of the rescue got out. "It was a nice feeling that I had done something good for that day."

AT THE B & B later that evening—shirt laundered by the owner, who offered to help after hearing what had happened—David called home and told his wife about the day's events. Then he turned in, figuring the next day would be business as usual. He woke to a buzzing phone. Video of the rescue had gone viral, and everyone wanted to hear, first-hand, what had happened. He did interviews with Washington media, with local papers and television back in Charlottetown, with national news in

Canada, and even with some overseas outlets. The five minutes of glory, he jokes, was nice. "People in Charlottetown that heard the story or saw it in the local newspaper were very proud that one of theirs had done something worth a modicum of notoriety."

He was happy enough, though, to get back home and get back to normal life—to being a husband and a father, to his work, and to the community he calls home. These days, David spends his time windsurfing, playing the cello, and studying developments in neurology. The subway rescue has become just what he assured the man on the track that it would be: an amusing story he recounts every now and again, usually when someone else brings it up.

Speaking of that man, David never did learn his name, or the name of the other commuters who pitched in to make sure this story had a happy ending. When it comes to that remarkable day, it's the only thing he regrets.

ERIK BROWN

Diving in the Dark

"You'll never see a dive like this again, that's for sure."

ON A NORMAL DAY, THAILAND'S Tham Luang Nang Non cave system isn't particularly difficult to navigate—which explains its popularity with the local Wild Boar soccer team. The seventeen-year-olds and their coach enjoyed exploring the complex under the mountain range that straddles the Thailand–Myanmar border. On a few occasions, they had even used the ten-kilometre complex as the setting for an initiation of sorts, in which a new team member's name would be inscribed on a cave wall. So it was nothing out of the ordinary, really, when the team decided to head to the caves on June 23, 2018, following a Saturday practice. Once there, they left their bikes and bags outside the entrance to the cave and made their way in on foot, carrying nothing more than their flashlights. They weren't planning to be there for long.

· · · ·

ERIK BROWN HAD JUST RETURNED to his dive shop in Koh Tao, about four hundred kilometres south of Tham Luang, when he heard that there was a situation unfolding in the cave system. Twelve members of a soccer team, along with their coach, had become trapped when a monsoon blew in, bringing with it torrential rains and massive flooding. What had started as an adventure for the boys had quickly taken a dangerous and potentially deadly turn, and a search and rescue mission was underway. Erik reached out to a friend involved in the rescue efforts to see if divers were needed, and when the reply came in—yes—the thirty-five-year-old didn't hesitate. He and a friend were on a plane the next morning. "If they need help, and there's anything I can do, I'm going," he said in a phone call to his mother.

Born in Langley, British Columbia, Erik was a surfer before a shoulder injury took him out of the sport. He loved the water, though, and wanted to find another hobby that would keep him near it and in it. Diving answered the call. His first experience came on a trip to Australia in 2004, and Erik quickly fell in love. In the years that followed, he received certification in various disciplines, including deep diving, technical diving, and cave diving. In 2010, he moved to Egypt and cofounded a technical diving school—Team Blue Immersion (TBI)—near the Red Sea's infamous "Blue Hole," widely considered one of the most dangerous diving spots in the world. The work was never dull: TBI offered training seminars, completed world-record dives, and provided logistics services for documentaries. In August 2013, Erik took part in Expedition Alexander Hamilton, one of a team of four divers who placed a memorial plaque on the first American ship to be sunk during the Second World War. With the ship resting in nearly a hundred metres of water, just off the coast of Reykjavik, it was a dangerous mission.

For divers with Erik's training and experience, cave rescues are part of the work, although the results are often grim. "Ninety per cent of the stuff I go out on unfortunately on these occasions is [body recovery]," he says.

As Erik headed north toward Tham Luang, he hoped that this time would be different.

THE EARLY DAYS OF the Thai search and rescue mission didn't offer much reason for optimism.

On Sunday, June 24, a crew located the boys' bags and sandals about three kilometres inside the cave, but rising waters quickly forced them to suspend the search. The following day, a team of Thai Royal Navy SEALs reached an inner cave, where they found handprints on the wall. Again, though, flooding sent them back.

By Sunday, July 1, a small army—literal and figurative— had gathered outside of the cave entrance. Thai army and navy troops, on the scene from the outset, had been joined by local volunteers as well as rescue specialists from the United States, the United Kingdom, China, and Australia. Efforts to pump water out of the caves were well underway, with additional heavy-duty equipment being flown in by plane.

But so far, it had all been for naught. As the world watched and waited, hopes for a successful rescue began to fade.

The breakthrough came on Monday, July 2, when British divers John Volanthen and Rick Stanton managed to make their way through nearly three thousand kilometres of tunnels and caves—nearly half of which required diving in treacherous conditions—to a ledge where the boys and their coach were perched above the floodwaters. They had been in the cave for nine days.

July 2 was also the day that Erik arrived on the scene, and he was quickly pressed into action. With the boys finally found, the search and rescue efforts swung into full "rescue" mode. The first priority was bringing fresh water, food, blankets, and medical supplies to the boys, whose coach had taught them to meditate as a way of staying calm and preserving precious oxygen. At one point, the rescuers hoped to bring oxygen tanks to the team, which would have allowed them to stay in the cave until the flood waters receded, but the tunnels were too narrow in places to bring the tanks through. On Friday, July 6, Saman Kunan, a former Thai SEAL who had been attempting to bring oxygen to the team, died when his own tank ran out. The only option left was to get the boys out.

Given what he'd heard about the cave system, Erik knew it wouldn't be an easy rescue.

"Every single challenge you can throw at a diver was there," he says. "We have zero visibility, we had long hikes in, we had super-narrow channels, we had no communication from one [diver] to the other. . . . It's large stretches of passages and by-passages, and with the quick currents and the visibility, it's definitely up there for some of the most challenging dives I've done, for sure."

The rescue team devised an elaborate system for bringing the team out—one they practised at a local swimming school with boys roughly the same age and size to ensure that nothing was left to chance. The initial plan involved a buddy system—two divers to each boy, one leading from the front while the other followed behind with a flashlight—but conditions in the caves made that impossible. Approximately 40 percent of the journey out would be underwater and in extreme circumstances. "[There are] cracks 30 centimetres big that you have to squeeze through to get back there," Erik says, "and you really can't see your hand in front of your face. . . . When they say zero visibility, they mean zero visibility—you can't see anything." In a message home to his family, he described the diving like "swimming in coffee."

In the end, a streamlined system was devised: an oxygen cylinder was strapped to the front of the boy and a handle was attached to his back; then he was outfitted with a full face mask and essentially clipped to a diver who swam behind. Speaking to the media after the rescue, diver John Volanthen described the arrangement as resembling a "shopping bag that sometimes you would hold close to your chest if the passage was narrow and deep. If the passage was low and wide you would hold them out to the side and essentially manoeuvre them around any obstacles that were in the way." The divers themselves found their way through the dark passages by holding on to dive lines that had been laid ahead of time.

Even for an experienced diver like Erik, it was a daring operation. "I got told from the previous divers sort of what it was like, but when I arrived here and went in the first dive and saw even the first section, which is the 25-minute underwater swim and navigation through pretty much mud . . . I won't lie—in my head I was [thinking] there's very little chance this would work," Erik says.

On Sunday, July 8, with oxygen levels in the cave dipping to dangerously low levels, it was finally time to start bringing the boys out. Support divers were stationed along the route with fresh oxygen tanks, ready to assist those travelling with the boys, who were sedated to keep them calm during the ordeal. Erik was positioned a few hours into the cave—unable to see in the almost total darkness, and unable to communicate with any of the divers moving in what seemed like slow-motion around him. For hours at a time, he knew only what was happening in his small section of the cave.

"So you're not really sure how successful it is to be honest," he says. "It was successful up to me but they still had two hours to get [out] to where the US and Thai medical teams were. . . . That's the hardest part. You've got to wait another three hours, swim yourself back out, then pop your head up." Each shift lasted about ten hours, including the hike to the mouth of the cave, and rescuers needed to be ready at a moment's notice. "You had to have your boots on, wetsuit on, 24 hours a day."

Under the circumstances, staying calm was sometimes a challenge. He had to turn his "brain off a little bit." He says, "You have to focus on the minor task you have, try to put the sort of grand scale off to the side a little bit. Nothing prepares you for something like this. You'll never see a dive like this again, that's for sure."

Over the course of three days—July 8, 9, and 10—and against all odds, the rescuers safely brought out all twelve boys and their coach. On his Facebook page, Erik shared a photo of himself with two other divers, along with a short update for family and friends: "9 days, 7 missions, and 63 hours inside. Success."

WITH SO MUCH ATTENTION FOCUSED on the rescue during the two weeks that it played out, it's not surprising that interest remained high in the aftermath. Books and documentaries were quickly in the works, and Erik found himself in the somewhat uncomfortable position of being interviewed by news outlets from Canada and around the world. "I find it fairly awkward," he said at the time. "I'm used to being behind the camera rather than in front of it."

Back home in British Columbia, he received the Silver Medal for Bravery from the lieutenant governor. At the ceremony, his mom wondered out loud what it might take to get a gold medal. The gentleman sitting next to them—who had saved a family from a burning building—answered: "Die." Erik quickly decided he was "more than happy" with the silver.

He's also been asked who he would like to play him in the inevitable movie about the rescue. It's a question he tries to shrug off with jokes. "I don't think I'll have a character," he told one local newspaper. "I think I'll be support worker number four." He did, however, offer a slightly more glamorous option to an interviewer from *Diver* magazine: "Some of the Thai news had me labeled as Thor with long hair covered in mud," he said, referring to photos that had circulated of him after he emerged from one of his shifts in the cave. "If Chris Hemsworth wants to gain 20 pounds and have a non-speaking role then it's all his!"

Joking aside, Erik knows the experience was nothing short of remarkable. He cherishes the memories and the friends he made during those days in the caves. "You literally couldn't write this. It's extraordinary what some of these guys pulled off, and I'm happy that I could help in whatever way I could to support them and make their job a little easier along the way."

BILL AYOTTE
Battle with a Bear

"It was either me or nothing."

CHURCHILL, MANITOBA, IS PROUD OF its polar bears. Situated on the shore of Hudson Bay, in the province's far north, the town has long been known as the polar bear capital of the world. Thousands of the majestic white creatures summer nearby, awaiting the winter freeze that will allow them to venture out onto the ice to hunt seals. For Churchill, the bears are a welcome tourist attraction, bringing an estimated ten thousand people to town during the five or six weeks in October and November when bear activity is at its height. That influx of people—and the tourism dollars they bring—help keep the local economy churning. That's a good thing, certainly, but co-existing with the largest land carnivores on Earth requires a delicate balancing act. Signs around town recommend caution and display the number of the bear-sighting hotline; a polar bear patrol is on standby for emergency calls; and school children are taught what to do, and what not to do, in case of an encounter. Running, it's generally agreed, is bad.

Looking back on the events of November 1, 2013, Erin Greene might well wish for a do-over. The Montreal native had been a visitor to Churchill in the summer of 2012 and had so enjoyed the experience that she made the decision to move to the community the following year. She'd been in town long enough to absorb the bear-encounter rules that the local school children are taught. But when a polar bear is charging down the street toward you in the early morning hours, your first instinct—your only instinct—is to run.

ON OCTOBER 31, 2013, CHURCHILL celebrated Halloween along with the rest of the country. Kids here follow the same safety measures as everywhere else: wear something reflective after dark; travel in groups; don't eat candy that comes without a wrapper. But in a northern community like this, extra precautions are taken. Early in the evening, when the trick-or-treating is in full swing, many of Churchill's adults form a protective ring around the town. The goal? To make sure polar bears don't enter while the children are out.

But by 5 a.m. the following morning, when thirty-year-old Erin and her friends were making their way home from a late-night party, that human chain was long gone. The streets were quiet, at least until one of Erin's friends looked back and saw the polar bear running toward them in the dark.

"She said, 'Guys, watch out, there's a bear,'" Erin says, "and then we literally had seconds from when we saw the bear and when the bear was on my head."

As her friends ran to safety, Erin wrapped her arms around her head, doing what little she could to protect herself from the attack. It wasn't nearly enough. "I definitely remember it biting my head and thinking oh my god this is happening, this is a bear," she says. She figured this was it, that she was dying. "I just became very weak because I was losing a lot of blood and I'd come to terms with the fact that this was going to be how I died."

In the house across the street, Bill Ayotte was up and about. He's an early riser—always has been—and that morning was no different. The sixty-nine-year-old was working on a crossword puzzle when the screaming started. At first, he thought the noise was coming from the television, but he quickly realized the commotion was outside the house, not inside. He opened his front door and squinted through the dark.

"Sitting on his haunches was a polar bear," he recalls, "and he had a woman by the head and was wagging her around in the air like a rag doll. I couldn't believe what I was seeing."

For a split second, Bill froze. He didn't own a gun, and he knew there wasn't time to call the bear patrol. "She was out there by herself, and it was either me or nothing," he says.

His eyes scanned the front porch, looking for something— anything—he could use as a weapon. There, leaning up again the wall of the house, was a snow shovel, standard equipment in Churchill, where snowfall can happen pretty much any time, save July and August.

"I thought, 'If I'm going to save her, I have to do it now,'" he says. And so, clad only in his socks, pyjama pants, and a sweater, he ran down the front steps, across the street, and straight toward the bear. At first, he wasn't sure he'd be able to help; with the bear shaking the young woman violently from side to side, he couldn't get a clear swing at its snout or eyes, where he knew it would be most vulnerable to a hit. But his arrival momentarily distracted the animal, and it stopped its shaking. Bill saw his chance and wound up as hard as he could.

Miraculously, it worked. The shovel made contact and the bear dropped the woman, who made a beeline for the safety of Bill's house. He'd turned to follow her when he felt something grab the back of his leg. Instantly, he was on the ground with the bear on top, mauling him now instead of the young woman he'd raced out to rescue.

The next few minutes were a blur. Again and again he felt the animal's giant paws come down on his back. At one point, he heard his right ear being ripped off. He knew, in his heart, that the bear was aiming to kill him. To this day, he believes the only thing that saved his life was the fact that he'd fallen forward onto his stomach when the bear grabbed his leg. If he'd landed the other way around, the 180-kilogram predator would have had unfettered access to his chest and would likely have crushed his rib cage and internal organs as he continued to maul.

"I was thinking, 'That son-of-a-bitchin' bear has killed me,'" he says.

By this point, the commotion in the street had woken several of Bill's neighbours. Flare guns and cracker shells were set off, and in the house next door, Didier Foubert-Allen grabbed his shotgun and fired at the bear—all to no avail. Knowing he needed to get closer if Bill were to have any chance of survival,

Didier scrambled into his truck. He drove straight toward his neighbour, blaring the horn and flashing his headlights as he went. This last-ditch effort did the trick: spooked, the bear dropped Bill and ran off into the dark.

The entire attack lasted maybe four or five minutes, a long time to feel helpless.

"I was on the ground and all I can remember is feeling how really cold I was," Bill says. "I'm not sure I said anything but if I did utter words, I would have said 'I don't want to die on the street like an animal. I'm cold. Get me off the ground. Get me on my feet. I want to die on my feet like a man.'"

IN THE EMERGENCY ROOM AT the local hospital, conscious despite severe injuries to his head, stomach, legs, and back, Bill's thoughts were on the young woman he'd rescued. "I wanted to know she was all right before I died," he says.

He asked after her again later, after being airlifted to the Winnipeg Health Sciences Centre for treatment. The nurse told him Erin was in the next room. Later than night, she visited to thank her "angel in disguise" for saving her life.

It was then that Bill learned the extent of the Erin's injuries. The bear had pulled off most of her scalp, severed three arteries in her head, and bitten her in the arm and on the leg. She needed blood transfusions, twenty-eight staples, and countless stitches to repair the damage, and she is still missing part of her left ear. She was, she said, grateful to have escaped the attack alive.

Bill was also worse for the wear, with wounds to his head, stomach, legs, and back. He spent a week in the hospital, and three more weeks recovering in Winnipeg, so the plastic surgeon who reattached his right ear could make sure it was healing properly. Once he was given the all-clear, he made his way back to Churchill, eager to put the nightmare behind him.

Others, however, weren't quite as ready to move on. In October 2014, nearly a year after the attack, Bill received the Order of the Buffalo Hunt. One of Manitoba's highest honours, it's awarded to those who demonstrate outstanding skills in the areas of leadership, service, and community commitment. "He risked his own life to save a neighbour," wrote Conservation Minister Gord Mackintosh, "and that courage should be recognized and rewarded."

In addition to recognizing Bill's "heroic intervention," the province also made presentations to Erin, Didier Foubert-Allen, and the polar bear alert team who captured the animal after the attack.

Six months later, it was the federal government's turn to pay tribute. At a ceremony in Ottawa, Governor General David Johnston awarded Bill the Star of Courage, which recognizes acts of conspicuous courage in circumstances of peril and is the second highest of Canada's three bravery awards.

Although he readily admits that the awards are an honour, he also balks at the idea that what he did was brave. "It was either do something or I'd have to live with consequences after if I didn't help the woman," he says.

Erin has her own thoughts on the matter—thoughts that go beyond issues of bravery and courage. "When we think about bravery and people who have courage, there's also a huge element of softness and compassion that has to be there in order for somebody to make that move," she says. "If you don't have compassion for another human being then you're not going to put your life at risk."

SEVERAL YEARS HAVE PASSED SINCE the attack that brought Bill Ayotte out onto his street in his socks and pyjamas to brandish a shovel against one of nature's most deadly predators. He still has that shovel and has added a folding shotgun to his arsenal—a bit of extra security on the bike rides he often takes to the outskirts of town. So far, he hasn't needed it. The lifelong resident of Churchill had never had a close encounter with a polar bear before that night in 2013, and he hasn't had one since. He's happy enough to keep it that way. "They don't bother me. As long as they're at a distance."

Although Erin briefly returned to Montreal to recuperate from her injuries, she's back in Churchill now. She teaches yoga classes, manages a local gift shop, and, during the summer, when beluga sightings are common, leads stand-up paddleboard tours on the Churchill River. Despite her Quebec roots, this town is now home—a community that looks after its own, even if that means raising money to help pay for out-of-province medical expenses. That effort, undertaken on her behalf, was a helping hand she won't ever forget, and it speaks volumes about the people she's lucky enough to call neighbours. "Knowing that this community produced someone who would risk their life to save another person's, I definitely wanted to be somewhere where humans turned out like that."

Erin has stayed in touch with Bill and his wife, Kathleen Bouvier, even joining the couple for a special reunion dinner. She once sent Bill an angel figurine as a gift. He still has it, along with a scrapbook of clippings that Kathleen compiled about the incident. His grandkids thumb through it occasionally and are convinced they have "the greatest grandpa in the world."

Erin agrees. "If that bear had a minute more, thirty seconds more," she says, "if Bill hadn't come out, I wouldn't be here."

MONA PARSONS
The Role of a Lifetime

*"I was determined not to humble
myself before any of them."*

WOLFVILLE, NOVA SCOTIA, IS A pleasant place to visit.
Restaurants and cafés abound, all serving food and drink from
the bountiful Annapolis Valley. The waterfront park offers a
perfect spot from which to view the red clay cliffs of Cape
Blomidon, not to mention the comings and goings of the
famous Bay of Fundy tides. Bed and breakfasts are housed in
stunning mansions, some once owned by sea captains. And
the nearby Grand-Pré National Historic Site tells the story of
the Acadian people, including the infamous deportation that
began in 1755.

There's history here, clearly, some of it visible, and some less
so. Just down the road from the main drag, for example, is the
74th Branch of the Royal Canadian Legion. It's a nice building—pale blue clapboard siding, white trim, bright blue door,
and a Canadian flag planted proudly out front—but it's easy

to walk past without a second glance. Inside, though, in the room where veterans meet to share stories and maybe a glass of beer, hangs a black-and-white photo. It seems somewhat out of place among the commemorative plaques and war memorabilia that line the walls. The young woman is movie-star glamorous: dark hair, dark eyes, smooth complexion, and painted lips. This is Mona Parsons—and while she's not a veteran in the typical sense of the word, she's as much of a war hero as any who gather here.

BORN IN MIDDLETON, NOVA SCOTIA, in 1901 and raised in nearby Wolfville, Mona was the youngest child of Colonel Norval and Mary Parsons. In her teens, she announced that she wanted to be an actress and then set about making it so. She travelled south of the border to hone her craft, returning home briefly to attend Acadia University and take part in the various drama activities on campus. Then it was south again—where she landed work as a chorus girl with Ziegfeld Follies in New York. It wasn't quite the dramatic star turn she'd hoped for, but she was on her way.

She might well have continued down the starlet path had her mother not fallen ill in 1927. When Mona got word, she returned to Nova Scotia to care for Mary, who died in 1930. In the wake of her mother's death, Mona realized she needed a more stable career. Back to New York she went, but this time to study nursing. She'd completed her training and was working as a private nurse in the office of a Park Avenue specialist when her brother wrote to ask a favour: a business associate from Amsterdam was touring the United States and Mexico and would soon be in New York. Could Mona perhaps show him around?

Five months later, in late 1937, the actress-turned-nurse married the business associate—Dutch millionaire Willem Leonhardt. The newlyweds settled in Laren, just outside of Amsterdam, where they built their dream home, "Ingleside," and settled in. For two years, life was good: the Leonhardts were fixtures in Amsterdam's social scene, attending dinners and balls and often hosting evenings at their home. The festivities continued even in the early days of the Second World War, when life in the city played out in much the same way it had before the fighting began. But in May of 1940, Germany invaded Holland, and everything changed.

The early days of the occupation were challenging. Many Dutch citizens were forced into work at German factories, curfews were imposed, and food rationing became a fact of life. Amsterdam also had a large Jewish population, and soon everyone had a story about a friend or neighbour who'd been rounded up and deported. Some chose to conform, to throw in with the Nazi occupiers and safeguard their own futures. Others—Willem and Mona among them—chose to resist.

The resistance cells were small, and trust and secrecy imperative. Discovery meant imprisonment at the very least and likely execution. For Mona and Willem, it was a risk worth taking. All around them, Dutch citizens were standing up to the Nazi invaders: hiding Jews and escaped prisoners of war, organizing strikes, setting up an underground press. The Leonhardts wanted to contribute too.

Perhaps realizing that their home was their greatest asset, they joined a cell that was helping to repatriate British airmen who had been downed over Holland on their way home from the front. In many ways, Ingleside was the safest of safe houses: large, set back from the road, and surrounded by ample land and many trees. The servants were dismissed and their attic quarters turned into a room for the men the Leonhardts would soon host. A secret hiding spot was added behind a bedroom closet in case the home was searched. The men would stay for only a day or two, just long enough to make arrangements for a late-night rendezvous between a local fishing boat and a British submarine waiting off the coast.

It was a risky venture, but it worked for a time. In September 1941, however, the cell was infiltrated. A fellow resistance worker was arrested mid-mission and executed. Desperate to avoid detection, Willem went underground. Mona, who believed her gender would protect her, prepared to throw the Gestapo off her husband's trail. She'd tell them Willem was on a fishing trip, and when they didn't find him or anything else suspicious in the house, they'd leave her be. It didn't work. Mona quickly found herself on the way to prison.

As she surveyed her new surroundings and tried to tamp down the worry she felt for Willem's future and her own, she knew she needed to stay strong, to not give up anything that would lead to her husband's capture. And so, for three months, she drew on the acting skills she'd left behind after her mother's death. She played a role: strong, silent, even contemptuous. She held on through countless attempts at interrogation, never letting her captors see how scared she was. She stayed in character when she found herself on trial, and even when the guilty verdict—complete with a sentence of death by firing squad—was read out.

"I knew all eyes were on me, expecting me to burst into tears," she wrote later. "I was determined not to humble myself before any of them. As I left the courtroom, I put my heels together and bowed toward the judge, the prosecutor and my German counsel . . . . *Guten morgen, meine herren*, I said. My action took them by surprise. They stared at me with their mouths open."

Impressed by this unexpected show of strength, the judge followed Mona from the courtroom and suggested she lodge an appeal. The death penalty, he suggested, might be lessened to life in prison. Mona took his advice. After a month in a cell on death row, she received the good news: the appeal had been granted.

"PRISON," MONA WROTE TO HER father after the war, "was a hard, nasty, cold, hungry & demoralizing life. . . . The first year I was ill a lot, weighed only about 94 pounds & was green— night sweats, coughing & diarrhoea every day for 3½ months & often vomiting. Tears have run down my cheeks for hunger."

She knit socks for German troops, secretly working in bumps that would cause blisters. She spent time in solitary confinement when she was found out. She was moved several times, finally landing in the German town of Vechta, where she worked in the prison kitchen and befriended a young Dutch baroness, Wendeline van Boetzelaer. Wendy, whom Mona later described as her "companion and guardian angel," dreamed of escape. Together, the two women devised plan after plan, hoping for a chance to put one into action.

That chance came in the early hours of March 24, 1945, when Vechta—home to both an airfield and transfer point for German troop trains—was bombed by Allied planes. The building housing the male prisoners was levelled. The female guards, hoping to keep themselves and their charges alive, ushered the women into the nearby fields. Wendeline and Mona never looked back.

Getting out was one thing, staying out another. Wendy, at least, knew the country and the language. She could easily pass as German. But Mona? What little German she spoke was marred by her Canadian accent. No one would be fooled into thinking she belonged. And so, for a second time since she'd been arrested nearly four years ago, Mona would need to play a role. At twice Wendy's age, Mona would pass herself off as the younger woman's aunt—feeble-minded and with a cleft palate that led to a pronounced speech impediment. Looking back years later, Mona recalled thinking the whole plan might have been amusing if the stakes weren't so high. "We were far behind the Nazi lines and at any moment might be recaptured," she wrote. "If that happened, our lives wouldn't be worth a plugged pfennig."

For three weeks, and across more than 125 kilometres, the two women acted their parts. They worked in exchange for food and board, often sleeping in fields and barns. They spent one particularly tense night in the company of an SS policeman, whom they'd approached for help before realizing who he was. Finally, they made it to the Dutch border. When they couldn't find lodgings that would accommodate the two of them together, they said their goodbyes.

For several days, Mona stayed with a German family on their farm, hiding in the cellar when intensified Allied attacks and the German slash-and-burn retreat made it too difficult to be out in the open. When the fighting finally subsided and the Polish army marched through, they told anyone left alive to seek shelter in Holland. Mona could have cried with relief.

AS ECSTATIC AS MONA WAS to be back on Dutch soil, the road to Ingleside was far from smooth. She was severely malnourished, with only eighty-seven pounds on her five-foot-eight frame, and her bare feet were covered with infected blisters. Perhaps worst of all, after working so hard for weeks to convince people that she was German, she now had the opposite problem; she had to convince the liberating troops that she was not German, and, more importantly, not a spy. Spies were taken to prison, and the thought of having escaped one just to end up in another was almost too much to bear. The family she approached for help at a farmhouse near Vlagtwedde believed her, though, and passed along an incredible piece of news: the area was under the control of the North Nova Scotia Highlanders. They could take her to them, if she'd like.

Mona braced herself for what was to come. She needed the troops' help for food, medical attention, and shelter, but she knew she'd have to prove to them that she wasn't a spy. She prepared to answer the barrage of questions that would surely be coming her way. In the end, though, there was no need. At the Canadian Army Rear Headquarters in Oldenburg, Germany, where Mona had been taken to prove her identity, she encountered a miracle—familiar faces. The captain's father had treated Mona's own mother in her dying days; several soldiers were acquaintances from the drama program at Acadia; and Major General Harry Foster, who came to visit her in the hospital, was another friend from Wolfville. They vouched for her identity and listened, captivated, to her story: nearly four years in German prisons, and a harrowing escape on foot to safety. She was still in Germany, but for the first time since the Gestapo had led her out of Ingleside in September 1941, Mona Parsons was home.

MONA DID MAKE HER WAY back to Ingleside, where she was eventually reunited with Willem. But his health, always precarious, had suffered greatly during his own imprisonment. Shortly after Willem's death in 1956, Mona returned to Canada, where she once again met the kind major general who had visited her in the hospital in Germany. They married in 1959 and settled in Wolfville.

Parsons died of pneumonia in 1976. Today, visitors to Willowbank Cemetery can find her tombstone in the family plot. The inscription is simple, noting the date of her birth and death, and identifying her as the wife of Major General Harry Foster. Not a word of her work in the Dutch resistance, her long imprisonment, or of the commemorations she received from General Dwight D. Eisenhower, commander of the Allied

Expeditionary Forces, or from Air Chief Marshal Tedder of the Royal Air Force, both of which expressed gratitude for her efforts on behalf of Allied airmen. Aside from a few close friends and family, few knew of her remarkable history, and it had not ever been publicly acknowledged.

Prior to 2017, you'd likely have headed to the cemetery if you'd somehow come across Mona's story and wanted to pay your respects. These days, though, there's a much more fitting monument to her remarkable strength and courage. Under an oak tree in a park just outside of the post office stands a bronze statue of a woman quite literally kicking up her heels—or clogs, as a closer look reveals. Commissioned by the Wolfville Historical Society and the Women of Wolfville, and sculpted by local artist Nistal Prem de Boer, the statue depicts Mona Parsons dancing with joy. The title of the work—*The joy is almost too much to bear*—is taken from a letter Parsons wrote to her father from the Netherlands, just after the Nazi occupation ended. It is, at long last, a public acknowledgement of the woman who sacrificed her own freedom for helping others find theirs.

JAMES KITCHEN
AND WILLIAM WARD
On Thin Ice

"All I really did is go to work."

JAMES KITCHEN FIGURES IT'S DESTINY, the fact that he flies for a living. Born in Clandeboye, Manitoba, about an hour outside of Winnipeg, his first experience with aviation came at the ripe old age of two, when his aunt Sandy sat him in a helicopter. He doesn't remember that day specifically, but he has plenty of other memories to add to the story: building kites and model airplanes with his grandfather, and just the general sense that he was, from a young age, "groomed to appreciate aviation."

And who knows? Maybe destiny did play a role in the events of March 13, 2011—when James and his colleague William Ward found themselves in exactly the right place at exactly the right time to lend a lifesaving hand to two Inuit hunters in Nunavut.

••••

IT WAS MID-FEBRUARY WHEN PILOT James and aircraft maintenance engineer William left Calgary to join a team on a mission to fly two helicopters to Iqaluit on behalf of Peregrine Diamonds. The trip was a bit of a nightmare, plagued by mechanical problems and weather delays, but they eventually made it to Salluit, Quebec. Iqaluit lay just across the Hudson Strait—a relatively short flight, provided they could get clearance. Not for the first time on this trip, they found themselves in a holding pattern. At the local airport, they installed pop-out floats, which keep the helicopter afloat on water, and waited for the weather to clear. Early on the morning of March 13, they finally caught a break. After an uneventful flight, they landed in Iqaluit, and the pilots headed to the hotel for breakfast while the engineer stayed behind to remove the pop-out floats.

James and the others had barely sat down when his phone rang. It was Jennifer Burry, Peregrine's representative in Iqaluit, requesting that they stand by for a possible rescue. "There were two hunters stuck on their qumutiik [an Inuit hunting sled] sitting on an ice flow," James says, recalling the bits of information Burry passed along, and the local government was frantically trying to figure out a way to reach them. Helicopters don't typically hang around at the Iqaluit airport, and without one, a ground rescue would have been the only option. With eight or nine hours of travel time between Nunavut's capital city and the rescue site, the outlook was bleak. This, then, is where destiny comes in: James and Will—and their helicopter—had just touched down.

Shortly after that initial call from Burry, the order came through to push out for Chapell Inlet, in the southeastern tip of

Frobisher Bay. James hurried back to the helicopter while Will quickly reinstalled the floats he'd just removed. James considered the weather—low level overcast, about thirty-five below zero: a typical Arctic day—and shook his head. "My initial thoughts were that if they were in the water they would be hypothermic and likely dead. If they were alive, time was of the essence."

ROUGHLY TWO HUNDRED KILOMETRES AWAY, the two hunters, David Alexander and Jimmy Noble Jr., were indeed alive. David, though, was in dire straits. The pair had set out that morning in search of polar bears, a routine outing for the two experienced hunters—at least until David's snowmobile hit a soft patch of ice and went through.

"I couldn't tell how thick the ice was, and it was too late to turn around," David recalls.

Ninety metres away, and contrary to the information Jennifer Burry had initially received, Jimmy was still safe, the ice beneath his feet solid enough to hold him, his snowmobile, and his sled.

As David climbed onto his qumutiik and two empty jerry cans, struggling to stay afloat, he shouted instructions to his friend. "I told Jimmy, 'You got to call for help right away.' I was soaking wet, up to my chest. Gobbled a little bit of sea salt," he says.

Keeping an eye on his friend, Jimmy grabbed his satellite phone and reached out for help. Back in Iqaluit, GPS coordinates and other vital information was relayed to James by Louis Trottier and John Buckland at Great Slave Helicopters. The two men stayed in touch with both parties throughout the rescue. Also in town, pilot Malcolm Murray was now on standby with another helicopter loaded with extra fuel; the rescue that James and Will had set out on was at the outer limits of their nautical range, and they needed a Plan B just in case the two men were farther away than expected.

Out on the ice, David and Jimmy weren't aware of the flurry of activity in Iqaluit; they were just trying to survive.

"All kind of thoughts going through the mind," David says. "I mean, I didn't want to have to go through a slow pain. I had my rifle right beside me. If I didn't know there was help coming, I would have had my thought of going a quicker way."

As David held on to his gas cans for dear life, doing his best to keep his head above the frigid waters, Jimmy unfolded a big blue tarp and laid it across the ice—a decision that would soon make it much easier for James and Will to locate them in a vast expanse of white. After that, there was nothing to do but wait.

IT TOOK THREE AND A half hours for James and Will to reach the stranded hunters. With whiteout conditions on land due to high winds and blowing snow, they had to fly low level along the coast. James, in the pilot's seat, kept watch to the right; Will, on the bench seat in the back, looked to the left through the helicopter's sliding door.

When they first arrived at the GPS location given, they didn't see a thing. "We must have flown right over them," says Will, adding that the helicopter's GPS was a real lifesaver. "At one point, James banked to the right and we picked up tracks."

The next thing they noticed was David, still in the water, floating on his bright red jerry cans. Jimmy was a little ways away, near his snowmobile.

Amazed that David was still alive, James and Will quickly discussed a plan for pulling him out.

"We decided that Will would loosen his seatbelt and hang out the helicopter door as far as he could while I hovered. He would grab David by his jacket and pull him in."

The trick was getting close enough, and low enough, to pull it off.

"We had to come in backwards to get him," James explains, "and hover over right on top of him."

"When you're in a helicopter, there are two safety belts—a shoulder harness and a lap belt," Will explains. "I took the shoulder harness off and loosened the lap belt as far as it would go. Then I locked the sliding side door into the open position and waited for James to turn around."

Once the helicopter was in the best possible position, Will stepped out of the fuselage and stood on the landing skid tube.

"I was calling out to James—'Lower! Lower'—as I reached down to David with my hand," Will says, noting that they were maybe thirty centimetres above the surface of the water. "I could see his eyes, and they were as wide as saucers."

Somehow, miraculously, the plan worked on the first attempt, and with David safely in the helicopter, James manoeuvred so that they were hovering over Jimmy. Wearing what James recalls as an "amazing racoon-pelt coat," Jimmy carefully stepped over the ice toward them and joined his friend inside. The whole rescue, Will figures, took not much more than five minutes.

While James guided them back to Iqaluit, Will spent the return journey taking care of the two men. David was literally blue, too cold to speak, and with his legs like solid blocks of ice from sitting in the water for three hours.

"We got them into survival sleeping bags and put on headsets so we could ask them how they were doing," Will says. "I worked off David's Sorel boots and wrapped his feet. Our Canada Goose parkas come with handwarmers, so I had some of those. I grabbed one and crushed it up and cupped his hands around it."

Jimmy, thankfully, was in better shape than his friend. "I remember at one point he looked out of the window and said, 'I wish I had this view—you can see the break-up,'" Will says.

"When we got back to Iqaluit, there was an ambulance waiting for them," James add.

And just like that, it was over. The two men were whisked off to the hospital, and James and Will, along with everyone else who'd played a part in the dramatic rescue, went back to whatever it was they'd been doing when the call to help came through. William and Malcolm Murray—the backup pilot who'd been on standby in Iqaluit—left for a diamond camp north of Iqaluit the following day, but James stayed a bit longer on company business. By the time he flew out a few days later, he'd heard through the local grapevine that David and Jimmy were both doing well.

It was a happy ending for a story that could have turned out quite differently, and to this day, both men are grateful for the part they played. Flying, James says, is a rewarding career, one that allows him to see the country and avoid being tied to an office. "I don't think I could sit at a desk and do the same thing every day," he says. "But it's give and take in this industry. I get helped out all the time by local First Nations, so to give back is a good feeling. There have been many times where I'm in a small community and all the hotels are booked and someone takes you in. I've even been broken down in the middle of a snowstorm up north and someone comes in a Ski-Doo and helps me out."

In the North, he continues, anything can happen, and for pilots like him, rescue training is a necessity. Prior to the events on Frobisher Bay, he'd been involved in rescues in both Yellow-knife, NWT, and Whistler, BC. "When you fly in the bush, you can be the go-to guy in small communities," he says. If you're in the area, and you can help, you do so—no questions asked. In that sense, he says, March 13, 2011, was a pretty regular day. "All I really did is go to work."

IT WAS ABOUT A YEAR later that James and Will learned they'd both been nominated for the Governor General's Medal of Bravery. Will received his award in April 2014, with his family looking on. "It was a sombre and humbling experience," he recalls—except for the part when his son, Adrian, saw him at the front of the room and, in a moment where you'd otherwise have been able to hear a pin drop, said, "Me Daddy?" In March 2015, it was James's turn, and like Will before him, he travelled to Ottawa to receive his medal from Governor General David Johnston. Accompanying him on the trip were his uncle Gerry and aunt Sandy—the woman who put him in a helicopter for the first time when he was just a toddler.

The statement from Rideau Hall read: "While Mr. Kitchen skilfully kept his helicopter hovering over the water, Mr. Ward reached down to rescue the two victims, pulling them into the helicopter one after the other, all while battling the unforgiving Arctic winds."

James is incredibly honoured to have received the award. The ceremony, he says, was "amazing," and Rideau Hall is "something everyone should see; its architecture is worthy of the queen." But today, having tucked the medal away in a special place, the forty-three-year-old is happy enough to be back to his normal live, living and working in Calgary, Alberta.

"I still fly regularly," he says, "and life is still an adventure."

He keeps in touch, intermittently, with Will, and with Jimmy, who often writes emails and is active on social media—when he's not racing Ski-Doos across the Arctic. David is quieter, although James recently heard through Jennifer Burry that it's on David's bucket list to have coffee with the two men who pulled him from the ice.

"I just need to make that happen," James says.

CLARK WHITECALF
Into the Flames

"I guess God picked me to go and save her."

CLARK WHITECALF KNOWS A THING or two about fire. As a young man trying to find his way in the world after a stint in residential school, he left his home on Saskatchewan's Sweetgrass reserve and relocated to Saskatoon. He took odd jobs to pay the bills, including work with the "mop-up" crew of a forest-firefighting unit. Dropped onto scorched earth in the far reaches of northern Saskatchewan, he'd pick his way carefully through the debris, putting out spot fires wherever they threatened to flare up.

These days, the memories and scenery have a tendency to blend—scorched earth in one place looks pretty much like scorched earth in another—but there's one trip he remembers well. As he and his crew were being airlifted north, he looked down on the biggest fire he'd ever seen. Watching it carve its way through the forest was a surreal experience; the fire was like a living beast, chewing up everything in its path. The image stayed with him—a constant reminder of the damage fire can do, given half a chance.

BY THE TIME AUGUST 31, 2015, rolled around, a now forty-year-old Clark Whitecalf was back in Sweetgrass, married to Samantha Moccasin and father to five children. Life was good. Set in the rolling grasslands just west of North Battleford, the Cree reserve was a beautiful place to raise a family. Samantha had a job at the local daycare, and Clark worked construction, although a broken leg that hadn't completely healed had slowed him down a bit. Heading out for a drive wasn't on his list of things to do that particular evening, but when his newly licensed sixteen-year-old daughter, Masey, asked if she could practise her driving skills, he and Samantha agreed. At about 9:30 p.m., they all piled into the truck and hit the road—Masey, Clark, and Samantha squeezed into the front, and fifteen-year-old Hailey in the back.

They hadn't been out for long when Masey spotted the glow up ahead, a wavering light that was turning the night sky a faint orange. Not taking her eyes off the road, she alerted her mother and father: "I think Sonya's house is on fire."

Clark and Samantha knew the house, knew Sonya Fineday and her husband, Joe, knew that the couple had teenaged children. What they didn't know was whether or not anyone was home. Clark switched seats with Masey and drove as quickly as he could, arriving on the scene to find the bungalow already engulfed in flames—and a truck parked in the driveway. By the time the volunteer firefighters arrived, Clark knew, it would be too late to save anyone who might be in the house. They had to act, and they had to act now.

He and Samantha pounded at the locked front door, but it brought no response. Rather than taking that as a good sign—an indication that no one was home—Clark felt his sense of unease increase. If someone was inside, it was possible they'd been injured or overcome by smoke. Maybe they wouldn't be able to call out for help, or let him and Samantha know they were there. Forgetting all about his still-healing leg, he kicked in the door, intent on getting inside, but a black cloud of smoke stopped him in his tracks.

Leaving Samantha and Masey calling into the house through the open front door, and Hailey on the phone with emergency services, Clark ran to the garage, which contained a side entrance. He got into the house this time, and he made it as far as the kitchen before the smoke and the flames pushed him out again.

Back in front of the house, he was met by Samantha and his two daughters, both of whom were crying. Samantha told him that an orange cat had come out of the front door and started pacing on the lawn and meowing. They'd taken the animal's distress as a sign that someone was still inside, and she and Masey had crawled through the front door on their stomachs, taking care to stay beneath the billowing smoke. This time, when they'd called out, they heard a noise.

"Clark," Samantha said, "there's somebody inside."

He didn't hesitate. Once again he approached the front door. Like his wife and daughter had done, he stayed close to floor, pulling himself through the smoke on his stomach. Off and on, he could hear a girl's voice, though he couldn't tell where it was coming from. He peered through the smoke and the flames into the living room, where he saw an arm hanging over the edge of the couch. It belonged to a young woman, dressed in a tank top and shorts: Jolei Farness, the Fineday's eighteen-year-old daughter.

"That's when I stood up, and I walked towards her," he says. But when he reached out to grab her arm and pull her out of the room, the unthinkable happened. "Her skin peeled off and I fell over."

Gasping for breath, Clark ran outside for some fresh air before trying again. A second attempt to pull the young woman by the arm brought the same results—more damaged skin and another trip back through the door for a much-needed breath of fresh air. On the third attempt, Clark decided to try something different.

"I went back in, and this time I grabbed her by her armpits and I just dragged her out the house," he says. "And when I got to the steps I fell over, I kind of dropped her on the steps and I went rolling down the stairs."

Working with Samantha, Clark rolled Jolei onto her side. After a tense moment or two, when Samantha was sure the young woman wasn't breathing, Jolei started to cough. As Clark made one last trip into the house to check for anyone he might have missed, Samantha and the girls heeded Clark's warning to get away from the burning house—and the large propane tank sitting in the yard. Gently, they helped Jolei to stand and walk to her uncle's house, just across the road. Clark stayed behind, moving whatever he could out of the path of the flames, until the volunteer firefighters arrived.

As the paramedics took Clark to a local hospital, where he was treated for severe smoke inhalation, Jolei was transported two hours southeast to Saskatoon. The next day, the young woman struggled to put the pieces of the evening together. She remembered coming home, looking at Facebook on her iPad, and then nothing until she woke up at the house across the street from her own, screaming as Samantha poured cold water on the burned flesh of her arms. Now, suffering from smoke inhalation, a hole in her lung, and second- and third-degree burns, she listened as a nurse told her how close she'd come to dying.

"They said if I'd been in there for one or two minutes more, I wouldn't be alive," she recalls.

Three months later, she was out of the hospital and visiting a relative when Clark Whitecalf happened to stop by. At first, he didn't recognize her. She said hello, showed him the scars on her arms, and gave him a hug. For Clark, that's when the enormity of the situation began to sink in. "I'm starting to realize if we didn't drive by that night, she wouldn't be alive," he recalls.

The meeting left him feeling awkward, he says, "But I also felt really good."

SAMANTHA MOCCASIN-WHITECALF has always known that her husband is capable of extraordinary things. She has faith in him, she says, in part because of his work as a forest firefighter, but also just because of who he is. "He has always been responsive," she says. "I'm very proud of him. I love him for who he is. I feel protected by him."

It's no surprise, then, that she was happy to see Clark honoured for his bravery on the night Jolei Farness almost died. In October 2016, the couple travelled to Regina, where Lieutenant Governor Vaughn Solomon Schofield presented Clark with a Royal Canadian Humane Association Silver Medal for Bravery. In December of the same year, Clark was awarded a Carnegie Medal in recognition of the extraordinary risk he took in rescuing Jolei.

"The situation inside the building was a deadly situation," said Eric Zahren, executive director of the Carnegie Hero Fund Commission, "potentially deadly for even a very short exposure, and his exposure was not short."

More accolades followed. In 2017, Clark received a Queen's Certificate for Bravery and the Gold Stanhope Medal, awarded only once a year for the entire Commonwealth.

Clark is proud of the awards and humbled—"I don't take life for granted," he says—but mostly he's grateful he was able to help when help was needed. His memories of everything that happened that night are still a bit hazy, but he remembers the thought that was running through his head.

"I thought there's a person that's going to die if no one doesn't do anything about it, so I guess God picked me to go and save her, I don't know," he says.

He's not sure if it was his old firefighting instincts or something else, but from the moment he saw the flames, he knew he was going to try to help.

"I didn't even think of the dangers," he says. "I just reacted. I just did what I had to do."

And because he did, a young woman is alive and well.

ERICK MARCIANO
A Crash Course in Courage

"It only takes one gesture to make a difference."

ERICK MARCIANO WATCHES THE NEWS. Like so many others, the forty-eight-year-old general contractor and father of three is all too aware of the danger that lurks behind the scenes of everyday life: shootings in schools and places of worship, acts of terrorism in the nation's capital, and, lately, cars used as weapons. London Bridge was the site of one such attack in 2017; Paris's Champs-Élysées later the same month. And in 2018, a white van was driven into a crowd on busy Yonge Street in Toronto—just six hours down Highway 401 from Erick's hometown of Montreal. The attack killed ten and injured sixteen.

It was scenes of drivers mowing down pedestrians, replayed time and again on the nightly news, that raced through Erick's mind at 12:30 p.m. on Tuesday, November 12, 2019. He was sitting in his SUV at the corner of St. Hubert and René-Lévesque Boulevard, waiting to make a left-hand turn toward

Berri Street on his way to a meeting, when he saw some unusual activity just down the road. A westbound car on Réne-Lévesque, a white Honda, "burned a stop sign halfway, regretted it, backed up," Erick recalls, "but he was next to a policeman."

At first, it seemed like a routine traffic stop. The cops rolled down the window to chat with the nineteen-year-old driver—so far, so good. But then things went sideways. All at once the car took off, heading west down René-Lévesque.

Two blocks later, says Erick, "the policemen kind of cornered him into a snowbank. They got out of their car, pulled their guns; he managed to back up and make a really aggressive U-turn."

The police followed, and a dangerous situation was set into motion. As Erick watched from his stopped Mercedes, the Honda barrelled toward the intersection. Between pedestrians out on their lunch breaks, the normal foot traffic around the bustling Centre hospitalier de l'Université de Montréal, and a construction crew at work in the area, the sidewalks were teeming with pedestrians.

"It came into my mind, I said: 'this isn't going to happen here.'"

Without stopping to think about the risk to his own safety, he pulled into the intersection, honking "like crazy," and angled his car to block the path of the oncoming vehicle. He managed to jump out seconds before the Honda plowed into the passenger side of his SUV.

"I didn't want him to hurt anybody. I figured, sacrificing a car was really no big deal. And that's what I did," Erick says, adding that he was thinking about the pedestrians who might not make it home that night. "He had a Honda, and there was no way he was going over the median. For me, that was the safest thing to do."

While the Honda's nineteen-year-old driver was arrested and then taken to the hospital for treatment, Erick spent the next three hours in the back of a police car, waiting to be interviewed about the incident. The next day, when the young man appeared in court to face charges, Erick learned that he was intoxicated and had a history of mental illness. The driver's mother publicly thanked Erick for stepping in and preventing the situation from being any worse. The police, too, were grateful—almost embarrassingly so, in Erick's opinion.

"It was just a natural thing to do, and if I had to do it again, I would do it again," he says. "It only takes one gesture to make a difference."

ERICK WOULD HAVE BEEN HAPPY to leave it at that, but others weren't so willing to forget the split-second decision that saved dozens from serious injury or worse. Speaking to the media a few days after the dramatic episode, Montreal mayor Valerie Plante praised Erick's "remarkable heroism."

"To commit such a bold act, at the risk of his personal safety, to protect the life of pedestrians is among the most admirable acts of bravery," she said before presenting him with a certificate of honour and inviting him to sign the city's Golden Book.

As his wife, three teenagers, and parents looked on, Erick added his name to the book. The last person to sign, he noticed, was internationally renowned climate activist Greta Thunberg. Seeing his name in the book next to hers was, he admits, "pretty cool."

Erick's wife, Michelle, agreed with the mayor's assessment of her husband's actions. "He's always thinking about others and always puts others before himself, so it's just something he does," she said, while joking that she wouldn't be lending him her car any time soon.

Good thing, then, that Erick's car insurance company got in on the celebration of their client's actions. He hadn't given much thought to his Mercedes in the aftermath of the crash. In the grand scheme of things, he figured, a car—even a nice one—was pretty insignificant. "It's just metal. It really doesn't matter," he says. "Anything but life is replaceable."

"What matters is the outcome," he told a reporter, "and everybody could go home last night."

Even so, it was a nice surprise when the insurance company took a special interest in the case. "I called my insurance company, and they said that, considering the circumstances . . . they're going to absorb absolutely everything," he says. "The deductibles, the responsibility, and so on."

As appreciative as he is of the recognition he's received, Erick still balks at the use of the "h" word. "I'd omit the word 'hero' for now," he told a local radio station. "Some people had told me that not a lot of people would have done this, but I beg to differ. For me, it was an easy decision."

"I did what I had to do," he continues. "If I was put in that situation again, I would not hesitate to do it again."

SOPHIA LEBLANC
Small But Mighty

"I was a little scared but not that much scared."

SIX IS AN AGE FOR fun. It's a time for the new adventures of school, for learning to read and write, to count to one hundred, and to tell time. It's a time for friends, for colouring, for doing puzzles, for dancing, for tobogganing and skating in the winter, and swimming and building sand castles in the summer. Six is not typically a time for life-and-death situations, for dramatic rescues, and for Medals of Bravery—unless, that is, you are Sophia Grace LeBlanc.

ON NOVEMBER 1, 2018, Candice Hicks was at the wheel of the family minivan, on her way to Oxford, Nova Scotia, to pick up her father. Her three children—Sophia, four-year-old Ethan, and two-year-old Elise—were in the back, strapped safely into seatbelts and car seats. The drive should have been uneventful, just a thirty-minute trip from their home in Amherst, nothing out of the ordinary. But in Little River, with just a few minutes left to go, her tire hit a rut in the road. Candice lost control of the vehicle, and, in the blink of an eye, was careening across Highway 204, sailing over the guardrail, and plunging down an embankment into the river below.

"We hit the guardrail, it made a really loud noise—I think we all still have that noise in our head—and we flew off into the river," she says. "I just knew we were going into water."

With no way to stop what was about to happen, Candice braced for the inevitable impact and thought about her kids as horrible images raced through her mind: scenes from movies where submerged cars gradually fill up with water as the passengers are trapped inside.

But then, a bit of luck—if you can call it that: the van landed, nose-down, half in the water and half out. Candice and the kids were hanging upside down by their seatbelts, and there was glass and blood everywhere, but, miraculously, the worst-case scenario had been avoided. Now she just needed to figure out how to get herself and the kids out of the van and back up the embankment, where they would be able to flag down some help.

Ignoring the intense pain in her arm, she wiggled out of her seatbelt and through the van's window; Sophia did the same. With the two of them relatively safe on the riverbank, Candice turned her attention to her younger children. Elise was awake, but Ethan had gone quiet. A quick peek through the window confirmed that he was unconscious.

Still upside down in her car seat, Elise was positioned closer to Candice, on the side of the car that was easier to access. In order to get her son, Candice would have to get her second daughter out first. But that turned out to be easier said than done. The pain she'd felt as she extracted herself from the van turned out to be the result of a broken wrist; her hand flopped uselessly at the end of her arm, which made undoing the car seat's complicated system of safety harnesses impossible. With no other options available, Candice turned to Sophia for help. As calmly as she could manage, she walked her daughter through the necessary steps. It worked; the young girl was able to free her sister and help her get out of the van.

Even with three of them on the riverbank now, Candice knew the situation remained dire. Ethan was still unconscious, the van was still in the water, and the cars passing by on the road above couldn't see them. She'd have to climb up the embankment to get help, but that would mean leaving her kids—one unconscious and two near the water—unattended. As desperate as she was, that wasn't something she could imagine doing. And so, once again, she looked to her oldest daughter.

"I asked Sophia to climb up and wave down a car," she says.

"It was really hard because there was so much bushes," says Sophia, who had to first climb on to her mother's shoulders for a boost, because the embankment was so steep. "I was a little scared but not that much scared. I knew I could do, I could do something safely and save my family."

She clambered up the rocks and over the guardrail. And then, the six-year-old who had, only moments before, been hanging upside down in a minivan partially submerged in water, stood on the side of the road and waved for help.

Doug Patriquin was the first to stop. The retired firefighter wrapped the small girl in a blanket, made sure she was safe, and then headed down the hill to help. Anthony Terry—who'd been working in his garage nearby when the sound of the crash caught his attention—had put in a call to 911 before joining Candice at the river and using a knife to cut Ethan out of his car seat. With the help of the two good Samaritans and the RCMP that soon arrived on the scene, the family was quickly bundled into ambulances and on their way to the hospital.

It was, all told, a happy ending. Although Candice's arm was shattered and would eventually require surgery to insert metal plates, the kids were fine. Ethan came to in the ambulance, and no one had anything worse than cuts and bruises. And through it all, Sophia handled herself like a trooper. "She was by herself with first responders and the people who came to help, there were a lot of people," says Candice. "She was just having a great old conversation with them."

IT WAS MEMBERS OF the local RCMP branch who decided Sophia should be recognized for her bravery. Among the first to arrive on the scene that day, the officers were impressed with the little girl's actions. And so, in January 2019, just a few months after the accident, a then seven-year-old Sophia attended a small ceremony in Amherst where Staff Sergeant Craig Learning presented her with the Act of Heroism Award.

"I think it's important to recognize people when they contribute and Sophia is the real hero today," said Learning, while also thanking the first responders and good Samaritans who pitched in. "A big thanks to them. It kind of keeps that faith in humanity."

Along with a certificate—a bit of a disappointment for a young girl, as far as awards go—Sophia and her siblings also received some toys from the RCMP and the province's Emergency Health Services. And, although she didn't know it at the time, the wheels had been set in motion for further recognition. Constable Angela Downey nominated Sophia for the province's Medal of Bravery.

Nova Scotia had been presenting its bravery award for twelve years by the time Sophia's name crossed the desk of the award's administrators. It's been given to men and women who have performed a wide range of courageous and selfless acts: rescuing strangers from icy or dangerous waters; pulling neighbours out of burning buildings or cars; assisting in the aftermath of a plane crash; even disarming a gunman in a hostage situation. The province, it seems, doesn't lack for local heroes.

But on December 4, 2019, when Premier Stephen McNeil presided over that year's ceremony at Province House in Halifax, it nevertheless represented a first. At eight years old, Sophia was the youngest recipient in the award's history.

"Sophia, we're really proud that you're here," the premier said, addressing the young girl in the pink dress sitting in a chair made for much bigger humans. "What an extraordinary demonstration of courage you showed when you made sure that not only was your younger brother and sister [safe]—you went and got help for your family."

After the ceremony, Sophia met with reporters, carefully holding the blue box that contained her medal. Asked why she was receiving the award, she replied, simply: "I saved my family." When questioned about being called a hero, she explained that a hero "is someone that respects everyone and wants to be nice to everyone." She told reporters that this was the best day ever, and that the medal itself was "cool." Her plan? "I'm going to put it in my room where I can always see it."

"It was an exciting day," said Candice. "I'm so proud of her. I don't think she understands the significance of what happened. It was funny during the ceremony, she was sitting on her chair looking all around and taking it all in. She looked a little bored."

And hungry—or so she told her mother once the proceedings wrapped up.

Looking back on the events that led to Sophia receiving the awards, Candice marvels at her daughter's ability to remain calm under pressure.

"She said I was screaming like a crazy person. I was panicking and yelling for help. You could tell she was scared but she said, like, what do we do now. She got my daughter out and she climbed up my back."

Sophia still seems unfazed by the events of that November day in 2018. Although she was a bit of a nervous passenger in the months immediately after the crash—scared of bumps and rough roads and travelling too fast—she's fully recovered now. And she has some good advice for anyone who finds themselves in trouble at the side of the road: "If you see anyone else who has a car accident just make sure you have a seven-year-old or six-year-old to help."

TREVOR SMITH
Swept Away

"The first thing you feel is fear."

CENTRAL YUKON IS WILD COUNTRY. To the south, the stunning scenery of Kluane National Park and Reserve attracts roughly thirty-two thousand visitors each year. Whitehorse, the territory's capital city, pulls in ten times that. But by the time you get to Mayo—a village at the confluence of the Mayo and Stewart Rivers, roughly four hundred kilometres north of Whitehorse—those numbers drop. Folks who make it this far are likely intent on fly-in fishing expeditions, big-game hunting, or exploring the vast wilderness on foot or by canoe. Or they might be following the Silver Trail, exploring the territory's rich history of silver mining, gold mining, and mineral prospecting—activities that drive the Yukon's economy to this day.

On November 15, 2009, Trevor Smith and Rafe Etzel were carrying on that tradition, staking mineral claims about

123

a hundred and sixty kilometres north of Mayo. The helicopter that shuttled the men to the site dropped Rafe off first. There was snow on the side of the mountain—not unusual in an area that averages more than thirty centimetres of the stuff each November, and where frigid winter temperatures ensure that it sticks around—but it was nothing that set off alarm bells. Rafe set about his business, expecting the day to pass uneventfully, as so many others had.

And then the snow beneath his feet gave way.

Even buried up to his ankles, the twenty-three-year-old didn't think he was in trouble. "It didn't seem that steep at the time," he says. "I didn't expect anything."

Erring on the side of caution, he nevertheless reached for his radio to call for help. That's when he heard the noise—a rumbling, whooshing rush that definitely signalled trouble. He looked up. A big white wall of snow was racing toward him. Next thing he knew, he was part of it, careening head over heels down the mountain as he held his radio aloft, determined not to lose his grip on what could very well become his only lifeline. Again and again he tried to get to his feet, to jump out of the avalanche's path, but the momentum was simply too strong. When the rushing snow finally stopped, he was completely buried.

"I couldn't move and started freaking out," he says. As he struggled to fight the rising panic, he realized he could still move his wrist—the wrist that was attached to the hand that was, miraculously, still clutching his radio. The last thing he remembers is trying to send an SOS.

•••••

ABOUT FIFTEEN MINUTES AFTER THE avalanche swept
Rafe down the mountainside and buried him alive, twenty-
four-year-old Trevor Smith passed over the area in the helicopter. Right away, he noticed the path the snow had cut down
the mountain. Then he realized Rafe was nowhere to be seen.
Shaking off concerns about a second avalanche, he told the pilot
to set him down so he could start a search.

Finding someone who has been buried by an avalanche is no
easy task. The human body is three times denser than the mass
of snow, rock, ice, and soil that plunges down the side of a mountain, sweeping up everything in its path. Once the avalanche
stops, a body settles, and the snow settles and hardens on top of
it, making movement—and hence escape—almost impossible.
Skiers and snowboarders are taught to punch upwards if they
find themselves buried, but even that can be a challenge. After
tumbling head over heels, who can tell which way is up? Ava-
lanches kills more than 150 people each year worldwide, with
an average of fourteen deaths in Canada.

Trevor knew that Rafe's situation was dire and that he had
no time to waste in finding him. But he didn't have a ton to go
on. Rafe's SOS signal hadn't gotten through, and the mountainside was nothing but a white expanse. As it turned out, though,
that radio still helped to save Rafe's life. After about fifteen
minutes of searching, Trevor noticed something unusual: an
antenna, sticking up out of the snow. He dropped to his knees
and started to dig.

"The first thing you feel is fear," he says. "But once I started
working, I don't remember feeling anything—I was just
focused."

Trevor had cleared about a metre of snow when he finally got to Rafe's head. The man didn't look good—he was purple, and unconscious, and for a few scary moments, Trevor wondered if he was too late. He kept digging, frantically trying to remove the snow from around Rafe's head and chest. After ten minutes or so, Trevor noticed that his co-worker was breathing again.

"The first thing I said is just, 'If you can hear me, blink,' because his eyes just opened abruptly and he looked at me right in the eye and blinked," Trevor says. "I can't really recall the words that came to mind, but there were a bunch of them."

Trevor stayed with Rafe, in the snow, until the helicopter arrived to take the injured man to the nursing station in Mayo.

ON AUGUST 6, 2011, Trevor Smith stood in the Westmark Whitehorse Hotel alongside Commissioner Doug Phillips, receiving the Commissioner's Award for Bravery.

"I am proud to present this award to a very deserving Yukoner," said Phillips. "Trevor distinguished himself by acting with bravery and great strength of character in a very dangerous situation."

Rafe Etzel's life, he continued, "was saved as a direct result of Trevor acting quickly and decisively, putting his own life at risk."

Accepting the award, Trevor said he was "very humbled and grateful," but not sure that he deserved it.

"The award means a lot," he said. "Whether or not I'm totally deserving is hard for me to say, it's definitely made a difference in some people's lives and everybody got to go home safe and alive so, yeah, I'm glad to be getting it."

Amanda Workman, for one, believes wholeheartedly that Trevor deserves the award. As Rafe's former partner, and mother to his three children, she's beyond grateful that her children still have their father in their lives. She nominated Trevor for the honour, noting that he was "very quick to respond" and "very selfless" in the face of danger.

And as for Rafe? He needs absolutely no convincing: "He totally deserves this, he saved my life, there is no one better to get this award."

BEACHCOMBER
The Wings of War

"They just kept flapping their wings and just flapping their wings and heading off for home."

THE SECOND WORLD WAR WAS nearing the start of its third miserable year in the summer of 1942, and for the Allies, the outlook was bleak. The German Army had made huge advances, extending its reach well into Russia and forcing the British Army in North Africa back into Egypt. Closer to home, in Europe, the Allies had lost valuable ground along the Western Front and had seen their troops pushed back across the English Channel to Britain. Although the desire for a full-scale assault on Western Europe was unwavering, the Allied forces weren't in a strong enough position to mount it. And with each passing day, casualties continued to rise.

These were the circumstances when the Allies began to discuss a major raid on a French port town. The Americans—who had joined the war effort in December 1941, just after the Japanese attack on Pearl Harbor—were eager to contribute and adamant that a second front was needed to prevent further German expansion in the east. The Russians, who were almost singlehandedly defending the Eastern Front, were also on board. But it was perhaps the Canadians who were the most anxious to have the talk of a raid become a reality.

Canada joined the war effort on September 10, 1939, and troops had arrived on British soil shortly after. At home, politicians were eager to sell stories of heroism and courage to families who had sent their husbands and sons and brothers overseas. But with the British Army pushed off the Continent, those same men hadn't seen any action worth writing home about. They were restless and bored, tired of the endless training and preparations to defend England against an invasion that had yet to materialize. Corporal Robert Prouse of the Canadian Provost Corps represented the feelings of many when he recalled those days. "Like every other soldier," he wrote in an account of his war experiences, "I was bored to tears with the long inaction and was itching for battle."

On the ground with his men in England, Lieutenant General Harry Crerar was keenly aware of toll that boredom was taking. The commander of the Canadian Corps (while General Andrew McNaughton was in Canada on sick leave) worried about the "continued lack of participation" in operations and the difficulty of maintaining the "desired keenness and morale." So when Crerar heard rumours that the Combined Operations Headquarters, under the command of Vice Admiral Lord Louis Mountbatten, was considering a sizeable raid on the French port town of Dieppe, he immediately asked that Canadian troops be allowed to participate. As Crerar told one of his officers at the time, "It will be a tragic humiliation if American troops get into action . . . before Canadians, who have been waiting in England for three years."

The British agreed, and as plans for what came to be called Operation Rutter fell into place, the 2nd Canadian Division was actively involved. The raid, set for July 1, 1942, had two main goals: test new equipment and gain the experience and knowledge required to plan the much larger amphibious assault that would eventually be needed to defeat the Germans. The Canadian commanders, wrote Crerar, "expressed full confidence in being able to carry out their tasks," as long as luck and weather were in their favour.

As it turned out, neither luck nor weather went the Allies' way, and Operation Rutter was called off. Almost immediately, planning began for another attempt, scheduled this time for mid-August.

AS THE CANADIANS AND the British were gearing up for the summer raid on Dieppe, soldiers of an entirely different sort were also training hard. In the coastal town of Dover, a little more than a hundred kilometres southeast of London, a British "pigeon fancier" by the name of Jack Lovell was preparing an avian army for battle.

Animals of all shapes and sizes have been used in war efforts throughout history. Horses have carried men and supplies into battle. Elephants have cleared fields ahead of advancing armies. Dogs have served as guards, as bomb sniffers, and as company for war-weary troops. And birds have often acted as messengers.

Pigeons, in particular, function well in this capacity, thanks to the speed and altitude at which they can fly, and their amazing ability to find their way home over incredibly long distances. Not surprisingly, pigeons have often been an integral part of armed conflict, keeping channels of communication open between armies, spies, and towns. And when hostilities broke out in 1939, the British Secret Service was keen to use these remarkable birds to its advantage.

Throughout the course of the Second World War, thousands of British pigeon owners donated birds to the war effort. More than a million of the birds were used by the army, the Royal Air Force, the Home Guard, the police and fire services, and even by the code breakers at Bletchley Park. The National Pigeon Service volunteer organization was formed to coordinate the training and breeding of birds for service. Lovell was one such trainer and breeder, and after signing the Official Secrets Act, he set up four lofts in Dover and got to work. In the summer of 1942, one of Lovell's "soldiers"—NPS.41.NS.4230, also known as "Beachcomber"—would travel with his human Canadian counterparts into one of the most ill-fated battles of the Second World War.

THE RAID ON DIEPPE, CODENAMED Operation Jubilee, was scheduled to begin at 5 a.m. on August 19, 1942. On paper, the plan was simple enough: more than five thousand troops—the majority of which were Canadian—would land on the beaches in front of the port town. Cover would be provided by ten small ships offshore and by more than seventy squadrons of fighters and fighter-bombers overhead. The objectives were similar to the aborted Operation Rutter: seize and briefly hold the town, gather intelligence, and destroy defences during the retreat.

But absolutely nothing about Dieppe turned out to be simple. Although the town's shoreline was flat, steep white cliffs stood on either side, providing a natural advantage to the German artillery stationed there. British intelligence was also on high alert after a clue in the *Daily Telegraph*'s August 17 crossword—"French port (6)"—seemed designed to tip off the Germans about the location of the raid. And making matters worse, the weather was also a factor. As the raid began, poor conditions caused many landing craft to miss their mark and leave troops far from their designated spots, while the heavy fog made it next to impossible for the commanders stationed on ships just off the coast to maintain visual contact. Despite this, and perhaps because of the fear that the Germans might be aware of their plans, the planners of Operation Jubilee had ordered complete radio silence, effectively cutting the landing troops off from any kind of help, should things go wrong.

Things went wrong almost immediately. From their well-situated positions, German defences bombarded the incoming ships and vessels with artillery fire. The men who did manage to make it ashore were greeted with heavy machine-gun fire that stopped them before they could make any progress inland. Pinned down in the sand, with men dying all around them and radio communications cut off, they watched in horror as the ships from which they'd disembarked turned and retreated to the safety of more open waters. With no other way to get a message to their commanding officers, the men on the beach sent word of their predicament with the only means at their disposal—carrier pigeon.

Despite the horrific and rapidly deteriorating conditions, the soldiers followed the established protocol of releasing two message-carrying birds. The strategy was a hedge against the dangerous conditions in which the birds were flying; they could easily be shot down and were sometimes driven off-course by the noise of the battles on land and in the air. On this particular day, carrier pigeons #2707 and #4230—Beachcomber—were released from the Dieppe beach. Each carried a message from the brigadier in a small container on its leg. Flying through heavy artillery fire and a simultaneous air battle, Pigeon #2707 was killed almost immediately, but Beachcomber made it through. Covering an average of fifty miles per hour, the bird made it back to operational headquarters in less than three hours, and the message he carried about the dire situation on the ground contributed to the decision, made at 9 a.m., to withdraw.

Despite Beachcomber's heroic efforts, it was a decision that came too late for the nearly four thousand men who died in the raid.

ON MARCH 1944—A LITTLE MORE than a year and a half after the disastrous raid—Beachcomber received the Dickin Medal, awarded by the People's Dispensary for Sick Animals in London to animals that have served in military conflict. Noting that Pigeon NPS.41.NS.4230 was receiving the award "for bringing the first news to this country of the landing at

Dieppe, under hazardous conditions . . . while serving with the Canadian Army," Beachcomber's citation reads, in part, "Beachcomber brought the first detailed news of the landing at Dieppe beach, with a second pigeon which was shot down. Beachcomber homed to Army Headquarters in the UK at over 50 mph."

While Beachcomber may have been responsible for delivering the first horrible news about the events playing out on the beaches of Dieppe, he certainly wasn't the only one delivering messages. At 1:40 p.m., as the situation on the beach spiralled further out of control, Major General J. H. Roberts—the commander of the 2nd Canadian Division—composed a grim message to his superiors back in England from the deck of HMS *Calpe*: "Very heavy casualties in men and ships. Did everything possible to get men off but in order to get any home had to come to sad decision to abandon remainder. This was joint decision by Force Commanders. Obviously operation completely lacked surprise."

A pigeon was brought up from the hold, a small container containing the message was attached to its leg, and it was released. On the deck below, the men watched as the bird took flight.

"First one was shot down," recalled John Grand, a member of the Canadian Corps of Signals. "The Germans shot a shell, and he exploded right over the top of the ship. . . . the boys were watching with binoculars and they saw the pigeon go down. So, I went down and brought another pigeon and that one made it. And, you know, that pigeon, it's eighty miles from Dieppe to Portsmouth. There was no coffee breaks and there was no stop on the road, because it was just seawater. And so, they just kept flapping their wings and just flapping their wings and heading off for home."

In June 2010, nearly seventy years after Beachcomber's heroic flight, the *Pigeon Service Message Book 418B*—used to record that first report of Operation Jubilee's disastrous outcome—was put on display on Canadian soil, in Dieppe, New Brunswick.

RYAN BARNETT
AND JOSH MCSWEENEY
In the Nick of Time

*"At the end of the day, you want people
to go home to their families."*

PERCHED ON THE SHORES OF Lake Ontario, Toronto is
Canada's largest city—and the fourth largest in North America. It's home to 2.9 million people, although that number
balloons to nearly six million if the population of the Greater
Toronto Area is taken into account. No matter how you look at
it, Toronto is big, and that means big work for local law enforcement. Nothing much surprises the officers of the Toronto
Police Service. They're used to robberies and assaults, murders
and rapes, domestic disturbances and gang violence. There's
community outreach, too, along with the occasional holiday or
championship parade. Cops in this city are used to a little bit
of everything in their day-to-day work, but it's safe to say that
when Constables Ryan Barnett and Josh McSweeney clocked
in for the afternoon shift on August 7, 2018, the last thing they
expected was to rescue two men from drowning in an elevator.

····

THE STORMS ROLLED THROUGH the city between 9 and
11 p.m. that day, dumping a whopping 72.3 millimetres of rain
on the downtown core. It was all over the news, and all over
social media—pictures of streetcars with water halfway up the
sides; cars trapped in the tunnels that run under the Gardiner
Expressway; commuters slogging through water that cascaded
down subway station stairs and flooded the platforms. It had
been a busy evening for first responders, with fire trucks and
police cruisers answering calls for help that were coming in
from all over the city.

On the western edge of 11 Division's territory, Josh and Ryan
had just wrapped a routine call, nothing out of the ordinary.
They were in the cruiser writing up their notes when a new call
crackled over the radio. A situation was unfolding at a com-
mercial building on Alliance Avenue near Rockcliffe Boulevard, where two men were stuck in an elevator that was quickly
flooding with water. The call was actually from 12 Division—
officially not their turf—but Ryan was pretty sure they were
close. And given how busy the night had been, it wasn't likely
anyone else was going to get there before them. They responded,
and dispatch quickly aired over the call. Within four minutes of
the initial call, Josh and Ryan were on their way. They arrived on
the scene two minutes later, around 11 p.m.

A few people were waiting outside the building—a grey
four-storey structure with a glassed-in stairwell visible from the
parking lot. The officers quickly made their way into the lobby,
where it was immediately apparent that people had already
been trying to help.

"They have a set of [elevator] doors pried open," Josh says. "We can see the elevator at the bottom of the basement. The hatch could only be opened about four or five inches—you could not get out—so we immediately went to the stairs where we could see a high level of water [at the bottom]."

That water in the concrete stairwell was murky and dirty, likely overflow from nearby Black Creek, and only about two inches of the metal doorframe at the bottom of the stairs was visible. With no time to waste, the two men stripped off their vests and gun belts and started to make their way down.

"So as we're going down the gentleman passes us a key, because the door [to the parking garage] was locked . . . of course," says Josh. "We get down to the door and are feeling around because we obviously can't see the lock. We find the keyhole and get it unlocked and then we're both pulling on the door because the water pressure's now pushing on both ends."

With the door finally open, and the garage mercifully lit, Josh and Ryan were able to see the two elevators. They knew the men were trapped in the second elevator, and they could now hear them screaming for help. They swam across the fifteen to twenty feet between the staircase and the elevator bank—the water was high enough that neither man could stand—and pounded on the door. "We're banging on it saying, 'We're here, we're here, we're trying to help you out,'" says Ryan.

But pulling on the elevator door made no difference; they'd need something to help them pry it open. Josh swam back to the stairs, ran to the top, and asked if anyone had a crowbar. A minute later he was downstairs again, a long crowbar in hand.

He swam the tool over to Ryan, who almost immediately realized it wasn't going to do the trick.

"There's too much length," Josh recalls, "and we couldn't get the leverage we needed in there with us kind of floating, basically, and bracing as best we could."

Back upstairs he went, this time looking for a shorter crowbar. Someone handed it to him, and he made his way back down. A quick look around told him that the situation had deteriorated. "I'd say between the time we first got there and then by the time I got back with the second crowbar the water had risen maybe six-plus inches—within a few minutes."

INSIDE THE ELEVATOR, KLEVER FREIRE, thirty-four, and Gabriel Otrin, twenty-seven, were getting increasingly desperate as the space between the water line and the top of the elevator car decreased with each passing moment.

The two men—an aerospace engineer and an industrial designer, respectively—had been working late at Klever's drone-design company, which had offices on the building's fourth floor. As the rain poured down on Toronto that evening, the building's custodian had reached out to tenants to suggest that they check on their cars in the underground parking lot. Klever's SUV was there, so he and Gabriel hopped in the elevator, hit the button for the garage, and waited. The first sign of trouble was the splash-landing; the second was the murky water that immediately began to seep into the car.

Within the first five minutes, Gabriel says, it was "pretty clear" what was going to happen. At first, they tried to force the doors to open, but they wouldn't budge. They thought about calling for help, but neither could get a cell signal.

"We were trying to find emergency latches, instructions on how to get out and we were looking for things we could use for leverage to force the doors open but we weren't able to find any instructions inside the elevator and the emergency phone was dead because of the water coming through, so our last hope was finding a way to get a cell signal," Klever says. "At some point we just decided that this wasn't going to be it and we started punching through the panels."

By now, they two men were standing on the car's handrails and were still chin-deep in water. When they finally managed to knock loose a panel, they could tell immediately that it wasn't enough space for a person to wiggle through. They did, however, manage to push a cellphone out and make a 911 call.

And then they waited. As Gabriel quietly prayed, Klever thought about his thirteen-year-old daughter; he'd planned to take her to a movie that night before discovering he needed to work late. "I was using the elevator buttons as a reference for how quickly the water was rising. We probably had three or four minutes left before it was full," he says. "In that moment you do think about the people that are going to be affected if something happens to you."

A bit more than six minutes after Klever and Gabriel placed the call, they heard Constables Barnett and McSweeney banging on the other side of the elevator door. It was, says Klever, the first moment of relief they'd had since the ordeal began.

••••

BACK IN THE PARKING GARAGE, Josh passed the shorter crowbar to his partner. At first, the two men tried to pry open the door from the right-hand side, but it wasn't working. "We're talking with the two guys on the other side and asking them if they can recall which way the door opens up," says Josh, who at this point was standing on some sort of railing outside the elevator doors. "It turned out it was a left-to-right motion. Luckily, Ryan had the crowbar, because he's a little taller than me, so he's got a little more leverage."

"We just kind of jammed it in the corner and I kind of squished myself in the frame and used the leverage," Ryan adds. "Both of us were reefing on it pretty good and got it open. It's just lucky—we happened to work together and got it open."

Klever and Gabriel wasted no time getting out of the elevator. Gabriel began to swim for the stairwell, but Klever—who'd had lifeguard training as a teenager—needed help. "Once we knew we'd be OK, I gave myself the freedom to relax for a bit and forget how to swim," he says.

Ryan and Josh, realizing the man was likely in shock, grabbed a hold of him and swam him to safety. Once upstairs, dripping wet and still severely shaken, Klever accepted a shot of vodka from one the building's other tenants, and then turned around and gave Ryan a giant bear hug. It was, all told, the happiest ending imaginable, and it happened in the nick of time. As best as Josh can figure, they'd had maybe five more minutes before it would have been too late.

••••

THE NEXT DAY, JOSH AND RYAN found themselves in front of the media answering questions about the dramatic rescue. Yes, they'd been allowed to clock out a bit early—they both needed to shower, and the jury was out on whether their uniforms would survive the ordeal (Josh had already written off his boots). No, they'd never had to pry open an elevator door in the line of duty before, and while they hadn't had any specific training for this type of situation, they'd followed protocol by taking a goal-oriented approach and solving one problem at a time. And no—definitely no—they didn't think of themselves as heroes.

"It's nice to be called a hero, but that's what we're supposed to be doing," said Josh, who'd been on the job for thirteen years at the time. "It's nice to help them out."

"It's what we're here for," Ryan added. "At the end of the day, you want people to go home to their families. It's what we want to do. . . . I think any officer in that situation would have done the exact same thing. Police officers do this for a reason: to save people."

While it's certainly true that police officers and other first responders routinely put themselves in danger as part of their job, it's still nice to be recognized for the effort. Ryan and Josh shared officer of the month honours in August 2018, and in May 2019, nearly nine months to the day after the rescue on Alliance Avenue, they shared another award: officer of the year.

Speaking to a capacity crowd at the awards ceremony, Ryan acknowledged that this particular call was unique in his twenty-one years of service. "Nothing else comes close," he said, before adding that every other officer nominated was equally deserving.

"As far as I'm concerned, there should be twelve winners; there were some amazing stories."

While Ryan's assessment is no doubt true—there's no shortage of courage among Toronto's finest—it's a pretty safe bet which officers Klever and Gabriel would have voted for, given a chance.

REBECKA BLACKBURN
Right Place, Right Time

"You can never underestimate the current."

JUNE 20, 2018. IT HAD been a pretty typical day for eighteen-year-old Rebecka Blackburn. A thirty-minute drive from her home in Leduc, Alberta, to the Devon Community Pool, stopping for a coffee on the way. Six hours on deck as a lifeguard, and another hour in the water teaching swimming lessons. She'd clocked out, showered off, and was thinking about what the evening might hold when she checked her phone and saw the message from her mom. Irene Blackburn and a few of her friends were close by, enjoying the warm evening at the shore of the North Saskatchewan River. Would Rebecka stop by and say hello?

Why not? She didn't have any pressing plans, the weather was beautiful, and it would be nice to dip her toes in the water and relax for a bit after a busy day at work. A few minutes later, Rebecka was dressed and on her way.

••••

THE NORTH SASKATCHEWAN RIVER STARTS its eastward flow in the Columbia Icefields, high in the Rocky Mountains. It cuts through Alberta and Saskatchewan before draining into Lake Winnipeg, the Nelson River, and eventually Hudson Bay—a thirteen-hundred-kilometre journey in all. Forty-five minutes southwest of Edmonton, the town of Devon is perched on its banks. The shoreline and river bottom are rocky here, and the currents often swift, which makes the North Saskatchewan a less than ideal spot for a swim. Still, locals and visitors come to the water when the weather cooperates, eager to catch a breeze, wade in up to their knees, or, on calm days, inflate a raft and float for a bit.

Rebecka arrived at the river at about 7:15 p.m. She quickly found her mother at the water's edge—there weren't too many others at the shore that night—pulled up a lawn chair and sat down. They'd been chatting for fifteen minutes or so when something out on the water caught Rebecka's eye.

"I looked out at the river and noticed a man quite far out splashing awkwardly," she recalls. "I brought it to my mother's attention and asked if she thought he was okay."

At first, Rebecka didn't think there was anything to worry about. The man's friends were nearby, pointing and laughing and making fun of his awkward-looking swimming techniques. It seemed likely that this was all a joke, that they were just fooling around. Within a few minutes, though, the current pushed him closer, and Rebecka heard him yell for help. Her instincts instantly took over.

"I kicked off my flip-flops and started running into the river in his direction," she says. Her mother's friend Sommer King followed her in, along with one of the man's friends, but the strong current made them both think twice about going out past the point where they could stand.

"One of his buddies—he admitted he wasn't the greatest swimmer," Rebecka recalls. "I was like, 'You stay here, I'm going out.' I would say it was about seventy-five metres, trying to go diagonally across the river."

She swam in a "head-up" front crawl toward the man, keeping her eyes on him the entire time. She was just over a metre away when he stopped struggling and went under. She remembers thinking, "Oh my gosh, here we go." Once again, she didn't hesitate. Drawing on the lessons she'd learned while training to become a lifeguard three years earlier, she dove down, grabbed his body, and performed a hip carry as she turned to make her way back to shore.

Like Sommer and the man's friend, Rebecka had noticed the strong current as she swam out to where the man was flailing in the water, but it wasn't until she was pulling him to safety that she really felt the effects. "At this point, my legs were numb from exhaustion," she recalls. "The man was pushing down on me for support, and I had never felt so weak and vulnerable in the water."

She kept going, though, pushing herself forward until she was finally able to touch down. As Rebecka struggled to regain her footing on the rocky bottom, Sommer was there to assist. Together, they brought the man to shore, where he regained his breath. The whole rescue, Rebecka figures, took ten minutes at most.

Because he was conscious and breathing, emergency responders were not called, though Rebecka suggested he seek medical attention in case of secondary drowning—a potentially fatal condition that can occur when water has been inhaled into the lungs. Later that night, one of the man's friends reached out on Facebook to say that the man hadn't gone to the hospital, but that he seemed to be fine. "Thanks," the message concluded, "you were a hero today."

WATER HAS ALWAYS BEEN REBECKA'S safe place, the place she finds peace. For as long as she can remember, she's been happiest in or on the water. Ocean, lake, swimming pool—it hardly matters. Her family calls her a mermaid, and the joke is that if they are on vacation and Rebecka can't be found, she's probably swimming somewhere.

No surprise, then, that she joined a swim club when she was four or five years old. She remembers that she was too young, technically, to start public swimming lessons, but she still wanted to be at the pool. For eight years, she swam competitively for the Leduc Otters, and when she was fifteen, signed up for a collaborative aquatic leadership program between the local recreation centre and her high school, where she earned certifications as a Red Cross Lifeguard, as a Water Safety Instructor, and in First Aid. She was hired as a lifeguard and instructor by the Leduc Recreation Centre pool in 2015, when she was sixteen. Two years later, after completing her National Lifeguard certification, she took on a second job in the same capacity at the Devon Community Pool.

She is without a doubt comfortable in the water—"very strong and well-trained," she acknowledges—which is why she didn't hesitate to wade into the North Saskatchewan River to rescue a drowning man. Even with all of her training, though, the day's events were shocking.

"I have never experienced a rescue that was as scary or intense as this one," she says, "and I'm thankful my training kicked in to autopilot. I was completely taken aback when I fatigued so quickly . . . even with the immense adrenaline that I had pumping through my body, I still have never felt so exhausted swimming in such a short period of time."

It was overwhelming to feel so "attacked" by water—the element that usually brings her peace—and to wonder, in the midst of her rescue effort, whether she'd be able to make it back to safety. "It just goes to show that no matter how strong of a swimmer you are, how confident you are in your swimming skills, you can never underestimate the current and the strength of it."

In the weeks and months following the rescue, Rebecka's actions were recognized with numerous awards and honours. The Red Cross Rescuer Award was, she says, "surreal," given that she'd been a member of the organization since she was fifteen years old. The Carnegie Hero Award—which Sommer King also received—was especially humbling, as it's given to only a few Canadians each year, men and women who have done extraordinary things. The Leduc Citizen of Distinction Award was special, too, and made her feel that the people in the city she calls home supported and were proud of her. But it was the Lifesaving Society Rescue Award that really stood out. Awarded by Lois Mitchell, the lieutenant governor of Alberta, and presented to Rebecka in a formal ceremony alongside members of the RCMP, it helped her recognize that her calm and professional response to a dangerous situation had indeed been special. While she's deeply honoured by the attention—especially since it shone a spotlight on issues around water safety—she still has trouble thinking of herself as a hero.

"It's been difficult for me to view myself as worthy of all the recognition and praise I have received, as I often feel like what I did was so small in comparison to what others have done and continue to do," she says. "I truly feel like I was just in the right place at the right time and I did not even think about what I was doing. I just reacted and did what needed to be done."

In fact, it wasn't until she got home that evening that the gravity of the situation hit her, she says. "I was very emotional as I replayed the incident over and over again in my head and thought of all the ways it could have ended differently."

These days, Rebecka is a kinesiology student at the University of Alberta, on her way to pursuing a graduate degree in chiropractic or physical therapy. She no longer works at the pool in Devon, having given that job up to focus on her studies and on her new position as aquatic supervisor at the outdoor pool in Leduc. The riverside rescue is well in the past now, but she thinks about it every time she crosses the High Level Bridge on her way into Edmonton and looks down on the churning waters of the North Saskatchewan River. She knows that her quick thinking and strength led to a happy ending, but not a day goes by that she doesn't remember the strength of the current, the weight of the man she carried on her hip, and how weak she felt in the water. "Every time I drive across that river I am brought back to that moment of pure exhaustion and fear," she says. "It was definitely a scary situation, but I am proud of myself for not hesitating and for trusting my training to save a life."

LES LEHMANN
Shots in the Dark

"There's luck and then there's something beyond luck."

THE CONDO COMPLEX ON the beach was a retirement plan of sorts. For Les and Lynda Lehmann, the idea was to earn a bit of income by running the place while also benefiting from a lifestyle change. Puerto Plata doesn't have a lot in common with Winnipeg: sand instead of snow, balmy ocean breezes instead of frigid winter gales, a laidback atmosphere instead of the hustle and bustle of a busy Canadian city.

The ads went up on TripAdvisor and other accommodation-rental sites, tempting travellers with pictures of lush gardens and a tranquil pool, and descriptions of the beach known for its calm waters and breezy weather—perfect conditions for wind-surfing, kiteboarding, and sailing. And people came. Soon, the couple's days were busy. Lynda looked after the bookings while Les took care of the property. In the evenings, he could often be found playing his guitar and singing at a local watering hole. Life was good.

January 30, 2014, was a typical day at the complex. The Lehmanns welcomed a school group from Winnipeg's Division Scolaire Franco-Manitobaine, who were in the Dominican Republic for a week of humanitarian work at a nearby school and orphanage. With the twenty-two students and four chaperones settled in, Les retired for the evening. But at 1 a.m., a strange noise and barking dogs got him up and out of bed. The sixty-four-year-old reached for a machete before heading out into the night to check the gated property for signs of trouble.

Within moments, he found it.

THE LADDER WAS THE FIRST clue that something was amiss. It was leaning up against a balcony, and the screen to that unit had been cut. Les looked around but found no one. Figuring that perhaps the dogs had scared the would-be intruders off, he decided to head home.

It was on his way back to his own bungalow that things took a turn for the worse. Out of the darkness, two men appeared. Towels covered their faces, making them impossible to identify, but there was no mistaking the raised pistol each man held, pointed directly at Les. Using the only weapon he had at his disposal, Les banged the machete on a nearby table and began to yell at the top of his lungs, hoping that the noise would alert his guests and neighbours and possibly spook the two men.

It didn't work. Shots were fired, one of which hit Les's left arm. Numb to the pain—perhaps due to shock, perhaps due to the adrenaline that was surging through his system—he kept banging the machete until it broke. Then he made a mad dash for home. The two men followed him inside and delivered a savage ten-minute beating, kicking and stomping and pistol-whipping the man who had interrupted their plans. With Les crumpled on the floor, the burglars left.

Still conscious despite the violence, Les watched the two men make their way across the complex, turning on lights to guide them. He knew exactly where they were heading—to the rooms housing the school kids and their chaperones. A single thought circled in his mind.

"I was responsible for these young kids," he says, "a lot of them were sixteen-, seventeen-year-old girls and it was their first time away in a strange country and, oh my God, if one of these guys had happened to have hurt one, you know, or fired a gun and one of them accidentally gets killed, that would have been horrible."

What happened to him, he decided, didn't matter. He had to do something.

Dragging himself to his feet, he grabbed a hammer—the first weapon he could find—and followed the two men. Quickly, though, he changed his mind, returned to the bungalow, and emerged again with a baseball bat in hand.

Security camera footage tells the rest of the horrific tale: the intruders kicking in a door, one of them entering the apartment while the other keeps watch; Les arriving on the scene and hitting the look-out in the head with the bat; the second intruder coming back out of the apartment and shooting Les twice and trying to pull his unconscious partner away at the same time; Les coming at him a second time, taking additional shots, stumbling now but raising the baseball bat again, and then falling under a third round of gunfire; the intruders escaping through a hole they'd cut in the property's chain-link fence; Les fashioning a tourniquet out of his shirt, wrapping it around his arm before collapsing.

The damage was extensive. In addition to the injuries sustained during the beating, Les had been shot nine times at close range, and a tenth bullet grazed his knee. His left arm and right knee were broken; a nerve in his left arm was severed. Bullets ripped across his chest and through his scrotum. And then there was the blood loss. By the time he arrived at a local hospital, he had just 1.5 litres left. Although none of the bullets stayed in his body, he nevertheless needed four hours of emergency surgery to repair the immediate damage, and he would require additional surgeries, and months of rehab and physical therapy, to heal.

The fact that he was still alive is, says his daughter-in-law Eugenia Lehmann, a miracle. "The doctors in the Dominican Republic have never seen anyone survive nine gun shots."

For his part, Les puts it down to luck.

"The first thought through my mind was, 'You're one lucky person.' I can see holes all over me but there was no blood spurting out of them. Any one of those bullets could've opened up an artery or something. I was still breathing okay. I didn't get one in the head. I thought, 'Hell, you're okay.'

"When you get shot from ten feet away and you get hit ten

times and you basically don't really get hurt that badly, it makes you wonder why," he says. "There's luck and then there's something beyond luck.

"Even 30 seconds after it happened, as I was laying there, I thought, 'You are one lucky person, because you're going to walk away from this,'" he says.

Looking back on the incident, Les knows that he wasn't thinking rationally, that he was acting purely on instinct.

"There was two guns pointed at me and I thought I'll just go crazy and be totally irrational," he says. "I thought they wouldn't shoot at me because I didn't have a gun, or a weapon, so my logic was they won't shoot me."

Les concedes that things didn't work out quite the way he'd planned, but he doesn't regret the actions he took. Although four students and a teacher were briefly held at gunpoint, none of Les and Lynda's guests were injured, and the Canadian embassy helped to get them home safely the next day.

ON OCTOBER 28, 2016, the Lehmann family travelled to Ottawa's Rideau Hall to watch Les—husband, father, and grandfather—receive the Star of Courage from Governor General David Johnston. The second highest of Canada's bravery awards, it recognizes "acts of conspicuous courage in circumstances of peril."

Les's family knows he's deserving of the recognition, as do the teachers and students from Division Scolaire Franco-Manitobaine. Les, though, isn't so sure.

"He doesn't feel what he did was heroic," says his son Sean. "He felt what he did, he had to do, and that anyone in that situation would do the same thing."

"It's something that happened," says Les, who admits to being humbled by the award. "It's ten minutes of my life that it occurred. First responders run into danger all the time and don't get thanked for it nearly enough . . . I just reacted in an irrational way and got away with it. I'm a lucky person."

Les is almost fully healed. He spent weeks in the hospital, both in the Dominican Republic and back in Canada, used a wheelchair for more than two months, and had numerous surgeries to repair the damage to his knee and arm. Rehab was gruelling, but he now walks with almost no limp and can once again play the guitar. He and Lynda still run the condo complex on the beach—where the chain-link fence has been replaced with a ten-foot concrete wall—and they still enjoy their life in this tropical paradise. If someone offered them a good enough price, they might be tempted to sell and leave, but they're not in any hurry. What happened to him, Les says, could have happened anywhere.

"I don't live in fear," he says. "If it had happened in Winnipeg, what would I do? Leave Winnipeg? Move where? You can always have a home invasion or a break-in any place in the world."

And, after all, he's got luck on his side.

RALPH JOYCE
Out on the Edge

"I got ya buddy, I got ya."

LARK HARBOUR, NEWFOUNDLAND, IS A pretty place to call home—although less than a thousand people do. Could be that's one of the charms of living in this small fishing community on the province's west coast. No crowds on streets or in shops, no hustle and bustle on the daily commute, and just about an hour from Corner Brook, if the desire to be in a city should strike. But the scenery is definitely the main draw. The Bay of Islands—where Lark Harbour and neighbouring York Harbour can both be found—is considered one of Newfoundland's best kept secrets, and a popular network of hiking trails offers visitors plenty of opportunities to explore the area's nooks, coves, and crannies. The remote beaches, towering cliffs, and panoramic views of the Gulf of St. Lawrence never fail to impress.

Even the folk lucky enough to see it all every day aren't immune. Which is exactly why John Parsons and Ralph Joyce were out on the Bottle Cove trail on the morning of February 7, 2019. John had been puttering in the kitchen of his house, not too far from the beach, when he glanced through the window and noticed a seal out on the ice. He figured it would make a great picture—something to show the grandkids, maybe—so he grabbed his camera, bundled up against the cold, and headed out, hoping he'd be able to get a good shot from the trailhead. In the parking lot, he happened to meet up with Ralph Joyce, not an unusual occurrence since Ralph walks twice a day in the area, sometimes with John and sometimes without. On this particular day, the men got to talking and decided to hike to the trailhead together.

A good decision if ever there was one.

ALTHOUGH THE MORNING OF FEBRUARY 7 was plenty chilly, the week before had been on the mild side, and Lark Harbour had had its fair share of rain. As the two men made their way up toward the trailhead, they noticed that the snow-covered path had grass showing through here and there. Same thing out on the point, which overlooks the cove from atop a rugged thirty-metre cliff. Stepping carefully, John inched out past where the grass left off, trying for a better view. He didn't notice that the ground—normally a mixture of sand, rock, and gravel—was covered by a solid sheet of ice.

"My feet came out from under me, I went on my back. And I was on my back sliding down, down over the cliff into the water on the ice," Parsons says. "About two feet from the edge, there was a small rock sticking out. And that rock held up against my foot on the left side—my boot—and I was there on my back. And Ralph was standing there and he said, 'My God, don't move, don't move.'"

Ralph had been a few feet behind John on the trail when John lost his footing. It was a terrifying sight, watching his friend slip toward the edge of the cliff, and for a moment, Ralph feared the worst. But when he realized that John had somehow managed to stop his slide, he knew he needed to do something. And fast. He turned tail and headed back toward the car as quickly as he could go, shouting to John to stay calm as he went. He knew that he likely didn't have time to get all the way to the parking lot and drive out to get help, so he wracked his brain for another plan. He pictured himself having to tell John's wife, Sharon, that her husband had gone over the cliff and immediately banished the thought from his head. That's not how this was going to end—not if he could help it.

The trail had rope along some of the walkways, so that was an option—and the best one he could come up with at first—but he knew that even getting to the rope might take longer than John had. Desperate for another idea, Ralph stopped to catch his breath and looked around for a tool he could use. There were plenty of trees nearby, but any branches that happened to be on the ground were frozen into the earth. Nevertheless, Ralph knew it was his best hope. He found a strong-looking stick, twelve or so feet long, and set to digging it out. Eventually, he was able to pry it loose.

Ralph dashed back to the point and, with some trepidation, checked to see if his friend had managed to hang on.

"I peeped down to make sure that he was still there," he says. Miraculously, John was just where he'd been when Ralph took off running for help, left foot still wedged against the small rock sticking out of the ice—the only thing stopping him from plunging over the edge of the cliff and into the icy waters below.

John had never been so glad to see another person in his life. "I said, 'Ralph, my God don't let me go, don't let me go,'" he says.

"I got ya buddy, I got ya," Ralph replied as he extended the branch out to his friend.

The next part was tricky. Ralph was a smaller man than John, and he knew that pulling John to safety was going to require leverage—which was in short supply on the icy surface of the point. A nearby rock looked like his best hope, so he shoved his foot against it, braced himself, and started to pull.

"As he was pulling me up, when my foot came off the rock, that was a scary moment because there was nothing to hold me," Parsons says. "If the tree broke or Ralph couldn't hold me or didn't have the strength I was probably gone."

He needn't have worried. A few moments later, both men were back on solid ground.

AFTER MAKING HIS WAY HOME and telling his wife all that had happened, John Parsons went back to the trail and hung a sign, warning fellow hikers of the danger lurking at the cliff's edge. Later that day, Ralph came by to check on his friend. Sharon Parsons recalls practically lifting him through the door in a bear hug, and how she spent much of the next two days in tears.

It took both Sharon and John a while to process the events of that day, and to come to terms with how lucky they were that it had turned out as well as it did. One thing they knew right away, though, was that Ralph deserved to be recognized for his efforts. The couple didn't waste any time in filling out a nomination form for the province's bravery award. And in July of 2020, in the midst of the COVID-19 pandemic that caused lockdowns and physical distancing all over the country, a small ceremony was held on the Parsonses' deck overlooking the spectacular scenery of Bottle Cove. Member of House Assembly Eddie Joyce, standing in for Lieutenant Governor Judy May Foote, presented Ralph with his award—a framed certificate and a medal featuring a stylized image of the province's trademark rugged cliffs and ocean waves.

Ralph was honoured to receive the award, but more thankful, really, for the fact that he was able to help when it counted.

"The main thing was I got him out of it," he says.

For his part, John was thrilled when he and Sharon learned that their nomination had been successful.

"It's absolutely wonderful to know that his bravery on that day and his courage and his strength literally saved my life," he says. "I just don't know how to thank the man for it other than to live the best life I can and maybe help someone down the road at some point in time."

JOHN PARSONS HAS DONE HIS best to put the events of February 7, 2019, behind him. The outdoors is a big part of his life, and he has no intention of locking himself inside on cold or rainy days. He still hikes, although he's promised Sharon to use a tether if he ever finds himself on the cliffs in less than ideal weather.

Ralph hasn't been so quick to get back on the trails. There are too many memories, he says, too many reminders that it could just as easily have ended badly, or that it could have been him instead of John teetering on the edge.

"I could have went on just as well as him," he says. "I didn't think about that at the time."

Although they don't meet up on the trails as often as they used to, there's no question that Ralph and John's relationship has changed.

"Every time I see Ralph, there's something inside of me that says, 'This chap saved my life,'" John says. "We're connected," he adds, "and we will be connected for the rest of our lives because of what happened that day."

LIAM BERNARD
AND SHANE BERNARD
Playing with Fire

*"I just gathered enough energy and
something just came into me."*

YOU CAN CATCH HIGHWAY 105 in Port Hastings, Nova
Scotia, just over the causeway that separates Cape Breton from
the rest of the province. For the first fifty or so kilometres, up
to the rural community of Whycocomagh, the two-lane road
cuts more or less through the centre of the island, carving a
path amid the rolling hills and green valleys that give way, the
farther north you go, to the spectacular Cape Breton Highlands
that have made this area such a popular destination with locals
and tourists alike.

But on the morning of September 16, 2016, sightseeing was
the last thing on Shane Bernard's mind. He and his best friend
Liam—also a Bernard, though not related—were heading south
off the island toward Halifax in search of work. The two thirty-
seven-year-olds from Waycobah First Nation were somewhere

between Melford and Glendale when their plans for the day took an unexpected turn.

It was clear the accident had just happened. A southbound pickup truck pulling a camper had collided with a northbound SUV. "We arrived there moments after the collision," Shane says. "Smoke everywhere, shrapnel, plastic, people screaming . . ." Despite everything that would happen over the next several minutes, it's the sense of utter chaos that has stayed with him. That, and the image of a hand pressed against the window of a smoke-filled truck.

BY THE TIME SHANE AND LIAM took in what they were seeing and pulled over to help, others had stopped as well. When the two men got out of their own vehicle and approached the scene, they learned that the woman in the SUV had died. But the two men and the dog trapped in the truck, which was now on its side in a ditch, on fire, were still alive. They quickly helped the first man slide out of the truck, and the dog figured out how to escape on its own. But with the second man, the driver, it wouldn't be as easy.

"He couldn't move," says Liam, and the fire was getting worse by the moment. "I was thinking that I probably had another minute or two to get him out of there."

Realizing that the man was trapped, and that they were in a race against time, he asked Shane to go find a fire extinguisher—fast. Then he turned back to the driver. In his mind, he ticked off the challenges one by one. With the driver's side of the vehicle up in the air, the man would have to be lifted out.

Given the man's height—over six feet, Liam estimated—and the fact that the dashboard was crushing his legs, the manoeuvre wouldn't be simple.

Even so, Liam knew exactly what he had to do. "I went in the truck and got the seatbelt off him and I told him I was going to try to get him out of there. I'm pulling at him and he's screaming, and underneath the dash part where the wheel is, it was pinned against his leg and I knew his leg was broken," he says. "So I had to rip out the stereo and rip out underneath the dash so I can get his legs free. Then I started pulling at him and I couldn't get at him and I am pulling as hard as I can and the flames are just getting bigger. Someone came with a fire extinguisher but they couldn't douse it out."

Nothing Liam tried worked, and with smoke rapidly filling the cab of the truck, the driver seemed to give up.

"He noticed I couldn't do it and it was getting too dangerous for me," Liam says. "He kind of pushed away from me and said: 'It's OK. Everything's going to be OK. Just get out. It's too dangerous.'"

With his lungs filling with smoke, Liam took the man's advice. He got out of the truck, but he had no intention of staying out. He gave himself enough time to quickly catch his breath and then headed back in.

"I just gathered enough energy and something just came into me—they tried to stop me," he says of the others who had gathered at the scene, "but I could hear him screaming for his life. I told them, get out of my way."

Liam climbed back on top of the truck and then right into the cramped and damaged cab. Shane and a few other men grabbed him by his belt loops and made sure the door stayed open. Liam pulled desperately on the driver, and Shane and the men pulled on Liam as the flames grew higher.

"It must have been pretty hot in there because I remember when I was holding the door, like, I could literally feel the hair burning on the side of my head, curling up and smelling that stink," Shane says.

Finally, they wrenched the man free of the truck—just in time.

"A minute or two later, that thing just started blowing up and it was in flames," says Liam. "If it wasn't for the help of those men and my friend Shane, that man wouldn't be here today . . . They didn't let go and we ended up saving his life."

"If it wasn't for those other men, I'd be dead too," he adds.

Although she wasn't on the scene that day, Shane's sister Nadine Bernard has a clear memory of the aftermath. Rather than continuing on to Halifax, the two men had made their way back to Whycocomagh, where Nadine had just hung up the phone with a co-worker who'd called to explain why she was late.

"She tells me she had witnessed this horrific car accident in Glendale," Nadine says. A pickup truck had gone into a ditch and was on fire, the woman told her, and "two men were in there burning and these two crazy guys ran up to the burning vehicle . . . jumped into the burning vehicle and dragged the men out to save them. 'I said are you kidding me? That's insane.'"

A few minutes later, her brother and Liam showed up, looking more than a little worse for the wear. It only took a few minutes for Nadine to connect the dots. Once she'd heard the whole story, she asked Liam what had possessed him to crawl into the cab of a burning truck. He told her that the driver was alive and a human being. "That's just what you do," he said.

THOSE ARE WORDS BOTH Shane and Liam choose to live by. "We are both the type of people who would do anything for you," says Liam. "We would give you the shirt off our back."

A few years before the accident on Highway 105, Liam helped rescue a toddler trapped in an overturned egg truck on the same road. In July 2011, Shane swam out into dangerous waters to rescue two girls who were drowning in the strong undertow off Mira Gut. (Shane, a father of two, didn't want to leave the stranded girls. "They looked pretty scared," he says. "They were young, like my daughter's size at the time.") And in 2010, in Glace Bay, he helped put out a fire on a fishing boat.

But even a track record of helping when help is needed doesn't prepare you for everything. A few years have passed since the fiery rescue, but it's still hard to shake the day's images.

"Cuts, scrapes, and bruises, they come and go," says Shane, "but the images from the accident, sometimes they bother me."

It helps to know that they prevented the situation from being any worse than it already was when they arrived on the scene and also that their actions were appreciated. At the time, Liam and Shane didn't know the name of the man they'd rescued; once the driver was free, they went on their way and left the first responders to their work. But later, the man they'd pulled from the cab of a burning truck—US resident Ralph Chrisman—put an ad in a local newspaper, trying to find them. Liam responded, and they've kept in touch.

Then came the awards. In June 2017, Liam received the Governor General's Star of Courage and Shane a letter of commemoration for their role in the fiery rescue. In November 2017, both men were awarded the provincial medal for bravery. And in late 2018, Liam became the sole Canadian in that year's class of Carnegie Hero Fund medal recipients.

"I don't know how to feel about that award," says Liam of the Star of Courage. "It's just for my kids really . . . something for them to have."

"I would have to do it again," he adds. "I wouldn't want to but I would have to if no one was going to do anything. It's in my nature I guess."

Liam was working in Alberta when the Nova Scotia Medals of Bravery were awarded, so his seventeen-year-old daughter, Nevada Francis, received the medal on his behalf. She told those gathered that she wished her father could have been there for the ceremony, and that she was proud of him. Afterward, Shane reflected on the events that had led to the award he never expected to receive.

"We showed up at those places at that time for those people. That's how an elder told me, one time, to look at it," he said.

It helps to think of it that way—to believe that there was some unseen hand guiding him and his best friend through that day—but he also knows there was no guarantee of a happy ending. "I recognize it was a high-risk situation and there's a possibility that I may have not made it home to my family that morning," he said. "So, I'm going to take this time to enjoy it with my family and just appreciate the simple things in life."

At least until the next time someone needs help.

COLLEEN O'REILLY
Everything for a Reason

"God gives you what you need, not what you want."

GROWING UP IN PLACENTIA, NEWFOUNDLAND, Colleen O'Reilly and her sister had the usual playthings to occupy their time: crayons and colouring books, dolls, bats and balls and other sports equipment, puzzles and games. But the O'Reilly house had something a bit different to throw into the mix—a lifesaving dummy.

At the time, Gerard "Whitey" O'Reilly was the province's only certified chemical firefighter. He was also a popular first-aid instructor for nearby colleges as well as local Scout, Girl Guide, and Brownie troops. The lifesaving dummy—which goes by the nickname "Annie"—often made its way home with him, and he never missed an opportunity to introduce his daughters to lifesaving techniques.

"I feel like I spent my whole life with this dummy," says Colleen, who admits that she used to find the big bag with a hole for a mouth more than a little terrifying. "But my father made a game out of teaching us how to do the Heimlich manoeuvre. Even so, we'd roll our eyes and complain about how boring it was, but he was just making sure we'd know what to do if we ever needed to help."

Perhaps not surprisingly, given her father's influence, Colleen kept up her first-aid training when she moved to St. John's and started a life of her own. As an employee of the province's Department of Finance and also as a staff supervisor at a local entertainment and catering company, she took workplace health and safety courses when they were offered and made sure her CPR and other lifesaving skills were current.

"You do this stuff because it's the right thing to do, and you just never know," she says, "but half the time you're thinking it's boring and that you're not actually getting it. But my advice is to do the course anyways, because it really does matter."

IT WAS DURING HER LUNCH break on July 13, 2016, that Colleen found out just how important first-aid training really is.

The finance department kept her busy between nine and five, but her evenings and weekends belonged to Spirit of Newfoundland. The food and entertainment company runs a St. John's dinner theatre out of the historic Masonic Temple on Cathedral Street, caters local events, and operates Marconi's, a popular lunch spot in the Johnson Geo Centre on Signal Hill. Spirit has been in operation for twenty-three years, and Colleen is proud to say she's been around for twenty of them. The company has produced and performed more than eighty-six original shows.

"There's seventy people on staff," she says, "and I'm like a mom or an aunt to all of them—it's more like family than work. There's always something to do: food and beverage planning, getting the cast on stage, sorting out the floor plans. Every bit of that changes every day, so it keeps you busy."

On this particular day, Colleen headed down to Marconi's on her lunch break, as she often did. Spirit of Newfoundland had an event that night at the Geo Centre, and she wanted to pop in to say hello and check on a few things, to make sure all of the necessary ducks were in a row. She was chatting with friends when the commotion started.

"Somebody was screaming, 'He's choking, he's choking,'" she says.

She looked around and saw a woman and a young boy—she put him somewhere between eight and ten—at a nearby table. As the other patrons looked on, horrified, Colleen ran over to the boy.

"He wasn't breathing and was holding his chest," she recalls. "With that, I grabbed him and did what I had to do. I hit him on the back, did two pumps of the Heimlich manoeuvre, and did it again and again. On the third time, six thrusts later, two pieces of watermelon flew out."

It was over in a matter of moments.

"The whole thing's a bit of a blur," she says, "but people told me I 'sprang into action.' I honestly couldn't say, because my mind was a blank. But all of that training—with my dad and with the courses I've taken since—I instantly came back to what I was supposed to do."

The aftermath of the incident is hazy as well. She remembers it being an emotional moment, with many of the ten or fifteen people in the café crying with relief. The little boy was crying, too, as was the woman with him. "He hugged me—they both hugged me. They were so appreciative," she says.

"She was his aunt, home from Australia for her wedding the next day, and the little boy was going to be part of the ceremony. They were out for some aunt-and-nephew time," she continues, admitting that she never did learn their names. "It was a really frightening moment."

She doesn't remember this specifically, but she's been told that she was "shaking like a leaf and as white as a ghost." What she does recall is that once the adrenaline wore off, she started to throw up—right in the middle of the café. "Not a pretty story," she jokes, "but there you have it! Someone brought a bucket and put it in front of me and gave me some water."

After a few moments, she pulled herself together and left. She still needed to stop by the dinner theatre, so she headed there next. When concerned colleagues took one look at her—still pale and shaky—and asked if she was okay, the throwing up started again.

"I took the rest of the day off from my government job and hung out with them and just talked. Spirit is my happy place, my comfort place—Spirit and the music. So I stayed there, working away, listening to music, until I went home that night, still in a little bit of shock."

Not wanting to call attention to herself ("I'm not the actress on the stage," she says), Colleen didn't tell anyone else about what had happened. But her co-workers had other ideas. They believed that her quick thinking and action—which had prevented a horrible tragedy—deserved recognition. And so, Paul

Bugge and Kara Noftle, both general managers at Spirit of Newfoundland, put her name forward for a St. John Ambulance Life-saving Award. On May 24, 2018, at the Anglican Cathedral in St. John's, Lieutenant Governor Judy May Foote presented the award to Colleen and several other deserving recipients.

"I didn't tell anyone at all about the award until about a week before," she says, but eventually she realized that the people who loved her would want to be there. "Once I told everybody . . . well . . . my whole department of finance came, friends came, family, Spirit of Newfoundland. There was a dinner reception at the lieutenant governor's house afterward. It was a very proud moment, but at the same time, it was very humbling."

A FEW YEARS HAVE PASSED since that day in the café, and Colleen has thought about it often. She didn't used to believe in that old adage about how everything happens for a reason. For a while there, she was too busy trying to sort out her own life to step back and wonder if there was some kind of meaning to it all.

"When the kids at Spirit are telling me that they're tired, or they have an exam, or they've got a sniffle, I joke and tell them, 'Don't go giving me your sob story,'" she says. "I tell them, 'I'm a forty-six-year-old gay alcoholic woman with Crohn's!'"

Six years sober now, she knows there were years when death was a very real possibility. Struggling to come to terms with her identity as a gay woman, she turned to alcohol and quickly developed a serious drinking problem. That, in turn, led to a perforated gallbladder and an eventual diagnosis of Crohn's disease.

"Twice in my life I could have died," she says. "Once because of alcohol abuse, and once because of Crohn's."

But she didn't. She hung in and got her life back on track. She focused on her work, her friends, and her family. Although she doesn't have children of her own, she's a highly involved aunt to her sisters' children—five nieces and one nephew in all—rarely missing a game or a performance. And on a summer day in 2016, she walked into Marconi's and saved a little boy's life.

"After the incident, a friend told me, 'God gives you what you need, not what you want,'" she says. "'If you were meant to die, this young fellow probably wouldn't have survived.'"

She thinks about that a lot, and how maybe she is indeed alive for a reason. The notion helped her accept the recognition and the award that followed—although she's still not entirely comfortable with being glorified just for doing "the right thing." But she's come around to believing that maybe she needed to get through everything she's been through so that she would be alive and well and ready to pitch in when her help was needed.

"I'm grateful that instead of being on the receiving end of help, like I was for so many years with the people who stuck by me, I was able to be the one giving it," she says.

These days, she finds herself aware of how much she loves her life—so much more now than in the darker days of her past. "I take so many photos," she says. "Moments and memories."

And every once in a while, she thinks about that little boy and his aunt, walking down the aisle to celebrate a wedding that might not have happened if it weren't for their chance encounter.

"It makes you realize," she says, "just how important and special life is."

RUSSELL FEE

Keeping the Wolf from the Door

"I felt like I had kind of punched someone that was way out of my weight class."

IF YOU'RE LOOKING FOR A scenic spot to pitch a tent and spend a few days, you can't go wrong with Alberta's Banff National Park. Nestled amid the awe-inspiring Rocky Mountains, the UNESCO World Heritage Site is a nature lover's dream: impossibly turquoise glacier-fed lakes to swim in or paddle on; trails to hike; canyons, caves, and fossil sites to explore. Whatever the season, there's always something to do and amazing sights to see. For more than a century now, visitors from all over the world have made the park a top travel destination, with an average of four million guests making their way through the gates each year.

In the summer of 2019, Matthew and Elisa Rispoli and their two boys counted themselves among those visitors. On August 9, the family from New Jersey had spent the day doing the things people do in Banff: swimming, skipping rocks, and just enjoying the great outdoors and taking in the beauty all around them. That night, they returned to the tent they'd pitched in the Rampart Creek Campground, worn out from all the fresh air and activity. By midnight, they were fast asleep.

One tent site over, Calgarian Russell Fee and his wife were also tucked in for the evening. The campground was quiet.

And then the screaming started.

AT FIRST, FUZZY WITH SLEEP, Russ figured a child had gone missing. But something about the desperation in the voices, the calls for help, told him otherwise. "The screams were so intense that I knew it was obviously a terrible situation," he says. "Panic immediately sets in."

Russ knew he had to help. He unzipped the flap of his tent and fumbled with his shoes as his wife handed him a lantern. Moments later, he was dashing in the direction of the screams. As he neared the neighbouring campsite, a strange and horrific scene came into view: the tent itself was a shredded and torn mess, and sticking out of it was the hind end of a wolf—larger than any dog Russ could ever recall seeing. The animal appeared to have something clamped in its jaws, something it was attempting to drag. "Just like he's pulling on a toy," Russ recalls. He quickly realized that that "toy" was the arm of the man in the tent.

Russ didn't even break stride.

"I had a good run going at the time . . . and it was just so quick and the screams were so intense . . . so I just kind of kept running at it and I just kicked it sort of in the back hip area."

More startled than hurt, the wolf backed out of the tent and let go of the man's arm. But it didn't run away. Staring at the animal as it stared back at him, Russ wondered, for the first time, if he was in over his head.

"I felt like I had kind of punched someone that was way out of my weight class," he says. Before he had time to think about his next move, Matt—scratched and bitten and covered in blood—charged out of the tent after the animal. "He was pretty amped up, too, so we both just started screaming at it."

As Matt and Russ threw rocks at the wolf in an attempt to scare it off, Elisa Rispoli and her boys looked on from inside the tent, where she'd lain down on top of the kids in an effort to protect them. It was, she wrote in a Facebook post after the attack, "like something out of a horror movie." When the wolf attacked, Matt had thrown himself between the animal and his family and had been doing his best to fight it off. As the wolf tried to drag Matt away, Elisa had grabbed hold of his legs in an attempt to pull him back. "We were screaming for help as he was fighting it and trying to save us, for what felt like an eternity (but I think was anywhere from 1–3 minutes)," she wrote. "I cannot and don't think I'll ever be able to properly describe the terror."

Russ's arrival—and his swift kick to the wolf's back end—created the distraction the family needed. Elisa and the boys made a frantic dash for the safety of the Fees' minivan as Russ and Matt kept an eye on the animal.

"It didn't even really seem terribly aggressive, which is a weird thing to say," Fee says. "I did make contact with a couple of rocks and it didn't even seem to care. It was just doing the perimeter of the site, back and forth, staring at us."

Eventually, the wolf backed off enough to enable Matt and Russ to join the others in the van. The Fees drove the traumatized family to a nearby hospital for medical attention. The rest of the evening, Elisa wrote, was a "blur of EMTs, good Samaritans, waiting for treatment, no phone service, and crying." Matt needed rabies shots, but was otherwise okay.

If not for their "guardian angel," she added, "it could have been so so much worse."

WOLF ATTACKS ON HUMANS ARE extremely rare. In fact, the Rispolis' experience was the first incident of its kind in a Canadian national park (there have been attacks reported in provincial parks, but only twice). In the aftermath of the attack, Parks Canada evacuated the campsite until they were able to track down and euthanize the wolf. It was, park officials reported, in extremely poor health, which was likely a factor in the strange behaviour it exhibited that evening. There was nothing found at the campsite that would have attracted or aggravated the animal.

Whatever led the wolf to behave in such an uncharacteristically aggressive way, there's no question that Russ's arrival on the scene prevented the evening from ending in tragedy. The Rispoli family certainly knows it, and on July 1, 2020, Governor General Julie Payette acknowledged it as well, announcing that Russ would be awarded the Medal of Bravery for the part he played in helping the Rispoli family to safety. Since ceremonies were not being held during the COVID-19 outbreak, Payette used her Facebook page to introduce followers to some of that year's award recipients. On August 13, it was Russ's turn. Under a summary of his actions on that terrifying night nearly a year before was a quote from Russ himself: "My advice would be to prepare for all of life's challenges, both the expected and the unforeseen. Rarely do you get a say in how they'll arrive, but we all must handle them eventually."

The Rispolis understand this better than most. Russ is prone to downplaying his actions that evening, telling those who ask that "it's never felt right to call it brave because I didn't know what I was getting into." He was, he says, "just going to help some people and didn't realize the severity of the situation."

But Elisa isn't willing to brush off the part Russ played in protecting her family. "We are forever grateful to Russ who came to our aid and likely saved Matt's life," she wrote. The family also isn't willing to let the attack colour their feelings about Banff and the wonderful adventure they'd been having before things took such a terrifying turn. In an Instagram post a few days after the encounter with the wolf, they wrote: "The Lakes in Alberta and BC are amazing, the mountains are dynamic, the wildlife is (well you know). Even though half of our trip has been focused on getting our lives back together I still find it stunning up here . . . I'm sure I'll be back someday but maybe in a camper van instead."

SHAUN DE GRANDPRÉ
Double Trouble

"All in a day's work."

MEDALS OF BRAVERY AREN'T EASY to come by. They are awarded to those deemed to have performed "acts of bravery in hazardous circumstances" and are given out sparingly. Receiving one is a high honour. But two? That's exceptionally rare. Check in with the staff at the governor general's office and they'll tell you that only twenty or so Canadians, all told, have received a second medal.

RCMP Constable Shaun De Grandpré can count himself among them.

From the time he was little, growing up on Montreal's South Shore, Shaun knew he wanted a career in law enforcement. For a time, he thought firefighting might be the thing, but he changed his mind while working as a chef at the RCMP National Headquarters in Ottawa. The men and women he met there were an inspiration, and after one member in particular encouraged him to make the leap, he started the "nerve-wracking" application process.

"There are several steps you have to take," he explains, "and after each step, I thought I was finished."

Far from it. In early 2009, he got the call to head to the RCMP Academy, Depot Division, in Regina for six months of training. It was intense but manageable. Years of martial arts training and outdoor activities—rock climbing, kayaking, snowboarding—had left him in great physical health. He relied on that to get him through, along with an ability to handle stressful situations he'd honed over thirteen years of working as a chef. When he graduated in January 2010, he was assigned, for field training, to the country's northernmost mainland post: Tuktoyaktuk, Northwest Territories.

TUKTOYAKTUK IS, AS FAR AS Canadian destinations go, off the beaten track. These days, a year-round highway will get you there, but it's still a bit of journey. You'll add nearly fourteen hundred kilometres to the ticker if you start in Whitehorse— never mind the distance you'd have to cover to get to the Yukon in the first place.

Back when Shaun made his way north, though, driving wasn't an option. The village on the shores of the Arctic Ocean was accessible only by boat, plane, or ice road, weather permitting. The newly minted Constable De Grandpré flew in on January 18, 2010. He quickly got used to the endless dark, the frigid temperatures—forty below, on average—and the necessity of keeping a shovel in the cold porch to dig yourself out from one blizzard after another. But when the sun finally began to creep back over the horizon a few weeks later, he set about exploring his new home.

Tuktoyaktuk is a small community: eight hundred or so people, maybe a hundred houses; dirt roads and one gas pump; two small grocery stores that sell overpriced and rarely fresh produce, and four-litre jugs of milk that will set you back nineteen dollars. Such is life in a fly-in community. But the summers were gorgeous, with twenty-four hours of sun, warm temperatures, and a bug season that lasted just two weeks. The people were welcoming and kind, and the village itself was strangely beautiful—wide open tundra dotted with small lakes to the south, and the Beaufort Sea to the west and north. If he looked out his office window at the right time of day, Shaun could sometimes see a herd of caribou running by or a pod of belugas. You couldn't get that in Montreal or Ottawa.

The work, too, was enjoyable. "There was never really a typical day in Tuk," he recalls. "One day I could be teaching a class at the school, then the next investigating an aggravated assault. There were often community events that we attended: potlucks, drum dances, sunshine festivals."

Twenty-hour rotations were typical—with one or two officers working from 8 a.m. until two the following morning. During those hours, calls would come straight to the office, but anything that came in between 2 a.m. and 8 a.m. would be diverted to a dispatch call centre at the RCMP headquarters in Yellowknife. Dispatch, in turn, would notify whichever officer happened to be on call at the time.

In the early morning hours of June 30, 2010, that officer was Shaun De Grandpré—still in the midst of his six-month field training. Scheduled to work the day shift, he was asleep when the call came in at around 5:15 a.m. "They told me that there was someone in the bay trying to commit suicide," he says. A group of friends had been partying on the beach when one of the men, highly intoxicated, got into an argument with his girlfriend. When the man started to swim out into the frigid water, one of his friends made the call for help.

The bay was just a few hundred metres west of the officers' housing compound, so Shaun knew he could get there quickly. He asked dispatch to call in Constable Richard Bushey, his backup for the day, and within minutes, the two officers were on their way.

The morning was bright; it was the beginning of the summer, and the sun was up for much of the day. Even so, there was a stiff wind coming off the sea, and the bay was choppy, with chunks of ice visible in the water. During the short drive over, the constables discussed a plan. "We thought of possibly using a canoe or launching the RCMP boat," Shaun says.

When they arrived at the shore, however, the situation had changed. A young woman ran up to them and pointed out into the bay, where not one but two heads could be seen bobbing in the waves. She explained that the man's girlfriend had gone in after him.

"I was able to see the male and female about a hundred metres offshore," Shaun says. "I could tell they were both struggling, as their heads were going under water and their arms were waving in the air. With the temperature of the water and the length of time the two had been exposed already, I knew we needed to act quickly."

With no time to deploy a boat or even to find a canoe, Shaun made a split-second decision. He dropped his duty belt and body armour and ran into the near-freezing water.

"It didn't really hit me how cold it was until I was about waist deep and started to swim," he says. "It felt like I was kicked in the chest." He kept going, though, and was able to reach the man and woman. "I grabbed the female first, as it seemed to me she was having the more difficult time staying above water. I helped her swim back close enough to shore so she could stand, and that's where Constable Bushey met her."

With one victim safely on shore, Shaun swam back out to get the other. This time, things didn't go quite as smoothly. "The man began to resist and tried to push me under as well as away from him," Shaun recalls. The struggle seemed to go on for several minutes—though Shaun figures it was more like a few seconds—before he finally got a good grip on the man and began the swim back to shore.

"At this point, I couldn't feel the cold anymore and my muscles were getting stiff," he says. "It was hard to swim."

Once again, Constable Bushey met him in waist-deep water to assist. As Bushey escorted the man to the RCMP truck—where the heater was already on full blast—two of the other people at the beach party ran out to help Shaun. With no EMTs in Tuktoyaktuk, it was up to the two constables to transport the man and woman to the health centre.

With that done, Shaun headed back to the station, where he was set up with dry clothing, a warm blanket, and fresh coffee—lots and lots of coffee. "I had a great sergeant at the time who kept checking in on me to make sure I was warming up okay and that nothing else was coming up," he says, and Constable Bushey was also on hand to help, both physically and mentally. Eventually, the sergeant told him to go home and rest. "So I went to my house and racked out for a few hours."

Shaun stayed in Tuktoyaktuk for another year and a half. He's not sure what happened to the man, but he'd occasionally run into the woman he pulled from the Beaufort Sea. "We would always talk about it," he says. "I try to make light of every situation, and we joked—in good humour—about it."

FAST-FORWARD A FEW YEARS TO June 5, 2015. Stationed in Yellowknife now, Shaun is working a night shift. It's about 3 a.m., but it's summer. So, as on that day in Tuktoyaktuk four years earlier, the sun is shining bright. Shaun and his partner are driving when they notice smoke coming from a building in the downtown core. Seconds later, Constable Ryan Gillis's voice comes over the radio: he'd seen flames coming out of a third-floor window in the nearby Ptarmingan apartment building.

"We were all just a block away and arrived at the same time," he recalls. "Constable Gillis, Constable Bryan Martell, and I managed to gain access from a side door to the apartment building and began going door to door, floor to floor evacuating everyone. The building was filling up with smoke and we could start to see flames while on the second floor."

The men continued to the third floor, where they ran into a problem. "There was a door that just would not open no matter how hard we tried," he say. "I gave it a final kick with everything I had left, and as the door flew open the flames burst out. I'm very fortunate that Constable Gillis was right behind me—and extremely quick. He was able to grab my vest and pull me out of harm's way."

As it turned out, the fire had originated in this apartment, and the entire space was engulfed in flames. When the fire department arrived on the scene, the constables directed them to the apartment, where they found an unconscious woman and got her out.

Once the scene was clear, "[our corporal] essentially dragged us to Emergency to be checked out," Shaun says. "They did some tests, mostly lungs and breathing, told us to self-monitor for a few days. In the end we were all healthy. I felt terrible because so many people lost everything that night. I had a few friends that lived in that building. However, by the grace of God, no one died." The woman who was pulled from the burning apartment stayed in the hospital for a few weeks but made a full recovery.

SHAUN REMEMBERS THE MEDAL OF Bravery ceremonies just as clearly as he remembers the incidents that led to his earning them. The first, in October 2012, was for the rescue in the Beaufort Sea (he received a Lifesaving Society medal for that incident as well).

"It was such a surreal event, being invited to Rideau Hall," he says. "It was an amazing experience. My parents were able to attend, and my now wife flew down as well. To be honest, while I sat there and had the honour of hearing the other recipients' stories, I felt like I didn't belong. I actually knew four other individuals that were at the event—firefighters from my brother's ladder house. When they began to read the details pertaining to my event, I became a little emotional." With a laugh, he adds that he "kept it together like a professional Mountie would."

The second time around, when he stood alongside Ryan Gillis and Bryan Martell to be recognized for the fire rescue, was just as meaningful. "There is a video of the ceremony and you can see that the Honourable Julie Payette leans in and says something and then I laugh a little," he says. Her message? "To stop risking my life or my wife will do it for me. And to take a break and let other people have a chance."

These days, Shaun figures, he's "working on a third." He's stationed in Ontario, part of the St. Lawrence Shiprider marine unit based out of Kingston. He and his wife—who have three children now—miss the North, but he enjoys the challenges of the new position. It's not often that he thinks of the rescues that earned him those Medals of Bravery, but when he does, he's inclined to consider his actions as "all in a day's work."

"I feel that if anyone else was in the position I was in, they would do the same thing."

AYMEN DERBALI

In the Line of Fire

"There is much more goodness than evil on this planet."

IT'S IRONIC THAT AYMEN DERBALI was likely one of the last people to learn the true extent of the horror that unfolded at the Centre Culturel Islamique de Québec on January 29, 2017. That was the day a twenty-seven-year-old man walked into the Quebec City mosque and began firing his semi-automatic weapon at the worshippers who had just finished their evening prayers. One hundred seconds and forty-eight bullets later, six men were dead and another nineteen injured. Although Aymen was there that night, he wouldn't hear the full story for another two months—when he woke up from the artificial coma doctors had induced in order to save his life and allow him to cope with the extreme pain of the injuries he sustained in the attack. That's when he learned the names of the men who had died, along with the names of the women who had been widowed and the children who had been orphaned. That's also when he learned that were it not for his own actions in the moments after the shooter entered the building, the outcome could have been much, much worse.

AYMEN DERBALI REMEMBERS A GREAT deal about the night of the shooting. He recalls, for instance, that he almost didn't go to the mosque. He'd lost track of time, and when he realized that it was already 7:30 p.m.—the time prayers were scheduled to begin—he briefly considered praying at home. Instead, he drove from his house to the mosque on the corner of chemin Sainte-Foy and route de l'Eglise. He arrived at about 7:45 p.m. and completed his prayers alone. He was in his usual spot in a back corner of the room when the shooter arrived a few minutes later. After that, things happened fast.

Aymen recalls the astonishment that rippled through the mosque as gunfire rang out near the front door. Cousins Ibrahima Barry and Mamadou Tanou Barry were heading home when they encountered the gunman. He killed them both and then made his way to the mihrab—the small niche from which the imam prays—where thirty or so worshippers huddled in fear. As the shooter came through the door, gun raised, people began to scream and run for cover. From his position nearest the shooter, Aymen made a split-second decision that would change his life: he made himself a target. "I thought if he shoots in my direction, he wouldn't use his bullets on anyone else."

He crouched down, as if readying himself to tackle the gunman. For a brief moment, their eyes met, and Aymen recalls seeing "determination, determination to kill us all."

"I tried not to panic or flee. I tried to concentrate so that he wouldn't fire on others," he says, explaining that, in that moment, he ran toward the shooter. "I would rather have been paralyzed for life than to have fled and been left unscathed, without having done something to help people."

Aymen's hastily conceived plan worked. In the space of just a few seconds, he tried to tackle the gunman three times. He was shot seven times: in the chin, in his spine, in his right leg, in his arms, and twice in his abdomen. One bullet cut through an artery near his heart. The gunman only stopped shooting when he needed to reload.

As Aymen lay bleeding profusely on the floor of the mosque, drifting into unconsciousness, he was aware of a few things. He remembers thinking that his plan had worked, that several people had been able to escape in the time it took the shooter to reload. He remembers screams coming from all around him, someone telling him to recite the Muslim statement of faith, and someone telling him to stay with them, to keep his eyes open. He remembers hearing someone else call an ambulance, and he has a vague memory of the police arriving on the scene. After that, nothing.

What Aymen is unable to recall from the time immediately after the attack, his wife, Nedra Zahouani, remembers in excruciating detail. When she arrived at Hôpital de l'Enfant-Jésus, she was told that her husband had been shot several times. His blood pressure was zero. As Aymen lay in the ICU in a medically induced coma, she was advised to consider taking him off life support. He would never have the kind of life he'd had before, the doctors said. He would not be able to walk; it was unlikely he'd regain the use of his arms; he would have no memories of his life prior to the attack.

It was difficult news to hear. Aymen was an active man, deeply involved with his family and his community. He'd moved to Canada from Tunisia in 2001 to study at Laval University, where he earned two MBAs. After graduation, he found work as an IT specialist, studied to improve his English, and even learned Spanish when he spent time in Bolivia as an IT consultant with Oxfam-Québec. He and Nedra married and had three children: two boys, who were eight and four at the time of the attack, and a girl who was eleven months old. Aymen played soccer on Sunday afternoons, drove his kids to various lessons, worked hard.

And now here he was, clinging to life in a hospital bed, the victim of a senseless act of violence.

"They said there was no hope," Nedra recalls. "A bullet has exploded in his spine. They said he wouldn't be able to move his four limbs, and it would be hard to live at home, or even in the hospital."

She heard what the doctors were telling her, and she fully understood the severity of Aymen's condition. But she refused to do what they were suggesting. Sitting at his bedside, she had a quiet conversation with her husband. "You'll stay with us and as long as you go down this road, I'll be with you," she remembers telling him. "Even if you never come to live at home with us, I'll always stay with you. I'll take you as you are."

....

TWO MONTHS PASSED BEFORE AYMEN opened his eyes. He had ten operations to remove the bullets and suffered four heart attacks. He spent six months in the hospital and another year in a rehab centre, fighting to regain some control over his broken body. With social workers, psychologists, physiotherapists, and occupational therapists at his side—and Nedra, always Nedra—he made slow but steady progress. But he was only able to spend part of one day a week with his family; their fourth-floor apartment wasn't wheelchair accessible, and doctors were concerned about releasing him before he had a more suitable place to live. That posed a significant financial challenge. Aymen had been the family's only breadwinner, and an accessible home wasn't going to come cheap.

Amira Elghawaby, a volunteer with the Canadian Muslim non-profit community organization DawaNet, remembers when she first heard about Aymen and the challenges he and his family were facing. In the days and weeks after the attack, she and other DawaNet volunteers raised money to support the victims and their families. They also made monthly trips to Quebec City to check in on the worshippers. In December 2017, during one such visit, the group asked what else the community needed. The answer was immediate: Aymen Derbali and his family needed a new place to live. Two days later, Elghawaby and the others started a crowdfunding campaign.

"This is a Canadian hero," she told CBC News. "This is a man who was about to sacrifice his life. . . . Now it's up to us and all of us as Canadians to help him and help his family."

The response was overwhelming. Over the course of the next several months, contributions poured in from across Canada and around the world—more than $400,000 donated by more than four thousand individuals. Aymen is incredibly grateful for the support he and his family have received, and he is especially touched that it came from across religions: Buddhists, Christians, Jews, and Muslims. It proves, he says, that "there is much more goodness than evil on this planet."

In August 2018, Aymen and his family moved into their new home, a bungalow not too far from their old apartment. It was important to Aymen to remain close to the community and to the mosque.

"There are people who would want to run from a place where they had an accident or where there was an attack," he says. "They want to flee, they want to forget it. That's not the case for me at all. I want to return often, pray at the mosque as usual, see my friends, so life goes on."

And life does go on—even if it will never be the same. Today, Aymen has regained the use of both arms, although he still has trouble using his fingers for fine tasks. He can operate his electric wheelchair, use a cellphone, and surf the internet using a wand on the keyboard. Most important to him, he can now touch and hold his children—something he wasn't sure he'd ever be able to do again.

"Sometimes I have to fight the sorrow I feel," he says, "but I compare my situation to how I was in hospital and it comforts me. I came out of a coma and I couldn't eat or drink. I couldn't speak. I've come a long way."

....

THE SHOOTER PLEADED GUILTY TO six counts of murder and six counts of attempted murder in what was Canada's deadliest attack on a place of worship. Aymen was in the courtroom that day, and again on February 8, 2019, for the sentencing hearing. In front of a room full of those affected by the gunman's actions, he recounted details of his life in Canada before the attack, the events of that horrible night, and the ways it had changed his life. He spoke of nightmares in which he could hear the screams of his fellow worshippers, and of recurring dreams in which he is able to walk again. He explained that thinking of his three children was what got him through days filled with pain and the difficult work of rehabilitation. "I thought of all my brothers [who died at the mosque]," he told the court, "who left seventeen orphans behind, who didn't have the chance that I had to see my children again."

When Aymen was finished, Justice François Huot acknowledged Aymen's "incredible demonstration of courage," and suggested that "we should take a lesson from you." At a follow-up hearing, Huot sentenced the accused to life in prison without the possibility of parole for forty years. It was the harshest prison sentence ever handed down in Quebec and one of the longest in Canada.

Aymen is glad that the trial is over. He very much wants to move on, to return to some sort of normal life. In the past year, he's started to hand out résumés, with the goal of returning to work part-time. He'd also like to get back into his humanitarian efforts (in 2009, along with a friend, he established the Canadian Relief Association for the Afflicted). Even more, though, he's eager to devote time to a new kind of work—speaking to high school students about the real-life costs of hatred, encouraging volunteer work among young men and women, and trying to build bridges between communities that have been separated for too long. In 2019, he received an award for good citizenship from the Quebec government, and in July 2020, he received the Governor General's Medal of Bravery.

Despite the dreams that still haunt him from time to time, he tries to stay positive. "When I think positively, I put things into perspective. It's true those thoughts take me back to images of the past, when I was playing soccer with my son, and it's true that I can't do that and it hurts, but at the same time I say, 'Okay, I can see my kids, they can see me, I'm still here, alive.'"

LIANE AND DANIEL WOOD
River Rescue

*"I just felt the sense that I was to go in the water.
There really wasn't any discussion about it."*

THE TRENT RIVER IS A constant presence in Frankford, Ontario, population 2,825. Making its way south toward the Bay of Quinte, it winds past the local legion hall and hardware store, around the tourist park, and through Lock 6 of the Trent-Severn Waterway. The fishing is good near the dam, and it's nice to watch the boats come and go, a pretty sight on a summer day when the sky is blue and the air is warm.

But on the bitter cold evening of February 6, 2013, no one was thinking of stopping by the shore to take in the view. At the Full Gospel Tabernacle Church, another successful family night was drawing to a close. Parishioners donned parkas, hats, and gloves, said their goodbyes, and headed out into the deep freeze. Eventually, only Reverend Daniel Wood, his wife, Liane, and another couple remained. Their daughters—two in the Wood family, one with the other couple—were already outside, waiting for their parents in cars left idling to warm. Everything about the night was perfectly ordinary, utterly routine. Until it wasn't.

The first sign of trouble was the noise, a crash "like somebody had run into the church with a car," says Dan. Moments later, the Woods' youngest daughter ran into the building with news that didn't, at first, make sense: "Megan," she said, referring to her friend—the daughter of the couple the Woods had been chatting with—"is in the river."

THE FULL GOSPEL TABERNACLE CHURCH stands on Trent Street South, an unassuming building faced in brown stone, with a double-door entryway, a bank of windows, and two crosses to mark it as a house of worship. If you were looking at the church from across the street, you'd notice the parking area to the left, and beyond it the Trent River. A retaining wall topped by a chain-link fence marks the end of the parking lot and the beginning of the embankment that drops roughly three metres to the water below.

It was down this embankment that the car carrying thirteen-year-old Megan tumbled into the icy river. To this day, no one knows how the Nissan Juke managed to roll backward through the fence. And in the moment, it hardly mattered. What mattered was getting to the girl.

A quick look over the embankment revealed a raging river, and an upside-down, half-submerged vehicle about ten metres downstream and five metres from shore. It had come to a stop against some boulders and seemed, for the time being, at least, stable.

As Megan's mother called 911, the others tried to sort out a plan. Dan, a forty-three-year-old former volunteer firefighter, was the obvious choice to go after Megan—and for a moment, he contemplated jumping into the water. But cooler heads prevailed. Still plagued by a recent shoulder injury, and wary of rendering himself useless in the jump, Dan ran back to the church for a ladder. Liane and her daughters prayed, and by the time Dan got back, her decision was made.

"While we were praying, I just felt the sense that I was to go in the water," she says. "There really wasn't any discussion about it."

A former competitive swimmer, the forty-two-year-old was comfortable in water, but this was different. The current was particularly strong that night and the rocky bottom was always tricky to navigate. Liane didn't relish the idea of descending into the total darkness on a ladder it was taking two men to hold steady, but she knew she had no choice and that speed was critical. She took a deep breath, lowered herself into the near-freezing water—up past her waist in some places—and inched her way along the shore and then out to the car.

That first icy trip was a frustrating exercise in futility. The SUV was locked, and with no way to break the submerged window or pry open a door, she had no choice but to return to the parking lot. Armed with an ice scraper—the nearest and most likely weapon she could lay her hands on—she made a second treacherous trip. At one point, she slipped and went under. When she surfaced, she was shocked to find herself still next to the car.

"The current was so strong there, the first responders were saying we can't believe you weren't swept downstream," she says.

Realizing that this was a two-person job, Dan had joined Liane in the water. Together, they came up with a new strategy. If the front of the car was submerged, perhaps the back was a better option? Through the pitch-black night, the couple worked their way around the vehicle.

"We were trying to feel where the window was on the back, to try and break it there," Liane says. "As we were feeling the bumper with our hands, trying to move down . . . our hands just kept going inside. I said to my husband, 'Are we inside the vehicle?'"

Liane's feet were so cold that they'd lost feeling; she had no idea she was standing in the hatch, which had likely opened when the car rolled down the embankment. It was the first break they'd gotten since the whole ordeal began, and they immediately began to call to Megan. After a few attempts, an "I'm here" could be heard from the front seat, where an air pocket had allowed the girl to keep her head above water.

Quickly, the Woods gave Megan instructions on how to get out. To do so safely, she'd have to swim over the tops of the upside-down seats and make her way to the back of the vehicle, where Dan and Liane were waiting with outstretched hands.

"She was incredible. She kept calm," says Dan. "We gave her instructions on how to get to us, she followed them. She made a very bad situation better. If she had panicked, it could have been much worse."

Miraculously, Megan made it out of the vehicle without getting her hair wet. It's something Liane still wonders about.

"In a 2013 Juke, the only space to move from the front . . . to high in the back seat is between the roof of the car and the top of the seat," she says. "That's only about twelve to fifteen inches. That was completely under the water, and Megan's hair was completely dry when she came out of that vehicle. It was something the first responders were talking about: 'How did she get out of that with her hair dry?'"

Miracles aside, the trip back to shore wasn't easy. Megan and Liane were both weak and suffering from hypothermia. As Dan helped Megan back to the ladder, Liane waited by the car, not trusting her failing limbs to carry her safely. After a few moments that seemed like forever, Dan was back. They made their way up the ladder and back to the parking lot as the first responders arrived on the scene.

THE RIVER RESCUE TOOK ABOUT ten minutes, all told, but the experience left a mark on all who were there.

In addition to being treated for hypothermia, Megan suffered from post-traumatic stress disorder severe enough to require a break from school. Although she's now graduated from high school, she still doesn't recall the details of what happened that night. For her, Dan believes, the time in the river is like "a big nightmare."

For Liane, though, the memories are clear. She remembers standing in the river waiting for Dan to come back and looking up at the parking lot to see her daughters staring down at her. "I just remember thinking, the last thing that I did with my girls was I prayed with them and the last thing my girls saw me do was try and help a friend and I was okay," she says. "I thought if it's my time to go, it's my time to go."

Like Megan, she suffers from and receives treatment for PTSD; she now has a service dog to help her manage. She also made a decision about her work as an insurance broker.

"It was a very good career in insurance," she says. "I just realized that nobody was going to get to the end of their lives and say, 'I'm so glad I've got an insurance policy from Liane.' I want to be someone that helps other people."

She went back to school and is now a registered psychotherapist.

In 2015, Liane and Daniel Wood travelled to Rideau Hall in Ottawa to receive the Medal of Bravery from Governor General David Johnston. Although the Woods were surprised to learn they'd be receiving a commendation for their actions that cold February night, the ceremony, says Liane, was a wonderful experience for their family.

"It was such an honour for Dan and I to be standing with so many people with such incredible stories themselves," she says. "Just to be in their company and to have the opportunity to meet the governor general was such an honour."

Megan's family has remained a part of the Full Gospel Tabernacle Church, so the Woods have stayed in touch with the young woman they saved. And despite the toll that night in the river has taken, Liane has never once questioned her actions. If the same situation were to arise again, she wouldn't hesitate to help.

"It was my automatic response," she says. "Nobody has a greater claim to being alive than anyone else. Looking back at it, would I do it again? Absolutely. The alternative is standing there and doing nothing. I don't think I could live with myself."

SERGEANT GANDER
A True Pal

"He gave his life defending his soldiers."

JULY 23, 2015, WAS A cold and wet day in Gander, Newfoundland and Labrador. Nevertheless, a small crowd had gathered under the protective covering of a tent in Gander Heritage Memorial Park. Some wore rain gear or long coats against the elements; others sported military berets and medals. A round of applause rang out as the statue of a soldier was unveiled, representing the men who had served with the Royal Rifles of Canada during the Second World War. The applause continued as the crowd's attention was directed to a second statue, smaller than the first and still draped in a black tarp.

"And now," came the announcement, "Mr. Wilson Hoffe and Philip Doddridge will unveil our hero's statue."

Together, Hoffe, chair of the Memorial Park, and veteran Doddridge removed the tarp, revealing the bronze statue of a large, shaggy working dog—a purebred Newfoundland named

Sergeant Gander who died in action during the Battle of Hong Kong, saving the lives of several Canadian soldiers in the process.

SERGEANT GANDER DIDN'T BEGIN HIS life as a hero. In fact, he didn't even begin his life as Sergeant Gander. "Pal" was the Hayden family's beloved pet—a furry ball of energy who loved nothing more than to play with the neighbourhood children, often pulling them on their sleds in winter. Eileen Chafe remembered racing across the snow behind Pal, and his fondness for greeting people by standing on his back two legs and putting his front paws on your shoulders. "He was very playful and gentle with us children," she recalled, "and often knocked us in the snow. . . . We all loved him."

But as the gentle giant continued to grow—reaching a massive 130 pounds—Rod Hayden began to doubt if the family could keep him. And in 1940, when Pal accidentally scratched the face of Eileen's sister, six-year-old Joan Chafe, Hayden knew he had to find another home for his cherished four-legged friend.

Luckily, a solution was close at hand. The nearby Royal Canadian Air Force (RCAF) base had been a hub of activity since the start of the war in 1939, serving as a crucial refuelling and staging area for planes on their way to the European front. From the time he was fully grown, Pal had been pitching in at the base, where the soldiers quickly came to appreciate his help. Using his size and strength, Pal would set to work moving fifty-gallon drums of petrol—two at a time—from the warehouse to the tarmac, earning bragging rights as the airport's first refuelling "vehicle." Not surprisingly, the soldiers stationed at Gander loved Pal just as much as the local children did, and when Rod Hayden asked, they were more than happy to adopt him.

Pal took to his new home well, frequently chasing after the landing airplanes—a habit that led more than one incoming pilot to radio that there was a bear on the runway. Pal soon became the regimental mascot for the 1st Battalion of the Royal Rifles of Canada. He was given a "promotion" and renamed Sergeant Gander.

The Royal Rifles were stationed in Gander to defend the RCAF base against a potential German attack and were not expected to face combat. But as the war expanded to the Far East—with Japan threatening the British colony of Hong Kong—the situation changed. In late 1941, the Royal Rifles were sent, along with other troops, to defend the island. Together, the men made a decision: Sergeant Gander, their beloved mascot, would go to war too.

He nearly didn't make it. The cross-Canada trip to Vancouver, where the Royal Rifles would board a ship for Hong Kong, started out well enough. Sergeant Gander marched proudly in a farewell parade in Quebec City, his sergeant's stripes displayed next to the regimental badge attached to his harness. But in Vancouver, as the battalion prepared to board the transport ship *Prince Robert*, a crew member made a mistake that pilots in Gander had been making for a year—and the captain quickly let the troops know that a "bear" could not be brought on the boat. The situation was eventually sorted out, and when the Royal Rifles set sail, Sergeant Gander was with them.

The regiment arrived in Hong Kong in mid-November 1941 and began to adapt to life on the island. It was a much warmer climate than they were used to—with temperatures typically in the low- to mid-twenties, compared to the near freezing conditions at home in Gander. It was a hard enough adjustment for men, but for a 135-pound dog covered in thick, heavy fur, the weather was a particular challenge. Rifleman Fred Kelly had been given the task of looking after Sergeant Gander, and he did his best to make the dog as comfortable as possible. He gave Gander long, cool showers, and let him drink beer straight out of the sink. At night, when Gander howled in his doghouse, unhappy at being left alone, Kelly brought the dog inside to sleep next to his own bed.

As he had done back at home, Gander quickly made himself useful. In a memoir of his time in Hong Kong—more than three years of which were spent as a prisoner of war—Rifleman Andrew "Ando" Flanagan recalled that the dog displayed "no fear of guns or bombs." Rifleman Reginald Law remembered that the normally friendly giant "growled and ran at the enemy soldiers, biting at their heels." With most battles taking place at night, Gander's black coat made him difficult to see, and his size made him terrifying. In the midst of one skirmish, when several injured Canadian soldiers found themselves trapped by the approaching Japanese, Gander drove off the enemy with a ferocious display of barks and growls. Weeks later, in a prisoner-of-war camp, the Japanese questioned Canadian POWs about the "black beast" they had encountered that evening. Were the Allies training giant animals to do battle alongside soldiers?

On the night of December 19—a little over a week after the Japanese attacked Pearl Harbor, bringing the United States into the war and setting off the Battle of Hong Kong—the soldiers of the 1st Battalion of the Royal Rifles of Canada engaged in the Battle of Lye Mun. Before the fighting began, Sergeant Kelly had put Gander in a concrete shelter, hoping the dog would be cool and safe for the evening. But when the attack came, Gander escaped.

"Gander must have seen the hand grenades landing," said Jeremy Swanson, former commemorations and programs officer of the Canadian War Museum. "He must have seen the men furiously throwing them back. He must have sensed their terror."

Gander headed straight for the action, making his way to a group of wounded soldiers lying on a nearby hill. When a grenade landed in their midst, Gander didn't hesitate. He took it in his mouth and dashed away. He made it only a short distance before the grenade exploded.

Interviewed in 2011 about Sergeant Gander, Reginald Law clearly remembered the moment. Seven soldiers had been saved, but the cost was steep. "When the firing eased up, I saw Gander lying dead in the road," he said. The next morning, as the Canadians were marched to the prisoner-of-war camp where many would remain for years, Fred Kelly also caught a glimpse of his fallen friend. "I didn't go near," he said. "I was so distraught."

The battalion's beloved mascot had died saving the men who had taken him in and made him one of their own.

••••

THE MEN OF THE ROYAL Rifles of Canada knew all too well the sacrifice Sergeant Gander had made on their behalf, but it took more than fifty years for others to begin hearing the story. In the mid-1990s, several Hong Kong veterans mentioned Gander to Jeremy Swanson during a Canadian War Museum event. Along with a group of volunteers, office staff, and interested vets, Swanson set about filling in the blanks in Gander's story. So impressed was Swanson by what he learned that he eventually contacted the People's Dispensary for Sick Animals in England, which awards the Dickin Medal—known as the "animal Victoria Cross"—to recognize animals who display "conspicuous gallantry or devotion to duty." In October 2000, Sergeant Gander became the first animal in fifty years to be presented with the award. Making the occasion particularly special, it was Fred Kelly—Gander's guardian during his time with the Royal Rifles—who accepted the medal, with a Newfoundland dog named Rimshot representing Gander at his side. The citation reads, in part: "For saving the lives of Canadian infantrymen during the Battle of Lye Mun on Hong Kong Island in December 1941. . . . Twice Gander's attacks halted the enemy's advance and protected groups of wounded soldiers. In a final act of bravery, the war dog was killed in action gathering a grenade. Without Gander's intervention many more lives would have been lost in the assault."

The medal was the first of its kind to be awarded to a Canadian animal and now resides at the Canadian War Museum in Ottawa.

More honours followed. In August 2009, when the Hong Kong War Memorial was unveiled in Ottawa, Sergeant Gander's name was listed alongside those of the 1,975 men and two women who fought for Canada against the Japanese. Following a tradition that had started during their days in the prisoner-of-war camps, when they shared any food that came their way, the veterans insisted that any recognition of their contributions to the war effort be shared with their mascot as well. And in 2012, when what began as a school project by eleven-year-old Noah Trembley culminated in the establishment of a "Forgotten Heroes" monument in Bass River, Nova Scotia—honouring animals who have lost their lives during military service—a statue of Gander was included.

And then, of course, there's the statue in Gander itself, the unveiling of which brought back difficult memories for some of those on hand that rainy day.

"It's very emotional, even talking about it, it's very close to my heart," said Philip Doddridge. The Royal Rifles vet served in the 1st Battalion, alongside Sergeant Gander, before spending three years in a POW camp. "He was very much loved by all of us."

"He gave his life defending his soldiers," added Wilson Hoffe. "We thought on the committee that this would be an appropriate [way to] recognize a hero, not human—but certainly a hero."

PART 3
Courage in the Face of Injustice

LEESEE PAPATSIE
Fighting for Food

"All I wanted was to have one protest."

LEESEE PAPATSIE WAS OUT RUNNING errands the day she saw the man with the sign. He was standing outside the grocery store holding it up for all to see. "Lower food prices! Remove expired products!" It was, she thought, a familiar story. Food prices in Iqaluit and surrounding areas were exorbitant—nearly $10 for a can of concentrated frozen orange juice, and $100 for a twenty-four-pack of water. A chicken could cost as much as $60, and a bag of apples $15. It wasn't unusual for her weekly grocery bill to top $500—for herself, her husband, and her one child still living at home.

She wanted to stand with the man but continued with her errands, anxious to get on with her day. But he and his sign stayed with her, setting off a train of thought that she just couldn't shake. Yes, food in Canada's northernmost communities was often more expensive than in the south due to shipping costs, but there was more to it than that. In 2011, the federal government replaced the Food Mail Program, which had subsidized the cost of a wide range of items, with Nutrition North, which covered only healthier foods, such as produce, dairy, and eggs. Not only had that made many staple food items more expensive, but the federal government's definition of "healthy" didn't always match the needs of a typical northern diet. Add in price gouging on the part of retailers, and the fact that more than 40 percent of the population in northern communities depended on social assistance, and being able to put food on the table was getting harder and harder.

Over the next little while, Leesee continued to think about the man with the sign and about the struggles she and her neighbours in Iqaluit—and others all across Canada's North—faced when it came to feeding their families: higher-than-average cost of living, higher-than-average unemployment—it all contributed to the problem, and the problem was creating problems of its own. The harder it was for families to put food on the table, the harder it was to ensure that kids didn't go hungry, that food banks weren't broken into, that basic nutritional needs were being met. More and more, she regretted not joining that man, regretted not making a sign of her own and standing beside him in his small protest. And although that moment had passed, Leesee soon realized that there could be others.

AS THE MOTHER OF FIVE kids, and an active grandmother as well, Leesee was no stranger to social media. In fact, many in Canada's isolated northern communities rely on platforms such as Facebook to stay in touch and connect with the wider world. And so, on May 29, 2012, Leesee sat down at her computer, opened Facebook, and created a group called Feeding My Family. Her plan? To use the group to organize a one-day food-price protest, similar to the ones that had taken place recently in Coral Harbour and Iqaluit.

The response was immediate—and astonishing. By June 4, two thousand members had joined. On June 6, it was four thousand. And on June 9, the date Leesee had chosen for her protest, membership was sitting at about fourteen thousand. Many of those people turned out for peaceful demonstrations in Iqaluit, Arctic Bay, Cambridge Bay, Clyde River, Grise Fiord, Igloolik, Pond Inlet, Pangnirtung, and at Parliament Hill in Ottawa to express their frustration over the high costs and low incomes in their territory.

The signs spoke volumes—"2 Many People R Going Hungry," read one; "Food Is Too Expensive in Nunavut," said another—and the message was heard. Local and national media covered the initial protests and others that followed, and by the end of June 2012, Nunavut officials had formed a Food Security Coalition and were planning meetings. In September 2012, Facebook itself took note, featuring Leesee and her group in a Facebook Story—an editorial initiative that recognized people who used the platform in inspiring ways. Clearly, her message was striking a chord.

Speaking to a reporter at the time, Leesee called the response humbling, scary, and amazing. "My main target is [getting] other Nunavummiut to stand up," she said. "That's my main target. Because this is not [the] Inuit traditional way of doing things." At that time, protesting was not something Inuit had done before, and some Inuit didn't agree with the approach. They would ask Leesee, "Why are you doing this, this is not the Inuit way." But she knew there were kids that were still hungry, and that made her stick with it. And soon enough, other Nunavummiut joined her.

Although Leesee had started the Feeding My Family group with a one-day protest in mind, things soon took on a life of their own. By the time of the Facebook profile, the group had attracted upward of twenty-one thousand members, more than half of the population of Nunavut itself. People began using the page to post pictures of high-priced items on local store shelves: $29 jars of Cheez Whiz, $77 chicken, $27 margarine, and $40 baby formula, among others. Mothers fed their babies canned Carnation milk because they couldn't afford regular milk. Before Leesee knew it, a movement was born.

"I think the reason it got so much traction is because a lot of Inuit—a lot of Northerners—have some understanding of hunger," she told a reporter. "Hunger is something Inuit relate to from the past. A lot of Inuit know hunger exists in the smaller communities, but it's not something that people talk openly about. Feeding My Family has been successful because people are now being more open about the problem. It is what I often refer to as 'speaking the same language,' or having a common understanding of hunger."

On May 21, 2013—nearly a year after she created the group—Leesee tried to sum up the previous twelve months:

. . . we were not sure how this site would have turned out, but it has been almost a year now since this facebook group was created, May 29, 2012, yup, yup and yup. We totally believed in and still believe in Northerners coming together to stand together as one and to say one thing, "high cost of food in the north."

Wow, it has only been a year, but man, things happen . . . FMF has been invited to several meetings, to bring aware-ness of what we have heard here, we have been interviewed about this site, there has been some amazing and really good stories and articles about hunger in the north. We have had some real amazing support from the media as well.

She ended the post by thanking supporters and asking for more suggestions on how to raise awareness in a "northerner way." "We cannot stop this," she concluded. "We need to keep it going."

LEESEE HAS KEPT IT GOING. In the years that have passed since she founded Feeding My Family, she has changed the focus of the Facebook group from an organizing forum for protests to an advocacy group with clear objectives—includ-ing encouraging northerners to empower themselves to create independence from within, urging government policymakers and retailers to find better ways to lower the cost of food, and advocating for new food suppliers to operate in the North in order to increase competition and lower prices. She's also taken on the task of educating others about the differences between a traditional northern diet of "country food"—anything that can be hunted, fished, or harvested from the land—and the fruit-and-vegetable-heavy diet deemed healthy by Canada's government. She'd like to see the government review the Nutrition North program and subsidize foods that fit the needs of northerners. She also speaks to local and national media whenever she can, trying to raise awareness.

In 2015, Leesee found out just how many people were listening. Nearly three thousand kilometres away, in Calgary, Chris Lihou, a writer at WAX Partnership creative agency, came across internet photos posted by people in Nunavut, highlighting the exorbitant costs of everyday food items. Surprised by what he learned, Lihou took the photos to his colleagues. They agreed that they wanted to do something to spread awareness of the issue in southern Canada, and they contacted Leesee for input. After speaking with her, the agency came up with a concept—a fake ad for a fictional grocery store called Way North Foods that would air on YouTube. The slogan? "Nobody offers you less for more."

Lihou describes the concept as a "shareable, relatable" way of informing southern Canadians about the issue of food insecurity in the North. "By using the really familiar grocery store ads that we all see, where you have smiling people and cheery jingles and all the rest of it and they're all touting how great their deals are, we thought it would be interesting to invert that and have them be really excited about these high deals," he told the CBC in 2016, just after the ads went public.

"Way North Foods isn't real," reads the ad's final caption. "But for families in Nunavut, its prices are."

Leesee loved it—and, as an awareness-raiser, it did the trick. The Way North Foods ad has more than thirty-seven thousand views on YouTube.

TODAY, LEESEE WORKS IN the same field as she did back in 2012—an educator for the territory's parks—but she's not about to give up the work she does on behalf of hungry families in the North. She knows that there are still many families who simply can't afford three meals a day, and many children who go to school hungry each morning.

But she also knows that Canadians are more aware today of the high price of food in the North than they were back in May 2012, when she sat down at her computer and created a Facebook page that turned into a movement.

"[What's surprised me is] people supporting our cause; northerners stepping up to post pictures when [taking photos] has been restricted by the stores; northerners speaking up about the hardship they are enduring. Southerners saying I can't believe this is happening in Canada," she told an interviewer in 2014. "I cannot believe this site has continued this far."

"I didn't expect it to go viral," she said in 2016, talking about both the ads and the Feeding My Family movement. "All I wanted was to have one protest."

VISHAL VIJAY
Never Too Young to Make a Difference

*"That was the idea: a vision of a world where
every child's rights are respected and protected."*

VISHAL VIJAY KNOWS EXACTLY the day his life changed.
It was March 2012, and he and his family were on a trip to
India. This was, in and of itself, not so unusual. The Vijays had
made several visits over the years for travel and to explore their
cultural roots, and eleven-year-old Vishal and his younger
brothers Ishan and Roshan were no strangers to the country's
hectic energy, to its cacophony of sights and sounds, or to the
poverty so often on display.

But this trip was different. During time spent in Andhra
Pradesh, in the southeastern part of India, Vishal's parents
made a point of visiting some of the region's poorer areas. They
wanted to show their children the different conditions that exist
in the world and, perhaps, to offer a reminder of how lucky
they were to be living a comfortable life in Canada. For the first
time, Vishal and his siblings saw what extreme poverty looks

like. "My heart broke as we drove through the slums and I saw children younger than me who were orphaned and abandoned, left to fend for themselves. They weren't in school, like I was, but instead were forced onto the streets," Vishal recalls. "While at the time I didn't understand the complex issues at hand, I knew that this was morally unjust, and something had to be done."

Those children were still on his mind a week later, in Faridabad. "After walking through slums on the outskirts of the city, I spent the day with many street kids who, with no schoolhouse and very few basic supplies, were studying under the shade of a tree," he says. "I talked with the students and teachers at this school and was moved by their courage and hope for a better future. After seeing firsthand the power education had to transform lives and lift children out of the cycle of poverty, I realized that there was something I could do. That was the turning point for me."

Once home, Vijay settled back into his typical preteen life. He was busy with school, with family and friends, with riding his bike around downtown Oakville, Ontario, and with karate— he was already well on his way to the black belt he would receive in 2014. Friday nights were family movie nights, and with each family member taking turns with the weekly "pick," the choices ranged from documentaries to Bollywood hits to current block-busters. And, of course, there was *Sky High*—a superhero comedy flick Vishal figures he and his brothers have watched at least twenty times.

But as spring inched closer to summer, he couldn't forget what he'd seen on his trip. Soon enough, he realized he didn't want to forget. What he wanted was to do something about it. He felt a calling and a responsibility to take action.

"Every summer, my dad would give my brother and me a challenge to stay busy," Vishal recalls. In 2011, he had built and published an app on the Apple App Store, and his brother, Ishan, had written a short film. "In 2012, as we were thinking about how we wanted to spend our summer, nothing felt as important or urgent as helping the street kids we had spent the day with and other kids just like them."

And so, once school let out, Vishal and Ishan started Children in Action, or CIA. Their goal? To help kids like the ones they'd seen in India.

With the full support of their parents, the brothers knocked on practically every door in the neighbourhood and asked if there were any kids who were interested in joining them. "Essentially, we were recruiting fellow kids who were interested in social impact and activism," Vishal explains. "Three of my neighbours were the first who agreed to join Ishan and me. We met biweekly that summer in my backyard or at my dining table. We didn't have a mission statement in the beginning, but we did have a strong desire to improve the lives of marginalized or underprivileged kids at home and around the world."

The group's first project was a fundraiser to build a clean water well in Sierra Leone. While researching water scarcity earlier that year for a grade six English project, Vishal had read all he could about the causes of poverty. "I pored through articles and UN reports and talked to everyone I could," he says. He learned that access to safe, clean drinking water was an important part of the solution. He shared his new knowledge with the others in the group, and together, they decided the well would be a great place to start. They got to work planning a bake sale, and a local toy shop, Pick of the Crop, agreed to let them set up in front of their store.

"Rather than putting a price on items, we simply said that all the food was free and donations were welcome," says Vishal. "From the very beginning we were trying to think of ways to change traditional fundraising—and it worked! We had people spending twenty dollars on a cookie, or people who spent two dollars for lemonade and spent time chatting with us about water scarcity and other issues that were contributing to child poverty."

At the end of the day, the group had raised $400 and were well on their way to building the development project in Sierra Leone. Children in Action was officially up and running and expanding by the day.

Vishal's karate school—No Limits Martial Arts, run by Adam Molnar and his siblings—was an early supporter, allowing the group to set up donation bins for their campaigns at the dojo and make announcements about their work in between classes. As their initiatives and campaigns expanded, they began to collaborate with other organizations too. Vishal recalls, "Our members collected thousands of food supplies, blankets and clothing items and distributed them to local charities like the Kerr Street food bank and Safetynet Children & Youth Charities. Our garage turned into a warehouse!"

Molnar also connected them with a designer who helped develop their first logo, and when Vishal began teaching at the school in 2013, many of the other young instructors also joined CIA.

"They invited their friends from school to join our group, and those friends brought their friends, and very quickly, we grew in an organic, word-of-mouth way. The group became a fun way for kids to have an impact and help other kids," Vishal says.

Those early days involved more fundraising efforts, as well as drives to collect canned goods, clothing, and other items that could be distributed locally in Halton or sent overseas to children in need. Soon, word of their work began to spread, and in 2013, Marc and Craig Kielburger, co-founders of WE Charity (then known as Free the Children), invited Vishal to participate in a cross-Canada speaking tour. During the 2013–2014 school year, he travelled to nine cities and spoke to 120,000 young people about children's rights and the importance of youth activism. It was a turning point for Vishal's fledgling non-profit. "[It brought] a lot of excitement to the work we were doing," says Vishal.

More opportunities followed: Children in Action was featured in a grade six social sciences textbook; Vishal collaborated with the new Canadian Museum for Human Rights on a permanent children's rights exhibit; and he was invited to serve on Free the Children's board of directors as a youth advisor. During his grade nine year, Vishal was selected by the We Are Family Foundation to attend Three Dot Dash's Just Peace Summit—a weeklong "incubator" in New York City for teen-led non-profits and projects. It was a transformative event. In addition to learning how to build and lead teams of volunteers, Vishal attended workshops on branding, collaboration, and organizational techniques. He also met mentors—including Herb Scannell (then president and CEO of BBC North America) and Pamela Bell (co-founder of Kate Spade and Prinkshop)—who were generous with their time and advice, and, in Bell's case, with food.

"She actually ended up inviting me to her house in New York," Vishal says, "and served me the best doughnuts!"

More importantly, these two mentors helped Vishal realize that it was time to change the name of his organization and his vision for its future.

"We didn't initially set out to launch a non-profit," he says. "We started this back when we were kids in middle school and we saw a need and wanted to do something to help. When we started out in 2012, we thought about calling ourselves 'Kids in Action.'" But the founding members eventually decided on Children in Action instead. "That way, our acronym could be the CIA. In middle school, this sounded like a great idea—we imagined that we'd be agents of social change and we'd wear suits and sunglasses at our events."

It didn't quite go according to plan. "It ended up being too hot to wear suits at our first bake sale," he says, and eventually, having kids sign up for the CIA didn't quite fly.

"Herb shared some valuable advice on transitioning from a grassroots youth-run community group—that met in my basement—to a well-organized non-profit that could have a global impact. And I remember Pamela sharing that our group name needs to quickly convey what we stand for. After a lot of thought, we decided on EveryChildNow, because we wanted every child to be receiving their basic needs now—that was the idea: a vision of a world where every child's rights are respected and protected."

In the years since, EveryChildNow, or ECN, has done much to begin turning that vision into a reality. Now a volunteer-led national organization with an impressive list of supporters and sponsors, ECN organizes its efforts around three pillars: Inspire,

Impact, and Advocate. They inspire and empower kids to get involved in social activism; sponsor sustainable development projects that provide basic needs for children and their families; mount campaigns that provide children with their basic needs in the short-term; and consider what can be done, politically, to fight for children's rights.

Take Skate it UP!, for example—a skate-a-thon that featured a silent auction and a raffle—or Chalk it UP!, a street chalk-drawing competition that included a carnival and competition around raising awareness about global and local issues affecting children. "I was initially inspired by the kids in India and wanted to improve their conditions," says Vishal, "but we quickly realized that there was need in our own backyard too." Care for Syria encouraged kids to create handwritten letters of support, collect clothing, and prepare hot meals for newly landed Syrian refugee families, while Read, Write, Repeat gathered school supplies and books to send to Indigenous children and local students. "And for our international development projects," Vishal adds, "we've partnered with aid agencies that have a field presence. For example, we collaborated with GlobalMedic to help package and assemble four thousand Ebola protection kits at their warehouse."

To date, ECN has raised $100,000 to support its initiatives, has collected more than thirty thousand supplies, and has helped more than a thousand families. "From large corporate sponsors noticing and supporting our work to children across Canada holding their own fundraisers—bake sales, selling rainbow loom bracelets, and crowdfunding—we've been very fortunate to have the work that we do resonate with so many people."

At the heart of this movement of social change is a belief in young people. Vishal's message to other youth: "We have the freedom to dream, the courage to stand up for what we believe in, and the power to make it happen."

SEVERAL YEARS HAVE PASSED SINCE that life-changing trip to India. The once eager middle-school student is now at Western University in London, Ontario, on his way to a business degree, or law school, or perhaps something else entirely; he wishes to "work at the intersection of social impact and strategy and leverage [his] skillset for good." There have been so many great moments on this journey, and so many things for him to be thankful for—a standing ovation at a WE Day event in Toronto, the sight of kids crowding into his backyard to assemble school care packages to send to Nepal, and the opportunity to interview Kofi Annan, who reminded Vishal, and all youth, to "always dream." But for Vishal, the best moment by far came in 2017, when he and his family returned to Faridabad and visited the spot where he'd met the children who changed his life in 2012. Back then, those wishing to study had to do so under the shade of a tree. Now, a schoolhouse stands nearby, largely made possible by ECN and its collaboration with local partners.

"I met many of the same children again that I'd first met five years earlier," says Vishal. "I learned about their goals of graduating school and eventually supporting their own families. I got to meet children like Riya and Gopal again, who remembered my brother and me and were so grateful—getting to see the look on their faces made it all worth it."

KRISTEN WORLEY
An Olympic Moment

"I didn't want to see harm coming to other athletes."

IT HAD TAKEN A LONG time—decades, in fact—but Kristen Worley was finally having her Olympic moment.

Walking into the offices of the International Olympic Committee (IOC) in Lausanne, Switzerland, on a Friday afternoon in late October 2019, Worley was struck by how surreal it all seemed. This was, after all, the same organization that had subjected her to humiliating and invasive testing to prove her gender; the same organization whose strict rules and regulations had made it impossible for her to continue her career as an elite-level cyclist. And yet, here she was, not pushing her way through the door in an effort to be heard, but invited—asked by the powers that be to join them at the table for a discussion about both reconciliation and the future of sport. Never in a million years had she expected to be here.

••••

KRISTEN WORLEY BEGAN HER LIFE as Chris Jackson—a baby boy adopted by a conservative family living in the tony Lorne Park neighbourhood just west of Toronto. It was, as Kristen wrote in her memoir, *Woman Enough*, the kind of place where "gender roles were clearly delineated—men were providers, women homemakers; parents knew best; and children behaved. 'Hell' was a serious swear word."

In other words, it was a difficult place to grow up if you knew, in the very heart of your being, that you weren't who you were supposed to be.

"When I was four, five, six years old, I knew I was living two lives," Kristen says. When Chris was four, he idolized his older sister and longed to hang out with her and her friends. They let him into their inner circle, dressing him up in girls' clothes. He loved it.

It was around about that time that Chris became aware of what he called "the switch." He didn't know precisely what it was, and most days, at least then, it was off. But when that switch flipped to the "on" position, the sensation was physical—an intense need to be among his sister's things. Eventually, "among" wasn't enough, and he began dressing up in her clothes whenever he could.

As Chris got older, the struggle to balance his two lives became acute. "We didn't talk about these things," Kristen says. "I grew up in the middle-class Canadian conservative triangle"—in Chris's life, the points were Lorne Park, Muskoka, and Collingwood, where everything and everyone that comprised the Jacksons' lives could be found. "I had nobody to talk to about it, but I did feel I had to do it. The double life became a survival mechanism, but it was a constant struggle."

Sports helped: running, international competitions in water-skiing, and, eventually, cycling.

"I had to create this kind of façade," Worley says. "Sports was a way of survival. Being 'Chris the athlete' gave me an identity and a bit of a breather. It enabled me to get away from my friends and family if I needed to. It was me trying to figure it out. I had no knowledge of gender identity or issues of intersex. I was just developing a Teflon persona."

But that protective coating only got Chris so far. His teens were difficult—too much drinking, too much confusion and alienation, two suicide attempts. Finally, in 2004, and with the help and support of Alison Worley—whom Chris fell in love with and married while living as a man—Chris underwent complete gender reassignment surgery.

The surgery took place at the same time that Chris—now Kristen—was thinking about making a run at the Olympics. Encouraged by Canada's national cycling coach, Kristen had spent the previous few years training—hard. She rode every day, regardless of the weather. She raced twice a week. She lost count of how many circuits she made around velodromes. But it was all worth it. Her coach believed she could qualify for competition in pursuit track racing. She just needed a licence. And for that, she needed the IOC.

In some ways, the timing was fortuitous. The next summer Olympic games were set for 2008, in Beijing. Worley had undergone her gender reassignment surgery in 2004. Under the recommendations of the Stockholm Consensus—released by the IOC in advance of the 2004 Athens Olympics to lay out rules governing the participation of transitioned athletes—an athlete needed to wait two full years following reassignment surgery before being eligible to compete. Worley would be eligible in 2006—plenty of time to submit to the gender verification process that was also a requirement of the Stockholm Consensus and be granted her licence.

And so, in April 2005, Worley became the first athlete in the world to be tested under the new policy. Facing four representatives of her own cycling association—none of whom possessed any special knowledge of gender issues or hormone science—she was questioned about the most intimate details of her surgeries, her body, and her life. It was an experience that left her feeling humiliated and angry; that much was clear right away. What didn't become clear until a bit later, when she'd had a chance to collect herself and think it all through, was how violated she felt. In ways that she wasn't immediately able to articulate, the experience changed her.

In the moment, though, the first hurdle had been cleared. On January 16, 2006, Kristen received approval to compete at the Olympic level. She dove into her training with renewed vigour, her eyes on the 2008 team, but the stepped-up training she undertook in an effort to get competition ready took a toll. The body of an XY female produces no sex hormones, and the lack of testosterone and other androgens essentially rendered Worley post-menopausal. For an elite athlete, the muscle deterioration, lower energy levels, and accelerated bone loss that comes along with that was devastating. She needed more testosterone and had no choice but to apply for a therapeutic use exemption (TUE). She subjected herself to another round of examinations in 2008—more poking, more prodding, more deeply personal questions. The TUE was eventually granted, but the amount was too little for her unique physiological needs, and her health continued to decline. The 2008 dream was in the rear-view mirror now, but she kept pushing. Year after year, Kristen fought every way she knew how for permission to receive more than the stipulated dose of testosterone, to no avail. She was rejected at every turn, often by officials who were far less informed than she was about the inner workings of the body, and what it needs to be healthy, to function properly.

The years between 2011 and 2014 were, Kristen says, dark times. Often during those long days, she recalled the violation she'd felt back in 2005, during that initial gender-verification test. Nothing that had happened since had done anything to make her feel less violated; in fact, things had just gotten worse. She couldn't shake her anger—and, eventually, she decided she didn't want to. What she wanted to do was change the system that had led to the feeling in the first place.

"The process they cooked up was barbaric, enraging and mortifying," Worley wrote in her memoir. "They gave no thought to respecting my rights or protecting me as an athlete or a person."

Not knowing quite what to do with the anger she was feeling, Kristen registered complaints with the Ontario Cycling Association and the Canadian Centre for Ethics in Sport; with Sport Canada, the Canadian Olympic Committee, and the World Anti-Doping Agency. She reached out to activists in other countries who encouraged her to keep going. She picked up the phone and called anyone she could get through to at the IOC, including then president Jacques Rogge and medical and scientific director Patrick Schamasch. She talked their ears off about diversity in sport and about how their gender-verification process was violating athletes.

By this time, Kristen says, she knew she was coming to the end of her career. Her health was failing her. "I wasn't actually looking to compete again, but I was looking to be healthy," she says. "I knew that I needed to move forward, and I didn't want to see harm coming to other athletes."

Over the years, her thinking about what had happened that day in April 2005 had coalesced: this wasn't a sports issue, it was a human rights issue. She shouldn't be allowed to compete because she was "woman enough"; she should be allowed to compete because she was human. And she—and all athletes—should have a right to the supports they need to do so in a healthy way.

With this in mind, she made a decision. In June of 2015, she lodged a complaint with the Human Rights Tribunal of Ontario. It argued that the IOC's gender testing policy—the one enforced by sporting commissions around the world, the one that had effectively derailed Kristen's own career—constituted a violation of human rights.

AS WITH MOST LEGAL ACTIONS, the outcome of the hearing and the mediation with Cycling Canada, the Ontario Cycling Association, and the International Cycling Union that took place over the next two years wasn't straightforward. "We gave a little," Kristen says, "and they gave a little." Policy revisions specific to TUEs were enacted. It was agreed that awareness and education programs around diversity and inclusion would be created. And in a turn of events that Kristen hadn't expected, she was asked to work with the Ontario Cycling Association and Cycling Canada to develop standards for XY female athletes. The guidelines they developed, released in July 2017, ensured that objective scientific research would drive the treatment of XY female athletes, and that medical personnel with appropriate expertise would be involved every step of the way. But there was still work to be done. Kristen recalls, for example, that in the decision at the initial hearing, the justice wrote that Kristen "identified as" an "XY transgendered athlete." "I don't 'identify as' that," she wrote. "I am that, an XY female." Nevertheless, the hearing and its aftermath represented a giant step forward. It marked a recognition of the fact that each athlete is unique, that cookie-cutter approaches to complex issues of biology and physiology do not exist, and that everyone has the right to compete. Most importantly, for Kristen, it ensured that no athlete would have to go through the humiliating process that she'd been subjected to not once but twice in her cycling career. It's not everything, Kristen admits, but perhaps it's enough—at least for now.

KRISTEN NEVER DID GET TO compete at the Olympic level— but you could say she's using her talents and skills on a much bigger stage now. Her advocacy work has taken her places her bike never could. Although the extent and parameters of her work with the IOC haven't been fully fleshed out, she knows that she's back where she belongs: in the world of sport. The position—whatever name it's given or shape it takes—will focus on issues of diversity, inclusion, and human-centric design, which will allow her to "crystalize" her identity as Kristen, she says. On the one hand, it will permit her to make use of her off-the-track skills as a design engineer, working to make the built environment around sport and sport events like the Olympics sustainable and ethical. "I am interested in building a more inclusive society—towns, cities, and spaces that are more climate positive, healthier, that don't leave host countries with mountains of debt and unusable infrastructure." The IOC shares that interest.

On the other hand, though—and perhaps more importantly—the opportunity will allow Worley to merge the two worlds that she's been living in: her professional life and her activism. Working with the IOC on issues of inclusivity takes her back to the time when she was Chris, "using sport as a protector." Except this time, Kristen won't be hiding or living a secret life. She'll be able to "take that personal experience—the good and the bad of it all—and turn it around to change lives of people around the world."

"I can help ensure that we are using sport for what it was meant to be used for—not just as sensational event that lasts for twelve or fourteen days," she says, but as "so much more than that. Sport is unique in many ways because it enables us to bring human beings together. It seems like a small thing, but sport is very influential. If we're able to change the behaviour, and the discussion and the language on the playing field, we can start to influence policy from the bottom up."

Kristen pauses for a moment, searching for the right words to sum up how she's feeling. "If I can be that influencer and have that as part of my legacy . . . I mean . . . wow! This really is my Olympic moment."

DAVID HOWARD
Supporting Our Soldiers

"It takes a village to grow a village."

DAVID HOWARD REMEMBERS HIS GRANDFATHER well. He served in the navy during the Second World War and came home, like so many others, suffering from what was then known as shell shock. He drank to cope, became abusive, and soon found himself cut off from his family and friends. "When I visited him," David recalls, "I saw this first-hand, but what I also saw was a veteran who had put his life on the line and was now sick and suffering because of this duty."

That image stuck with David. It was with him in the months after his grandfather's death, when, wanting to honour this man who had served his country, he reached out to a local veterans' group to determine what food support was on offer for veterans who might be struggling financially, and found the cupboard nearly bare. It was with him when he started a food drive to pitch in, and, a few years later, when he

243

and his family created the Canadian Legacy Project, a non-profit organization dedicated to supporting veterans living in poverty. It was with him, still, in 2016 when he and Murray McCann—the organizer behind Calgary's popular Field of Crosses memorial project—learned that homelessness was a growing problem among veterans, affecting nearly five thousand of those who had served. Armed with a belief that "for those who stood on guard for our country, that is five thousand too many," David and Murray started the Homes for Heroes Foundation to help.

And on October 28, 2019, standing on a snowy sidewalk outside of Calgary's 908 ATCO Village—the foundation's flagship project—David thought about his grandfather again, along with all of the veterans he'd met over the last decade. As he watched fifteen veterans of conflicts as far back as Korea and as recent as Afghanistan move into the "tiny home" village created specifically for them, he felt a sense of hope. Perhaps these men and women—and the others Homes for Heroes hoped to support in the months and years to come—would never know the isolation and despair that his grandfather had once experienced. Perhaps there really was a better way.

THE ATCO VETERANS' VILLAGE IN Calgary's Forest Lawn community is the first of its kind in Canada, and a testament to David Howard's vision and unwavering support for Canada's veterans. But David is quick to stress that Homes for Heroes is not an individual effort—far from it. "The villages belong to the local communities and cites that they are built in," he says. "We rely on the support of local companies and individuals to build the project. It takes a village to grow a village."

It was Murray McCann who came up with the idea of using tiny homes to help veterans experiencing homelessness. A tiny home, David explains, is just that: less than three hundred square feet in size, but fully equipped with all the features of a larger home. It seemed like a great idea, a way to approach the issue in both an environmentally conscious and economical way.

"I liked the idea," David says, "but before I could get behind the concept, I wanted to find out what our veterans needed and, more importantly, wanted in a program."

It soon became obvious that no one had a true grip on the problem. Government statistics suggested there were twenty-five hundred homeless veterans across the country, but groups directly involved in supporting Canada's homeless believed the number was much higher.

"The issue we saw was that veterans were not self-identifying," David explains, adding that he now believes nearly five thousand veterans were experiencing homelessness at the time he began looking into the stats. "They were proud and feared losing any VA (Veterans Affairs) benefits they were getting. They were also very resourceful. They couch-surfed with other veterans and did not use shelters that frequently."

Clearly, then, housing was a priority. That was a starting place. Next up was hearing from the veterans themselves. With the help of a researcher, David met with more than two hundred vets who were living in poverty, homeless, or struggling with their transition to civilian life.

"The veterans I spoke with were suffering or having a difficult time transitioning. Some had PTSD and went to the streets to live, and/or were struggling financially because they couldn't find work and their savings were running out. Some couldn't manage what little pension they were given or were having trouble accessing support from the VA," David says.

When he asked what type of housing would work for them, the common denominator in the answers he received was that they needed more than just housing: they needed support. "Getting someone in a home is a great first step," he says, "but what we determined was that there were reasons why our veterans were experiencing homelessness, and in order for them to integrate into civilian life and not end up back on the streets we need to address these issues."

These men and women needed help to get back on track, and they required individually tailored social service programs to do so. They also wanted to be in a community of peers. "As proud warriors they knew the only people who could understand what they have been through were other veterans," David explains. "Finally, they told us they wanted to come into a program—work on themselves, better themselves, find employment—and then move out. They were not looking for a forever home; they wanted to make room for the next veteran."

From the start, the veterans were on board with Murray McCann's tiny-home idea, but it wasn't until David spoke with the team at the Mustard Seed—a Calgary homeless shelter—that he discovered just how well the concept fit the Homes for Heroes mission.

"What I learned was that typically with the homeless population, they are moved into apartments, and that can make it too easy for them to cut themselves off from others," he says. "People coming off the streets have very few possessions, and when they go into these six- to eight-hundred-square-foot apartments it's overwhelming. They have a need to fill the space." That need can translate into a whole host of problems, from hoarding, isolation, and depression to drug and alcohol use.

As David pieced together all of the information he'd gathered, a vision began to take shape: not just tiny homes, but a village of tiny homes, complete with onsite counselling and support services, as well as community amenities, such as gardens, that would encourage integration and interaction over isolation. It sounded ideal—perfect, really—but there was still a long way to go.

What Homes for Heroes was proposing was unique, and as such, not the easiest pitch to make to the various groups that would need to be onside to get the project up and running.

"We needed the support of local municipal government, provincial governments, the federal government, Veterans Affairs, social service organizations, private enterprise, and Canadian citizens," David says. "It was not a program that a charity alone should be solving; we as Canadians owed it to the men and women who served to get this program off the ground."

Over the course of several years, David set about building the village that would help to build the village. His day job as president of The Event Group—which produces concerts, festivals, and keynote speaker events for a wide range of clients—prepared him well for the task of keeping multiple balls in the air. His wife, Jacqueline, an urban planner, was instrumental, helping to navigate various levels of government, social service groups, and sponsors. Rory Thompson, a veteran who works at CP Rail, was a key and early fundraiser, creating the Spin4Vets event that now contributes half a million dollars to Homes for Heroes each year. Working in partnership with the Mustard Seed, Veterans Affairs agreed to fund the onsite counsellor that would be such an integral part of the tiny-home village. And under the guidance of Nancy Southern, ATCO agreed to build and sponsor the project. Slowly, the pieces of the puzzle were coming together. The biggest question mark, though, was site.

There were several false starts—letters of intent offered and then rescinded—before the group won the bid on the Forest Lawn location. "It was a long and very drawn out process," David says, "and I now know why so many have tried to help their community in building projects and have failed."

The group stuck with it, though, and on March 12, 2019, ATCO broke ground. The idea that David and Murray McCann had cooked up back in 2016 was one step closer to becoming a reality.

THE HOMES FOR HEROES VILLAGE in Calgary is now fully operational. The fifteen veterans who took up residence in November 2019—all of whom underwent a needs assessment prior to moving in—immediately got the individual support they needed, with onsite services ranging from PTSD treatment, medical help, and mental health support to career planning, résumé writing, and more. Group therapy sessions take place once a week, and the residents work with both the onsite counsellors and each other to overcome hurdles. It is, says David, truly a "veteran helping veteran" program. "Once you have a veteran take possession of their home you see a dramatic change right away. The self-confidence comes back, and they have a great interest in changing their state of mind."

The positive impact on the veterans who call these villages home is clear—in March of 2020, two of the original tenants "graduated" from the program and are now living offsite and working full-time—but there are benefits beyond this as well.

From the start, the Forest Lawn community welcomed its new residents with open arms. It's not unusual for people to stop by the village with food or home supplies for the tenants, which creates a sense of belonging that's absent in many support programs for underserviced communities. It is, says David, an indication that people are willing to help, provided the opportunity to do so.

"Canadians may not shout from their rooftops their support of our veterans," he says, "but I can say that the majority are very thankful for their service and are more than willing to lend their support, if given the chance."

The village provides that chance, offering an opportunity for Forest Lawn residents, young and old, to connect with veterans in a real and meaningful way.

"The village was built to house our veterans who have fallen on tough times," David says, "but it also serves as a place to educate and get our youth involved in their community."

When school groups come to visit and interact with the veterans, they encounter one of the village's most touching features. "Each home is named after a fallen member of the Canadian Armed Forces," David explains. "Outside of each house is a plaque with a photo and bio of the soldier. The plaques not only serve as a memorial to our fallen, they also give us a chance to educate our youth about the sacrifices made by these men and women. Having schools come to the village and learn first-hand is a great part of this program."

In Calgary, Captain Nichola Goddard and Sapper Steven Marshall—both veterans of the war in Afghanistan—are among the honoured. When Murray Marshall learned that his son was going to be recognized in this way, the carpenter by trade asked to assist in the construction of the village. "I told them I would push a broom if I needed to," he said. "We can't change what happened, but if someone drives by these houses, Steven's friends or kids he went to school with or teachers, they'll think of him and smile. They'll think about Steve and there won't be tears; it will bring a smile to their face."

The idea puts a smile on David's face as well and encourages him to keep pushing ahead with the housing program. Villages are currently being planned for Edmonton and Winnipeg. Ultimately, he'd like to see Homes for Heroes villages in every major city across Canada.

"I never served but am now friends with hundreds that have," he says. "It is extremely rewarding work and I am proud of what our small team has accomplished. We are not done by any means, but we are headed in the right direction."

THE WOMEN OF IDLE NO MORE

Choosing Action

"Our silence is consent."

IT STARTED WITH A FEW Facebook messages and a tweet. Or maybe it began with Bill C-45. Quite possibly, its roots lie much deeper than any of that—somewhere in the hundreds of years of strong Indigenous resistance to colonization, environmental destruction, and systemic abuse. Ask any one of the four women credited with founding the Idle No More movement that swept across the country in late 2012 and early 2013 and they'll likely tell you that it doesn't matter where it began, or who started it. What matters is that it did, and in doing so, gave a collective voice to many who had been silent for too long.

Those four women, all from Saskatchewan—Jessica Gordon, Sylvia McAdam, Sheelah McLean, and Nina Wilson—didn't know each other at first, but they had something in common. Each one of them believed that Stephen Harper's Conservative government was poised to deliver a significant blow to

Indigenous people. The Jobs and Growth Act—the omnibus Bill C-45—proposed changes to more than sixty acts, including the Indian Act, the Navigable Waters Protection Act, and the Environmental Assessment Act. Anyone paying attention could see it was dangerous, that it removed protection for waterways, weakened environmental laws, and threatened the lands reserved for Indigenous peoples.

For Sylvia McAdam, the bill, and everything it stood for, hit a little too close to home.

"After I graduated from law school, I returned to my father's traditional land near the Whitefish reserve and to the water that I had been to when I was a child, and they were gone," explains the author and educator from the Nehiyaw (Cree) Nation. "The water had dried up. It was a terrible thing to witness. When my father and I went back to his traditional hunting lands, his cabin was gone. There was just a huge burn mark on the ground."

Eager to get to the root of the problem, Sylvia investigated. What she learned shocked her: not only were conservation officers blocking roads to keep Indigenous hunters away, but the land itself, Treaty 6 Territory, was being logged. Bill C-45, she knew, would make this type of abuse even easier to perpetrate. Fired up and eager to do something, she started an email chat with Jessica Gordon (Pasqua Treaty 4 Territory) and Nina Wilson (Nakota and Plains Cree from Kahkewistahaw Treaty 4). She shared what she'd seen on her father's traditional lands, and her concerns about what C-45 meant for their community.

"I told them there's something in law called acquiescence," she says. "That means that if you're silent, then your silence is taken as consent. All of us agreed that we couldn't be silent, that grassroots people have a right to know."

Sylvia soon added Sheelah McLean to the chat. A third-generation settler who is an anti-racist, anti-colonial teacher and activist, Sheelah was happy to help.

Facebook provided a convenient starting place. The women set up an events page and discussed what to call it. It was Jessica Gordon who came up with the name. "We were all sitting around, thinking how can we mobilize," Nina Wilson recalls. "She just said, 'We need to get off our asses and quit being idle. We can't be idle no more.' And we sat there and thought about that. There we go, that's how the name came up."

With an identity established, the women used the page, and a Twitter hashtag with the same name, to advertise their first event: a teach-in at Station 20 West, a community enterprise centre in Saskatoon. Set for November 10, 2012, the teach-in would provide information on the proposed bill, allow time for questions and the exchange of ideas, and present a petition for signing. The event notice ended with a nod to the acquiescence that Sylvia had spoken about with her fellow organizers: "Our silence is consent!"

THE STATION 20 WEST EVENT was a relatively quiet affair. Fifty or so people attended, including community activists, poets, artists, some academics, and a few politicians. It didn't seem like the beginning of an international movement, although that's exactly what it turned out to be.

The teach-in lit a fuse. With the help of social media, more events were planned. Many focused on the legislation, but others sought to address long-standing issues around healing, solidarity work, and Indigenous self-determination. On December 10, a Day of Action—organized to coincide with the United Nations' Human Rights Day—brought thousands to the streets in cities across Canada, protesting not only Bill C-45 but also murdered and missing Indigenous women, the rising number of Indigenous children in care, lack of revenue sharing and consultation on legislation, and a failure to deal with the residential school legacy. On December 11, Chief Theresa Spence of the Attawapiskat First Nation began a liquid fast in a teepee on the frozen Ottawa River, within sight of Parliament Hill. "I am in this resistance," she said, "because the pain is too heavy. . . . We want a life of freedom and not a life of pain and fear for the generation." On December 17, at Regina's Cornwall Centre, a flash mob performed a round dance, no doubt taking holiday shoppers by surprise. The following day, a similar scene unfolded at West Edmonton Mall.

And on December 21, a large Idle No More rally was held in Ottawa. Thousands walked the streets, flags raised in snowy skies, to make their voices heard. For Tori Cress, one of the organizers, it was the "most amazing day" she ever been a part of. "December 21st, 2012, to me, will always be remembered as the Day I stood up, with all of you, in a We rally," she wrote. "We did this. We set the stage for the world to listen and really hear us. Pride, Peace, Solidarity will forever be in my Heart and Mind when I look back upon this day. We, the Grassroots, our Leadership, & Non Natives shared a stage, shared our ideas, shared the Love of Our Peoples, and most importantly shared our Love of Turtle Island."

Nina Wilson remembers watching the movement take off and the feeling of being part of something bigger than herself, bigger than her own community. "We are trying to help people get their voices back so that we can make more change and we are able to have more of a First Nations voice," she said at one event. "Not just a First Nations, but an Indigenous voice, and not just an Indigenous voice but a grassroots voice, because it affects us all."

Somewhere in the midst of it all—when the rallies and the drum dances and the flash mobs were popping up everywhere—her son told her she had to check online, to look at the videos. "I was like wow! I started to cry. I couldn't believe it. I knew something was going on, but I just didn't have time to see the depth of what was happening. When I saw it, I was just stunned."

And it just kept going. Pressured, in part, by the peaceful, passionate voices being raised across the country, the prime minister agreed to meet with a delegation of Indigenous leaders in Ottawa on January 11. An Idle No More Global Day of Action was planned for the same date, with more than three hundred events taking place across Canada and the United States, and as far away as New Zealand and the Ukraine. Less than a week later, seven Cree youth, accompanied by two guides, left their community of Great Whale on the Hudson Bay to begin the Quest of Wisjinichu-Nishiyuu (Quest for Unity). They completed the eleven-hundred-kilometre trek and arrived in Ottawa on March 25.

"I think we were all completely blown away by how beautiful it was to see a movement spread across Canada, and then globally so quickly," says Sheelah. "The reason that it was so powerful is because everybody was a leader, everybody was working in the movement. Everybody was a part of it."

"The face of Idle No More is the face of all grassroots people, not specifically one person," Sylvia adds. "It's the face of the many who have fasted, and walked, and been part of rallies, who have been organizing from the very beginning."

IN SOME WAYS, IDLE NO MORE reached its peak in January 2013, on those snowy days in Ottawa. Despite the momentum, despite the protests both in Canada and around the world, despite the meetings between First Nations leaders and Stephen Harper's government, Bill C-45 was passed into law, and Idle No More shifted its focus from non-violent direct action to work in institutions and communities. Years later, Indigenous leaders and communities across the country are still battling to protect their lands from environmental degradation. The movement remains active, and its organizers believe its legacy lives on in important ways.

"Idle No More cannot be extinguished because it has grown so much that it's reached the homes of a lot of people," says Sylvia. "And when you get into homes, it's difficult to bring it out of there."

"A lot of people use it to motivate themselves and to feel, share in solidarity. They know they're not the only ones out there," Jessica adds. "Idle No More is still there, still strong— people are finding different ways to use the movement and empower themselves and others."

In 2018, for example, the movement supported calls for justice reform in the wake of acquittals in the fatal shootings of Colten Boushie (Red Pheasant Cree Nation) and Jon Styres (Six Nations), stating that "both cases highlight how Canadian [juries] across the country continue to send the message to Indigenous communities that [Canadians'] private property holds more value than the lives of Indigenous Peoples."

Idle No More has also been active in its opposition to Trans-Canada's Coastal GasLink project. The movement's Facebook page, which boasts more than 150,000 followers, is busy. Posts range from event notices (a "Cancel Canada" day of action set for July 1, 2018) to newsworthy items to fundraising efforts for those in need.

"Indigenous self-determination, sovereignty, protection of land and water . . . ," says Sylvia, "I think those are critical at this point, and we'll keep working toward that, until those things are in place."

If Idle No More is a movement that these four women somehow started, they are pleased that it no longer seems to need their leadership, that it can proceed under its own steam, carried forward by the women and men who have gathered under this umbrella and discovered their own voices.

"As more and more people come on board, it will take the shape that it needs to take," says Sheelah. "Each community has to decide how they're going to tackle the issues of sovereignty and rethinking what it means to live with the land and water. It is going to continue to grow, there's no doubt about that."

JULIUS KUHL
An Unsung Hero of the Holocaust

"He should be as well known as Schindler,
because he saved as many lives."

IN AUGUST 2017, the *Globe and Mail* published a lengthy article about Julius Kuhl. Not a household name, to be sure, although it would not have been entirely unfamiliar in Toronto. Prior to his death in 1985, Julius had lived and worked in the city for many years before retiring to Miami. He raised a family that included four children and many grandchildren and built a successful construction company from the ground up. A devout man, he was active in the Jewish community at home and abroad; in the early 1970s, he travelled to Israel when hostages were taken, offering to pay the ransom himself and staying to work with the survivors in the aftermath. Even so, the contents of that article would have taken many who knew Julius Kuhl by surprise. They likely had no idea that the man they knew—small in stature, friendly, often seen enjoying a cigar—was an unsung hero of the Holocaust.

....

JULIUS'S STORY BEGINS IN 1917, in the town of Sanok in southeastern Poland. The family was poor, and his mother—parenting her only child alone following the death of her husband—eventually made the difficult decision to send her nine-year-old son to Zurich to live with relatives.

Making the most of the opportunity his mother had given him, Julius put himself through college, earning a graduate degree in political science and law. According to Israel Singer—Kuhl's son-in-law and the former secretary-general of the World Jewish Congress—the young man was also granted *simicha* (ordination) and learned to be a *schochet*, or ritual slaughterer. "He was a *ba'al koreh* [a master of the reading] in an old folks' home from where he was fortunate enough to get food. He looked forward to one day being able to help other people."

The outbreak of the Second World War no doubt heightened the young man's desire to help. Following the German invasion of Poland on September 1, 1939, Kuhl's mother was deported to Siberia (she died shortly after the end of the war). Others faced even worse fates as the Nazis began rounding up Polish Jews and other minorities and sending them off to internment camps, where they were eventually slaughtered. In the face of the horrors unfolding around him, and perhaps figuring it was his best chance to make a difference, Julius decided to join the diplomatic corps. In 1940, he was hired by the Polish legation in Bern, which represented the London-based government-in-exile of his Nazi-occupied homeland. Part of his work would be to extend aid to Polish refugees.

"He was hired because they needed somebody who knew how to talk to Jews who were immigrants and who were coming to Switzerland," said Singer. "In that capacity, he was able to issue emergency visas and emergency passports to people who appeared at the border."

Passports, as it would turn out, became the centrepiece of Kuhl's work. At the time, holding a passport from a neutral country was a literal lifesaver for Jews in Nazi-occupied territory. A Jew holding a passport from Switzerland, for example, or any number of Latin American countries, was exempt from Nazi laws—including those that confined Jews to ghettos and forced them to identify themselves by wearing yellow stars. Perhaps more importantly, the document also made it possible for Jews to escape the occupied country.

What would eventually become a concerted and highly coordinated passport smuggling operation began simply enough. In October 1941, Eli Sturnbuch, a Polish Jew living in Bern, was desperate to save his fiancée, who was imprisoned in the Warsaw ghetto. He purchased a blank Paraguayan passport, carefully filled in her details by hand, and used it to secure her release.

As word of the rescue spread through the city's Jewish community, Julius realized that he might be able to use the same method to save many more Jews. He and others in his community set to work. With the help of a cooperative Paraguayan consulate, they bought hundreds of blank passports and repeated the process that had worked so well for Sturnbuch. The operation soon expanded, with additional passports being purchased from Haiti, Uruguay, Costa Rica, and other neutral countries.

Documents discovered in the postwar years shed some light on the operation's details and scope. Several times a week, Adolf Silberschein—a Polish Jew in exile and founder of the Committee for Relief of the War-Stricken Jewish Population—would send lists to Kuhl with the names, personal details, and photographs of Jews seeking to escape Nazi-occupied territories. Julius and his colleague Konstanty Rokicky would purchase the passports, fill each one in by hand, and paste in a black-and-white photo. Aleksander Lados, Poland's ambassador to Switzerland, provided protection and cooperation when needed. And bank records indicate that the entire effort was supported by American Jews, who sent money through the Polish consulate in New York. The work continued for two years, and while the exact number of passports issued is unknown, it's believed that Julius and his network saved hundreds, if not thousands of lives.

Much of what is now known about the work done by Julius Kuhl and his network is the result of a concerted effort by Markus Blechner, the grandson of Holocaust survivors and the honorary Polish consul in Zurich. After hearing of the passport network as a young man when Kuhl attended his bar mitzvah, Blechner spent years trying to prove that the story he'd heard was true.

"He should be as well known as Schindler, because he saved as many lives as Schindler," Blechner says, although he acknowledges that while thousands of passports were issued, not everyone who received one survived. The Germans eventually noticed the large number of South American passport holders in Switzerland and looked into the situation. All too quickly, Kuhl's operation was shut down, and Julius himself was asked to leave the country. With his wife, kids, and a suitcase of watches in tow, he headed to Toronto.

TODAY, JULIUS KUHL RESTS UNDER a tombstone near Bnei Brak in Israel. The inscription notes that he saved the lives of thousands of Jews. Shortly after his death, a number of photocopied passports and other documents were anonymously donated to the United States Holocaust Memorial Museum. Other records that detail the passport scheme are stored in the archives of the Yad Vashem museum in Jerusalem, including a 1945 letter from the Agudath Israel World Organization. Kuhl and his colleagues, it states, were critical in "rescuing many hundreds of Polish Jews."

It's strange, then, that before Markus Blechner's research and the newspaper article that followed, so few knew his story. Or perhaps it isn't. The father-in-law that Israel Singer knew wasn't the least bit interested in accolades or fame. "He did this for a certain period in time, then he was selling watches in Toronto, then he became a construction magnate," he says. "People say, 'Why didn't he promote his story?' Because he was busy. He was a man trying to build a new life, just like the [Holocaust] survivors were."

Even now, though, so many years after his death, Kuhl's influence is felt. Singer's wife (Kuhl's daughter) once met a teacher whose life had been saved by her father, and who allowed the entire high school to see the passport Kuhl had helped him get. "We've bumped into people whose grandchildren thank us . . . but it's not just for us," Singer said. "This belongs to the general history of the Jewish people."

Singer is certainly pleased that his father-in-law's story has finally been made public. It is, he feels, high time Julius Kuhl received the praise he so richly deserved. "My view is that Dr. Kuhl was in the right place at the right time, and instead of doing nothing—like most people—he did the right thing."

MARGARET BUTLER

Be Strong, Have Courage

"All you have to do is follow what pulls you."

THE REMOTE VILLAGE OF RWINKWAVU—about two hours east of Rwanda's capital city of Kigali—isn't exactly on the beaten path. Visitors to the country are far more likely to make a beeline for Volcanos National Park, with its stunning Great Rift Valley scenery, or explore the fishing villages and tropical islands of Lake Kivu. But when Margaret Butler arrived in Rwanda in 2007, sightseeing wasn't at the top of her to-do list. Instead of heading to one of the country's more popular tourist destinations, she made her way to Rwinkwavu.

Working with Partners in Health—a non-profit organization that fights social injustice by bringing the benefits of modern medical science to the world's most vulnerable communities—Margaret had come to Rwanda as a health educator while also completing the field work required for her master's degree in international education development. Rwinkwavu,

like so much of the country, was still picking up the pieces following the 1994 Rwandan Genocide against the Tutsi that had
left eight hundred thousand people dead in the span of a hundred days. The unspeakable violence was nearly a decade in the
past, but the scars remained: bullet holes in the walls of decrepit
buildings, hateful graffiti, and crushing poverty. There was good
work to be done here, helpful work, and she was excited to roll
up her sleeves and get started.

Margaret quickly settled into a routine. Before setting out
each day to visit the area's schools, the former elite athlete—
she was Canada's steeplechase champion in 2002—would go
for a run down Rwinkwavu's red dirt roads. At first, the village's children would just watch, not quite sure what to make
of the tall blond woman in their midst. "I was . . . scaring a lot
of children because I was so white they thought I was a ghost,"
she recalls.

Eventually, though, curiosity got the better of them, and they
began to join her on her runs. At least the boys did. Never the
girls. In Rwanda, it seemed, it wasn't normal for girls to run.

It also wasn't normal for girls here to attend school beyond
the primary level—something Margaret learned during her
daily classroom visits. Less than 15 percent of Rwandan girls
go on to secondary school, and less than 5 percent of that group
will attend university. For many families, the decision comes
down to money. In a country where the average yearly household income is about $400, day school costs roughly $200 a
year, boarding school runs to $500, and university requires a
whopping $3,000. If a family can afford to educate any of its
children, it's the boys who are chosen.

"The boys are seen as a better return," Margaret says. The girls? They're expected to stay home and help raise younger children or support the family by working in the fields. The situation struck her as incredibly unfair.

Raised on British Columbia's Bowen Island—just a twenty-minute ferry ride from West Vancouver—Margaret had, to some degree, taken her own education for granted: bachelor's degrees from the Universities of Washington and British Columbia, teacher's college at Columbia in New York. "As a young woman in North America, I never questioned whether or not I could or would go on to secondary school. It was a given," she says.

But for the girls she saw in Rwinkwavu each day, nothing could have been further from the truth. They weren't given the same chances their brothers were given, weren't able to envision a life for themselves beyond the village. In so many ways, they were stuck at the starting line of a race. And what's worse, they knew it.

"One day," Margaret recalls, "this girl said to me, 'I'm fourteen years old, and I know I'm not going to secondary school, and I'm feeling unmotivated to work in the classroom.' I sat there and thought, you know what? I would feel exactly the same way . . . I walked away from that conversation thinking I should—and can—do something."

When it came to figuring out what that "something" might be, Margaret found inspiration in her morning runs, and her own history as a competitor. At its core, athletics is about pushing yourself, about overcoming obstacles, and about the confidence you gain when you're able to finish a race or game or match despite the challenges in your way. Why not offer Rwinkwavu's girls a chance to feel that confidence? Why not encourage them to get into the race?

There it was: in partnership with the Partners in Health social workers, Margaret launched Rwanda's first-ever girls-only fun run. "It was," she says, "a great way of starting the conversation around girls' empowerment."

It was also a much bigger success than she'd dared to imagine. Four hundred girls from the local schools came out to the run, which was held in 2008 and organized to celebrate girls' education. As they dashed down the roads of the villages, kicking up red dust as they went, the boys stood off to the side, offering support with yells of "Komera!" In the local dialect, Margaret learned, the word means "be strong, have courage."

THE RACE WAS JUST the beginning—both for Margaret and the girls she was determined to support. Encouraged by the turnout, and the enthusiasm the event generated, she decided to keep pushing. She tapped her network of friends and families for donations in support of girls' education and raised $2,000. The funds would cover the cost of sending ten girls to day school for a year.

It was good, but not good enough. Getting girls to school was one thing; keeping them there was another. Time and time again, Margaret heard from eager, intelligent young women who wanted nothing more than to go to school, but who also knew that the minute there was work to be done at home, they'd be expected to help. There would be days missed, homework incomplete. What these girls needed, Margaret realized, was boarding school. And for that, she'd need more money.

In 2009, Margaret, who was by then living in New York City, started Komera, a non-profit scholarship fund dedicated to supporting the young women of Rwinkwavu. Her mother, Hilary, got the Canadian chapter off the ground and hosted a "Rotary Run for Rwanda" on Bowen Island. It was quickly supplemented by other "Komera Global Runs" that now happen every June in several US cities, including New York and Boston.

The fundraising worked, and Komera was soon supporting girls at local boarding schools, paying for tuition and rooming, uniforms, school supplies, and health products. "[It's] everything," wrote Hilary Butler in an article about her own visit to Rwinkwavu in 2015, "that an impoverished girl would need in order to complete her education."

By 2010, Komera had evolved along with Margaret's thinking about the type of investment these girls needed. Education was vital, but a more holistic approach was needed if Komera was to effect lasting change. Drawing on the expertise of board members and volunteers, both in North America and on the ground in Rwanda, Komera came up with an approach that would develop self-confident young women through the three prongs of education, community development, and sport.

In addition to attending school—just like the boys in the village—the girls Komera supports work with mentors, are given time to make health and exercise a priority, and take part in leadership workshops.

"During their school holidays, [students] attend camps with Komera where they learn about leadership development, health, and social entrepreneurship," Margaret explains. "They also participate in sport and explore positive ways that they can use their bodies."

The results are promising: 149 young woman supported with secondary school or university scholarships; 105 secondary school graduates (a 100 percent graduation rate); and 66 percent of those graduates now in university, training to be teachers, police officers, and pilots, among other career goals, or working toward running their own businesses.

Families are a hugely important part of the equation, as well, as Komera works to transfer leadership of the program to Rwandans. ("My goal," Margaret joked a few years ago, "is to work myself out of a job." In 2020, she did just that, stepping down from her day-to-day role with the organization.) When a student is accepted into the program, the family is asked to join the Komera Parent and Guardian Cooperative. Here, working with Komera mentors, they will receive financial advice, gain business skills, and be supported in starting small businesses and undertaking community improvement projects. The cooperative now includes more than a hundred families and fifty business ventures.

It's easy to see the difference that Komera's work is making. David Boehmer—a friend of Margaret's from high school who now serves on Komera's board of directors—has witnessed it first-hand.

"When I met the girls, they didn't look you in the eye or even say 'hello,'" he says. "They had no dreams whatsoever. Now, they're running businesses and giving back. That's because of Margaret."

Many of Komera's "fierce female leaders" are former Komera scholars, who have stayed with the organization out of a desire to give back. As Margaret always hoped it would, the community is embracing the program and making it their own. That's exactly the kind of success that organizations like Komera need in order to succeed and grow.

"Margaret's dream," says David Boehmer, "is that one of our girls runs Komera one day, that Margaret goes on to do something different and one of our girls takes that over."

News of Komera's successful work has spread beyond Rwanda's borders. In late 2015, then First Lady Michelle Obama recognized Komera's work with a shout-out from her Let Girls Learn initiative. And in 2016, Margaret was honoured by Boston mayor Martin J. Walsh as a winner of the EXTRAordinary Women Campaign.

The endorsements are wonderful, but they aren't what keeps Margaret focused on the task at hand. That drive and determination comes from a passion to help, to make a difference. Today, she puts that passion into AMPLIFY Girls, a collection of community-driven organizations working together to create a different model for development.

"When you're passionate about something, there's not much that will hold you back," she says. "Personally, I think it's all about following that gut. You're thinking, 'I know I want to do more but . . .' But really, all you have to do is follow what pulls you."

And what pulls Margaret Butler hasn't changed since 2007, when she found herself in a small Rwandan village where the girls were too shy to tag along on her morning runs. Her core goal has never wavered: it's about the girls, and the ways in which they can be empowered and inspired to succeed.

"Young women just need an opportunity," she says. "They have self-confidence but need someone to build it up."

"My hope for Komera is that they become leaders, presidents, mothers who send their daughters to school."

TOMAS JIROUSEK
Graduating with Honours

*"We've come a long way towards reconciliation,
and that makes me proud."*

THE LAST THING ON Tomas Jirousek's mind in June of
2020 was school. The COVID-19 virus that scuttled his final
semester as a political sciences undergraduate at Montreal's
McGill University had taken care of that. Classes and exams
went online, athletics and extracurriculars were cancelled, and
in-person commencement ceremonies were pushed to the fall.
So when he got the news that he had been voted valedictorian
for the Faculty of Arts, Tomas was, to say the least, surprised.

Quarantined with his family in Whitehorse at the time, the
twenty-two-year-old rushed to share the news. "I ran into my
parents' room and yelled, 'I'm valedictorian!'" he says.

The bit of news that came next was no less of a shock: he had
just twenty-four hours to write and record a brief speech that
would be shown during the school's virtual graduation ceremony four days later.

Many students would have gone into a full-blown panic at the thought of having to come up with a meaningful valedictorian address in less than a day. But Tomas didn't let the news faze him. In fact, he knew exactly what message he wanted to deliver to the graduating class of 2020.

THE FEELING WAS THERE RIGHT from the start—the alienation, the slight uneasiness. As a member of the varsity rowing team, Tomas spent a good deal of time in McGill's athletic buildings. It was hard to avoid the Redmen jerseys, banners, and flags that adorned the walls. Pick up a campus newspaper and there they were again, all over the sports pages. For an Indigenous student such as Tomas—a member of the Blackfoot Confederacy from the Kainai First Nation of southern Alberta—it was uncomfortable.

"Walking through McGill Athletics facilities, it can feel incredibly isolating, it can be insulting to see a slur like the Redmen printed on jerseys and printed on shirts and to see people proudly wearing this slur," Tomas says. "It can make you feel as if you don't belong in the space."

The name "Redmen" wasn't meant to be a racial slur. Dating from the 1920s, the team moniker was originally rendered "Red Men" and is widely believed to be a reference to the team's red uniforms and the red hair common among the Celts—an acknowledgement of founder James McGill's heritage.

But it didn't take long for things to slide into less benign territory. In the 1950s, the men's and women's varsity teams were commonly referred to as the Indians and the Squaws.

And by the time the eighties rolled around, several teams had chosen a stylized logo of an Indigenous man to adorn their jerseys.

To its credit, McGill was aware of the issue. In 2017, in response to the Truth and Reconciliation Committee's call for action, a university task force on Indigenous studies and education responded in kind, calling on its own administration to change the team name. As is so often the case with large bureaucratic organizations, however, nothing happens fast: a committee was struck to look into issues of "commemoration and renaming," and that was that. At least until Tomas Jirousek came along.

In the fall of 2018, Tomas—an established member of the rowing team and the Students' Society's Indigenous affairs commissioner—decided to speak up. "Being Indigenous, being an athlete," he says, he figured he could speak to the issue "from the heart."

He attended a campus town hall in early September and voiced his concern over the team name. His opinion was met with considerable resistance.

"Seeing fellow athletes who are supposed to be supporting each other in the capacity as athletes and then to know that they're so passionate about keeping [a name] that is detrimental to your mental health—it's terrible to say the least," Tomas said at the time.

In the wake of the town hall, an idea began to form. What was needed, Tomas figured, was a campaign—something that would educate and inform, that would show his fellow students, as well as the faculty and administration, that the desire for change was about so much more than being politically correct; it was about real people with real feelings, and the legacy of a systemic form of racism whose time had surely come.

"Listening to the experiences of other varsity athletes throughout the university and other Indigenous students on campus," he says, "I thought it was important to orchestrate a movement where we could demonstrate our discontent with the continued usage of the Redmen name."

And so the work began. Classes, of course, and rowing, but also many hours spent poring over archives and yearbooks and newspapers and reaching out to alumni to gather the evidence that would form the backbone of his campaign.

It wasn't easy.

In an old yearbook, he came across a gruesome picture of an Indigenous person being scalped. He was taken out to lunch by alumni and pressured to drop the whole thing. He received messages that suggested he was "just a dumb Indian who only got into McGill" by virtue of being Native. He met with the administration and the principal—all receptive, respectful, and open to ideas—but the process was, he says, still painful. "It's quite emotionally taxing when you have to describe over and over again . . . interactions you've had with other students, or other athletes at the gym."

Difficult or not, the campaign continued. An online petition calling for a name change collected more than ten thousand signatures, and a campus demonstration was planned for October 31. Carrying umbrellas to ward off the rain—and signs bearing slogans such as "Intent Doesn't Erase Impact," "Not Your Redmen," and "Racism Honours No One"—students stepped out of their classrooms and took their message to the streets around McGill's campus.

"This issue for me connects to everything that I have a problem with at McGill, in Canada," said Ella Martindale, a student from the Cowichan nation in British Columbia. "It connects to identity. Who am I? What am I doing here? Do I really belong here at McGill?"

Following the rally, Tomas and his fellow organizers kept the pressure up. In November, the Students' Society of McGill University held a referendum on the name change issue: 79 percent of students who cast a ballot voted in favour of a change.

The administration was listening. Following Tomas's successful campaign, and in the wake of the task force report that came out of the original response to the Truth and Reconciliation Committee call to action, McGill announced in April 2019 that the Redmen name would not be used during the 2019–2020 academic year and would be replaced by 2020–2021.

In a statement to the media, McGill principal Suzanne Fortier acknowledged that while the name was not meant to be derogatory, it was impossible to ignore the contemporary understanding of the term. The name, she said, "is not one the university would choose today, and it is not one that McGill should carry forward."

"I have learned about the true depths of the pain caused by the Redmen name," she continued. "I have heard from Indigenous students at McGill who feel alienated by the name. They feel disrespected and unconsidered. They feel conflicted over their rightful pride in being Indigenous people, and their pride in being McGill students."

Tomas, in Europe when the news broke, was ecstatic. But he knew better than to expect smooth sailing and braced himself for the backlash he figured would be inevitable when, in accordance with the change, all signs, banners, flags, and merchandise bearing the Redmen name were removed.

"Reconciliation, I think, will merit these type of difficult moments, these moments of critical self-reflection that will have plenty of people uncomfortable with the necessary steps we need to take in order to address the grievances of the past," he says. He believes the memorabilia itself has a role to play in that process and should be preserved rather than destroyed, so that "we can learn from the sins of our past."

FOR TOMAS AND MCGILL'S OTHER Indigenous students, the 2019–2020 academic year—the first without the Redmen name adorning team jerseys—was a time of healing.

"We went through this (past) year without being known as the Redmen," he says. "We were just the McGill team. It was easier, like a breath of fresh air. It felt more comfortable. You could feel the change among Indigenous students. You felt your place at McGill."

The recollections of the backlash and personal attacks were still there, of course, but better memories were layered overtop—memories of rallies in the rain and referendums, and of support from the administration, from faculty, and from non-Indigenous students whose allyship meant the world.

"We've come a long way towards reconciliation," he says, "and that makes me proud."

And then, of course, there was the valedictorian thing. That makes him proud too. Shortly after finding out he'd been voted to represent his graduating class, Tomas learned that he was the only First Nations student to have that honour for the Faculty of Arts, and one of only a few Indigenous students to ever serve as valedictorian in McGill's history.

It's knowledge like that that makes it impossible for Tomas to ignore the work that still needs to be done. "McGill is about to go into its third century," he says. "That it has only just now had its first First Nations valedictorian is an incredibly sad statement when you reflect on the history of Indigenous peoples in this country. Only a few decades ago, Indigenous people were not able to be doctors or lawyers or attend post-secondary schools without losing their status."

But the events of the last few years show that change— that progress—is possible, if only people are willing to put in the work. And that was the message Tomas was so eager to deliver in his abbreviated valedictorian address. In the spring of 2020, from his vantage point in Canada's North, he watched as COVID-19 laid bare inequalities, and as riots and calls for police reform tackled issues of systemic racism in both the United States and Canada. When presented with the chance to address his fellow graduates, Tomas decided to use it as a call to action—an opportunity to remind the class of 2020 that "the world needs McGill graduates to be willing and able to challenge systemic racism and other forms of oppression that persevere in our communities today."

For Tomas, law will be the path toward effecting further change. The next stop in his education is the University of

Toronto's Faculty of Law. "My passion to help people is what drove me toward law," he says. "I was raised to be giving back to my community, and I think I can do that in law in a way that other careers might not allow me to."

Whatever comes next, Tomas can look back with pride on his accomplishments at McGill. As the recipient of the university's first Moral Courage in Reconciliation Award, he knows he owes a debt of gratitude to the Indigenous students who came before him—those who were never recognized for their accomplishments but who nevertheless blazed a trail that he and others have followed. He hopes it will get easier for each successive graduating class, and he's cautiously optimistic about the future.

"As I graduate, I feel like the ball is rolling faster. We're seeing Indigenous students standing on that podium that we've collectively built over a couple of generations, and I feel like things are just getting better and better. I'm really proud to say I had a part in that."

VIOLA DESMOND
Standing Up by Sitting Down

"Every individual is equal before and under the law."

AS VIOLA DESMOND SANK INTO her seat in the Roseland Theatre on November 8, 1946, she must have felt a sense of relief. It was warm and dry—an improvement over the conditions outside—and for the time being, at least, her car problems were out of her hands. She'd hoped to be in Sydney, Nova Scotia, by now, conducting her business meetings, but fate had a different plan. The engine of her 1940 Dodge sedan had started acting up about 160 kilometres outside of Halifax. The nearest town was New Glasgow, so she'd pulled off the road there to find a service station. The mechanic assured her the car could be fixed, but not until the next day, when he'd be able to track down a part. It wasn't convenient, to be sure, but it wasn't the worst thing either. She was safe and sound—not stuck on a roadside somewhere—and the unexpected detour had provided something she rarely got on a typical night back home in

Halifax: free time. She'd arranged for a hotel room and decided
to take in a movie. The Roseland's marquee had promised *Dark
Mirror*, starring Olivia de Havilland and Lew Ayres. De Havilland was one of Viola's favourite actresses, and she was looking
forward to the show. But before the lights dimmed and the
opening credits rolled, Viola would find herself carried out of
theatre, quite literally kicking and screaming, and into Canada's
history books.

It started with a simple tap on the shoulder. It was the usher,
explaining that the ticket Viola had purchased was for the balcony, not the main floor; the woman asked Viola to move. Figuring that a mistake had been made, Viola quickly made her
way back to the cashier. She asked to exchange her ticket for
one that would allow her to sit downstairs.

"I'm sorry," the cashier replied, "but I'm not permitted to sell
downstairs tickets to you people."

You people. At that moment, standing in front of the ticket
window with her money in hand, Viola must have understood
what was really going on. This wasn't a mix-up about tickets or
seating arrangements. Although the usher hadn't mentioned it,
and neither, really, had the ticket seller, the message was coming
through loud and clear: Viola was Black, and at the Roseland,
Black patrons were required to sit upstairs.

AS A YOUNG BLACK WOMAN in Nova Scotia, Viola Desmond was no stranger to racial discrimination. In Halifax, she
lived and worked in the North End, a predominantly Black
neighbourhood. The daughter of James and Gwendolyn Davis,

she was descended from slaves who had come north from the United States in the aftermath of the War of 1812 and the American Revolutionary War. She was married to Jack Desmond, the first registered Black barber in Halifax. She'd taught at two racially segregated schools before leaving the teaching profession to train as a beautician. To do so, she had to travel to Montreal, and then to Atlantic City and New York City, as no beauty schools in her home province accepted Black women.

When she returned to Halifax in 1937, she opened Vi's Studio of Beauty Culture at the corner of Gerrish and Gottingen Street, in the North End, and catered to the Black women who were denied service in salons that welcomed the white community without question. Her shop was instantly successful and counted among its customers several influential Black women, including activist Carrie M. Best, opera singer Portia White, and Gwen Jenkins, one of the province's first Black nurses.

In 1940, she expanded her business and opened a beauty school—the Desmond School of Beauty Culture—so that other women like her wouldn't have to travel far from home to receive their training. Before long, women were travelling *to* Nova Scotia from New Brunswick and Quebec to attend. Building on what she'd achieved, Viola created a line of beauty products that were sold at venues owned and operated by graduates of her school. Despite the obstacles in her way, and despite the "unofficial" racism that she encountered every day of her life, she had become a successful businesswoman and an important booster of the Black community in her hometown.

And now here she was, 160 kilometres from home, at the end of a long and frustrating day, confronted yet again with the discrimination she'd faced so many times before. She tried to reason with the young woman behind the ticket counter, explaining that when she attended movies in Halifax, she always sat downstairs because of her poor eyesight. She tried, once again, to pay the extra ten cents that would have upgraded her balcony ticket. It was no use; the cashier refused to complete the exchange. And so, Viola took matters into her own hands. She turned away from the ticket counter, walked back into the theatre, and sat herself down in the same seat she'd been using before the usher tapped her on the shoulder.

It didn't take long for the usher to notice, and soon enough, the manager was called. He explained that the theatre could refuse admission to any "objectionable person." Viola argued that she hadn't been refused admission at all—she'd purchased a ticket, been allowed in, and had been more than willing to pay for a seat on the main floor. It was the ticket seller who had refused to take her money. But nothing Viola said made a difference to the manager, and nothing the manager said compelled Viola to move. The local police were called, and as astonished moviegoers looked on, Viola Desmond was dragged from the Roseland Theatre and taken to jail.

LATER, VIOLA TOLD HER YOUNGER sister, Wanda, that she "didn't go quietly." She tried to grab hold of a door jamb as the manager and a police officer, each holding one of her arms, pulled her into the street, bruising her hip and knee in the process. After an arrest warrant was issued, she spent the next twelve hours alone in a cell, sitting upright on her cot and trying not to lose her composure. "I took my purse out and dumped it out on the cot and sorted the items and worked on my appointment book," she told her sister. "I tried to kill time by keeping myself busy."

The next morning, she was escorted to the courthouse, where a hearing of sorts took place. Although she had no lawyer—and had not been told she was entitled to one—she was brought in front of a local judge and charged with a violation of the province's amusement tax law. The theatre manager, a Mr. Henry MacNeil, claimed that Viola had purchased a ticket for the balcony but sat downstairs. He explained to the judge that there was a ten-cent difference in the price of the two tickets and a one-cent difference in the provincial amusement tax.

Once again, Viola tried to explain: she told the judge that she'd originally asked for a downstairs ticket and, at the first sign of trouble, had tried to exchange the one she'd been issued. It made no difference. The judge quickly found her guilty and ordered her to either pay a twenty-dollar fine, plus six dollars in court charges (a sum equivalent to more than $350 today), or spend thirty days in jail. She paid the fine, although she told Wanda that she'd wanted to spend the thirty days in jail; it was only a sense of responsibility to her students that compelled her to hand over her money and return to Halifax.

It wasn't initially Viola's idea to get in touch with a lawyer. Her father—livid over the treatment his daughter had endured and the injuries she'd sustained—encouraged her to see a doctor. And the doctor, in turn, suggested she seek counsel. When she decided to contact a lawyer about having the charges against her reversed, the Black community she'd been serving and supporting for years rallied behind her. Carrie Best, founder of *The Clarion*—the province's second Black-owned newspaper— called Viola's arrest "Jim Crow-ism, at its basest" and covered her case closely. Pearleen and William Oliver, founding members of the Nova Scotia Association for the Advancement of Coloured People, took up her cause and provided funds to help her appeal her conviction.

Viola's lawyer, Frederick Bissett, chose not to address the violation of Viola's civil rights or right to a fair trial. Instead, he focused on getting compensation for the fact that she had been dragged from the theatre and the injuries she'd suffered as a result. But the Nova Scotia Supreme Court wasn't sympathetic. On January 20, 1947, Justice Maynard Brown Archibald ruled against Viola, saying that the original ruling should have been appealed to the county court. And since the deadline for filing such an appeal had lapsed, the conviction stood.

With that decision, Viola Desmond's act of resistance effectively ended. Throughout the entire ordeal, no one had mentioned the colour of her skin: not the cashier who refused to sell her a ticket to the main floor, not the usher who asked her to leave, not the manager and the police officers who dragged her out of the theatre, and not the local magistrate who had presided over her brief court appearance the following morning. It was only after the Nova Scotia Supreme Court rejected her appeal that one of the magistrates, Justice William Lorimer Hall, suggested that Viola's race might well have been behind all that had happened to her. "One wonders," he said, "if the manager of the theatre who laid the complaint was so zealous because of the bona fide belief that there had been an attempt to defraud the Province of Nova Scotia of the sum of one cent, or was it a surreptitious endeavour to enforce Jim Crow rule by misuse of a public statute?"

ON FEBRUARY 7, 1965, Viola Desmond died in New York City. She was fifty years old. Although she lived to see the end of segregation in Nova Scotia—it was legally dismantled in 1954—she never received acknowledgement of the racial discrimination behind her case, and she certainly had no idea that her actions would one day be heralded as a pivotal event in the quest for equality by the province's Black population. That recognition came about largely as a result of Wanda Robson's efforts to share her sister's story.

In 2003, at the age of seventy-three, and inspired by a course she was taking on race relations in North America, Wanda began to speak publicly about her sister Viola's life. She spoke to school children and university students, to reporters and politicians. In 2010, she published a book, *Sister to Courage*. That same year, Viola Desmond finally began to get the recognition she deserved.

On April 15, 2010, at a ceremony in Halifax, Viola was granted a pardon by Lieutenant Governor Mayann Francis. The initial charges should never have been laid, Francis acknowledged, calling the conviction a miscarriage of justice. Two years later, Canada Post issued a stamp bearing Viola's image, and in February 2016, a Heritage Minute was produced, bringing Viola's story to television viewers. Later that year, the Bank of Canada announced that Viola would be on the front of the new ten-dollar bill—the first non-royal woman to appear by herself on a Canadian banknote. On the back of the bill, along with an image of the Canadian Museum for Human Rights, is a quotation from the Canadian Charter of Rights and Freedoms: "Every individual is equal before and under the law and has the right to the equal protection and equal benefit of the law without discrimination."

On the day the bill was launched, Jennifer O'Connell, parliamentary secretary to the minister of finance, spoke about Viola's contributions to human rights in Canada. "Viola Desmond wasn't the first, or sadly, the last person to stand up to injustice," she said. "I hope with the daily reminder of her story, more of us will be encouraged to follow in her courageous footsteps and take a stand to do what's right."

Wanda Robson attended the ceremony that day and was the first to use the new bill to make a purchase—she bought her granddaughter a copy of a book about Viola's life. As a young woman, in a different time and place, Wanda had been embarrassed by her sister's act of civil disobedience—but no more.

"It's unbelievable to think that . . . my sister—a woman, a black woman—is on the ten-dollar bill," she said. "The Queen is in good company."

ACKNOWLEDGEMENTS

WRITING A BOOK ABOUT COURAGEOUS Canadians in the midst of a pandemic is, it turns out, just what the doctor ordered. As the world went a little crazy outside of my office, I got to focus on good news instead of bad, and on the many ways that people can be kind and brave and downright heroic, when the need arises.

This book quite literally would not have been possible without the many people who were willing to share their stories with me. While most of these stories have a happy ending, it's also true that some of the events described here were traumatic and life-changing for those involved. Letting someone else muck around with your memories and experiences is an act of trust, and I appreciate that more than I can say. I hope I've earned it.

I owe the fact that I'm capable of writing a book to my father and mother, Ron and Alice Pruessen. Each in their own way has taught me the importance of curiosity, of critical and careful thinking, of words, and of a well-turned phrase. They also instilled in me the idea that I am capable of almost anything I put my mind to—except math. Never math.

Thanks, also, to Janice Zawerbny at HarperCollins, who reached out with this idea and trusted that someone who usually sits on the other side of the desk could get it done. Who knew, all those years ago, that we'd still be in this crazy industry together? Copyeditor Canaan Chu saved me from some embarrassing errors with his meticulous work, and for that I'm grateful.

Finally, thanks to Terry, Michael, and Rachel—for putting up with stressed-out-on-deadline me, eating way more take-out dinners than is strictly healthy, and always reminding me of what's most important in life. I love you all to infinity and beyond.

SOURCES

PART 1: COURAGE IN THE FACE OF ADVERSITY

Ryan Straschnitzki: Keeping the Dream Alive

Canadian Press. "'I Couldn't Move My Body': Straschnitzki Recalls Humboldt Broncos Bus Crash," *Saskatoon StarPhoenix*, April 25, 2018, https://thestarphoenix.com/news/local-news/humboldt-broncos-bus-crash-ryan-straschnitzki-left-paralyzed-in-deadly-crash-says-survivors-bonding.

Graveland, Bill. "'I Was Bawling': Injured Bronco's Mother Stunned by His Progress after Surgery," CTV News, November 22, 2019, https://www.ctvnews.ca/sports/i-was-bawling-injured-bronco-s-mother-stunned-by-his-progress-after-surgery-1.4697389.

Graveland, Bill. "'What a Role Model': Paralyzed Bronce Makes Adidas Ad, Hall of Fame Nominee List," CBC News, September 30, 2019, https://www.cbc.ca/news/canada/saskatoon/ryan-straschnitzki-adidas-humboldt-broncos-1.5302726.

Hudes, Sammy. "A Family United Makes a Home in Airdrie Hotel," *Calgary Herald*, March 28, 2019, https://calgaryherald.com/news/local-news/bronco-unbroken-a-family-united/.

Hudes, Sammy. "Bronco Unbroken: Another Shot at Life and Hockey," *Calgary Herald*, March 29, 2019, https://calgaryherald.com/news/local-news/bronco-unbroken-another-shot/.

Hudes, Sammy. "Bronco Unbroken: From Tragedy to Tenacity, the Straz Strong Journey," *Calgary Herald*, March 27, 2019, https://calgaryherald.com/news/local-news/straz-strong-from-tragedy-comes-tenacity/.

Laing, Zach, and Vanessa Hrvatin. "A New Journey: Ryan Straschnitzki Hits
the Ice Once Again," *Calgary Herald*, July 22, 2018, https://calgaryherald
.com/news/local-news/a-new-journey-ryan-straschnitzki-hits-the-ice-
once-again/.

Ledingham, Britton. "Ryan Straschnitzki Is StrazStrong," *AirdrieLife*, Winter
2018/19, https://airdrielife.com/citylife/ryan-straschnitzki-is-strazstrong/.

Timea Nagy: One Girl at a Time

"Her Story." TimeaNagy.com, n.d., https://www.timeanagy.com.

Nagy, Timea E., and Shannon Moroney. *Out of the Shadows: A Memoir*. Toronto:
Penguin Random House Canada, 2019.

O'Brien, Cillian. "She Answered an Ad for Babysitting in Canada, Wound Up
a Sex Slave," CTV News, May 28, 2019, https://www.ctvnews.ca/canada/
she-answered-an-ad-for-babysitting-in-canada-wound-up-a-sex-
slave-1.4440327.

"Out of the Shadows: How Timea Nagy Survived International Human Traffickers,"
CBC News, July 2, 2019, https://www.cbc.ca/news/canada/hamilton/
out-of-the-shadows-how-timea-nagy-survived-international-human-
traffickers-1.5192342.

Reilly, Nicole. "Human Trafficking Survivor Timea Nagy Is 'Out of the Shadows'
with New Memoir," *Hamilton Spectator*, May 21, 2019, https://www.thespec
.com/news/hamilton-region/2019/05/21/human-trafficking-survivor-
timea-nagy-is-out-of-the-shadows-with-new-memoir.html.

"Timea Nagy, Human Trafficking: Interview," Speak Truth to Power Canada, n.d.,
https://sttpcanada.ctf-fce.ca/lessons/timea-nagy/interview/.

Luca "Lazylegz" Patuelli: No Excuses, No Limits

"B-boy Luca 'Lazylegz' Patuelli Smashes Stereotypes to the Beat," *Abilities*,
2018, https://www.abilities.ca/people/breaking-free/.

"Bio," n.d., Lucapatuelli.com, https://www.lucapatuelli.com/bio.

Bush, Jessica. "Inspiring People Who Have Overcome Adversity to Achieve
Wild Dreams," Buzzworthy, April 28, 2019, https://www.buzzworthy.
com/10-people-who-overcame-adversity-to-achieve-unbelievable-
things/.

Curran, Peggy. "Games Were Life-Changing Experience for Breakdancer," *Montreal Gazette*, March 24, 2010, https://www.pressreader.com/canada/montreal-gazette/20100324/283253094087650.

Dunlevy, T'Cha. "For Breakdance Crew ILL-Abilities, Physical Challenges Aren't Crutches," *Montreal Gazette*, November 13, 2018, https://montrealgazette.com/entertainment/local-arts/skys-the-limit-for-ill-abilities-breakdance-crew?.

Greenaway, Kathryn. "No Excuses, No Limits for Canadian Dance Ambassador Luca 'Lazylegz' Patuelli," *Montreal Gazette*, April 24, 2015, https://montrealgazette.com/entertainment/arts/no-excuses-no-limits-for-canadian-dance-ambassador-luca-lazylegz.

"Luca Patuelli," n.d., Concordia.ca, https://www.concordia.ca/alumni-friends/applause/search/luca-patuelli.html.

Mackrell, Judith. "ILL-Abilities: The B-Boy Supercrew Taking on the Able-Bodied," *The Guardian*, May 2, 2013, https://www.theguardian.com/stage/2013/may/02/ill-abilities-dance-breakin-convention.

News Staff. "Canadian Heroes Fox, Hansen Invoked to Open 2010 Paralympics," CityNews, March 13, 2010, https://toronto.citynews.ca/2010/03/13/canadian-heroes-fox-hansen-invoked-to-open-2010-paralympics/.

"Power of One: Dancing His Way over Disability," CTV News, August 14, 2012, https://montreal.ctvnews.ca/power-of-one-dancing-his-way-over-disability-1.683246.

Ramnanan, Marissa. "ILL-Abilities Celebrates Ten Years of Passion and Inspiration," *The Link*, November 20, 2018, https://thelinknewspaper.ca/article/ill-abilities-celebrates-10-years-of-passion-and-inspiration.

Sarkissian, Anna. "Glory Days at 2010 Paralympic Games," *The Journal*, March 18, 2010, http://cjournal.concordia.ca/archives/20100318/glory_days_at_2010_paralympic_games.php.

Tremblay, Alyssa. "Luca 'Lazylegz' Patuelli Dances on Ellen," September 17, 2013, Concordia.ca, http://www.concordia.ca/cunews/offices/vpaer/aar/2013/12/17/luca-lazylegz-patuellidancesonellen.html.

Terry Fox: Inspiring a Nation to Fight for a Cure

"By the Numbers: Terry Fox Edition," *The Province*, last updated June 15, 2016, https://theprovince.com/news/by-the-numbers-terry-fox-edition.

Marshall, Tabitha. "Terry Fox," *Canadian Encyclopedia*, last edited February 4, 2019.
https://www.thecanadianencyclopedia.ca/en/article/terry-fox.

McInroy, Ian. "This Dedicated Senior Has Raised $1 Million for Terry Fox,"
OrilliaMatters, September 13, 2019, https://www.orilliamatters.com/
local-news/this-dedicated-senior-has-raised-1-million-for-terry-
fox-1689023.

Milley, Danielle. "Terry Fox Exhibit on Display at Scarborough Civic Centre,"
Toronto.com, September 23, 2011, https://www.toronto.com/news-story/
68914-terry-fox-exhibit-on-display-at-scarborough-civic-centre/.

Scrivener, Leslie. *Terry Fox: His Story.* Toronto: McClelland & Stewart, 2000.

"Terry Fox's Marathon of Hope: The End of the Road," CBC Digital Archives,
September 2, 1980 (broadcast date), https://www.cbc.ca/archives/entry/
reliving-terry-foxs-marathon-of-hope-the-end-of-the-road.

"Terry's Story," Terry Fox Foundation, n.d., https://terryfox.org/terrys-story/
marathon-of-hope/.

"Timeline: Terry Fox," *Canadian Encyclopedia*, n.d., https://www
.thecanadianencyclopedia.ca/en/timeline/terry-fox.

Trottier, Maxine. *Terry Fox: A Story of Hope.* Toronto: Scholastic Canada, 2005.

Vogelsang, Glen. "Meet Ethan, an Incredible Young Man Following in Terry's
Footsteps," Terry Fox Foundation, November 18, 2019, https://terryfox.org/
meet-ethan_smallwood/.

John Cairns: Making Every Step Count

Cairns, John. Email correspondence with author, March 6, 2020.

Harrison, Sharon. "John Cairns: Profile," *Grapevine Magazine*, December 25, 2019,
https://grapevinemagazine.ca/articles/john-cairns-profile.

de la Harpe, David. "Everyday Hero: John Cairns, Wheelchair of Hope Founder,"
Global News, January 13, 2017, https://globalnews.ca/news/3180961/
everyday-hero-john-cairns-wheelchair-of-hope-founder/.

Staff. "Cairns to Be Named to Canada's Walk of Fame," Inquinte.ca, September 19, 2016, https://inquinte.ca/story/cairns-to-be-named-to-canadas-walk-of-fame.

Staff. "Unsung Hero: Meet John Cairns, the Double Amputee Who Climbed Kilimanjaro," CTV News, October 6, 2016, https://www.ctvnews.ca/canada/unsung-hero-meet-john-cairns-the-double-amputee-who-climbed-kilimanjaro-1.3104316.

John Westhaver: Turning Tragedy into Purpose

"About John," JohnWesthaver.com, n.d., https://www.johnwesthaver.com/about-john.html.

"Courage 2017 Recipient—John Westhaver," YouTube, June 15, 2017, 10:59, https://www.youtube.com/watch?v=WOSQTCRZd-E.

Kissinger, Michael. "Burn Survivor Credits Family in Overcoming Accident," *Vancouver Courier*, March 30, 2017, https://www.vancourier.com/news/burn-survivor-credits-family-in-overcoming-accident-1.13493095.

"Survivor Who Lost 3 Friends in Crash Shares Harrowing Story to Save Lives," CBC News, March 14, 2007, https://www.cbc.ca/news/canada/british-columbia/survivor-who-lost-3-friends-in-crash-shares-harrowing-story-to-save-lives-1.4574934.

Tafler, Sid. "Burn Victim's Story a Cautionary Tale for Students," *Globe and Mail*, May 31, 2007, https://www.theglobeandmail.com/news/national/burn-victims-story-a-cautionary-tale-for-students/article686328/.

Westhaver, John. "Rich in Live and Love," JohnWesthaver.com (blog entry), 2004, https://www.johnwesthaver.com/blog.

Westhaver, John. "What's Stopping You?" JohnWesthaver.com (blog entry), December 30, 2015, https://www.johnwesthaver.com/blog.

Westhaver, John. Zero Fatalities Tour PowerPoint Presentation, n.d., https://www.zerofatalities.ca/presentation.html.

Everyday Heroes: Conquering COVID-19

Croft, Dave. "Volunteers Step Forward in Yukon's Klondike to Help During COVID-19 Crisis," CBC News, April 9, 2020, https://www.cbc.ca/news/canada/north/yukon-dawson-city-volunteers-covid-19-1.5528089.

Grant, Kelly. "81% of COVID-19 Deaths in Canada Were in Long-Term Care—
Nearly Double the OECD Average," *Globe and Mail*, June 25, 2020,
https://www.theglobeandmail.com/canada/article-new-data-show-canada-
ranks-among-worlds-worst-for-ltc-deaths/.

Greenaway, Kathryn. "Nurse Infected with COVID-19 Reflects on Time Working
the CHSLD," *Montreal Gazette*, June 23, 2020, https://theprovince.com/
diseases-and-conditions/coronavirus/nurse-infected-with-covid-19-reflects-
on-time-working-in-chsld/.

Malik, Ghazala, and Sarah Bridge. "Essential Canadians: Meet the People on the
Front Lines of the Pandemic," CBC News, July 1, 2020, https://www.cbc
.ca/news/canada/front-line-essential-workers-1.5604776.

Ngabo, Gilbert. "Man Forgoes His 18th Birthday Celebrations to Spread Kindness
amid COVID-19," *Toronto Star*, April 27, 2020, https://www.thestar.com/
news/gta/2020/04/09/man-foregoes-his-18th-birthday-celebrations-to-
spread-kindness-amid-covid-19.html.

O'Connor, Joe. "Heroes of the Pandemic: Teen Celebrates 18th Birthday by Buying
(and Delivering) Groceries to the Blind," *National Post*, April 23, 2020,
https://nationalpost.com/news/canada/heroes-of-the-pandemic-teen-
celebrates-18th-birthday-by-buying-and-delivering-groceries-to-the-blind/.

Sponagle, Jane. "'Our Mission to Help': Whitehorse RV Park Opens Early for
Yukoners Self-Isolating," CBC News, April 8, 2020, https://www.cbc.ca/
news/canada/north/whitehorse-rv-park-opens-early-1.5525685.

PART 2: COURAGE IN THE FACE OF DANGER

David Silverberg: On the Wrong Track

Canadian Press. "PEI Doctor Rescues Man Who Fell onto Subway Tracks in
Washington," *Globe and Mail*, April 24, 2015, https://www.theglobeandmail

.com/news/national/pei-doctor-rescues-man-who-fell-onto-subway-tracks-in-washington/article24105891/.

Canadian Press. "P.E.I. Man Called a Hero for Jumping on Subway Tracks to Save Disabled Man in Rescue Caught on Video," *National Post*, April 24, 2015, https://nationalpost.com/news/canada/pei-man-called-a-hero-for-jumping-on-subway-tracks-to-save-disabled-man-in-rescue-caught-on-video.

"David Silverberg Describes Saving Man in Wheelchair from Subway Tracks," CBC News, April 23, 2015, https://www.cbc.ca/news/canada/prince-edward-island/david-silverberg-describes-saving-man-in-wheelchair-from-subway-tracks-1.3046687.

"P.E.I. Doctor Rescues Disabled Man from D.C. Subway Tracks," CTV News, April 24, 2015, https://www.ctvnews.ca/canada/p-e-i-doctor-rescues-disabled-man-from-d-c-subway-tracks-1.2343339.

Silverberg, David. Email correspondence with author, March 10–20, 2020.

Erik Brown: Diving in the Dark

Azpiri, Jon. "'9 days, 7 Missions and 63 Hours Inside,': B.C. Diver Part of Daring Thai Cave Rescue," Global News, July 10, 2018, https://globalnews.ca/news/4324139/b-c-diver-thai-cave-rescue/.

"B.C. Diver Describes Parts of Thai Cave Rescue as 'Zero Visibility—You Can't See Anything,'" CBC News, July 11, 2018, https://www.cbc.ca/news/canada/bc-diver-brown-thai-cave-rescue-1.4742158.

Clark, Russell. "Erik Brown: Accounts from Thailand Cave Rescue, Part 2," Diver, January 30, 2020, https://divermag.com/erik-brown-accounts-from-thailands-cave-rescue-part-2/.

Colpitts, Heather. "B.C. Diver at Thai Cave Rescue Won't Speculate on Which Actor Should Play Him in Movie," *Vernon Morning Star*, August 9, 2018, https://www.vernonmorningstar.com/home2/langley-diver-at-thai-cave-rescue-wont-speculate-on-which-actor-should-play-him-in-movie/.

"The Full Story of Thailand's Extraordinary Cave Rescue," BBC News, July 14, 2018, https://www.bbc.com/news/world-asia-44791998.

Ma, Alexandra. "One of the Thai Soccer Team Boys Described the Moment the First Cave Rescuer Found Them," Insider, July 18, 2018, https://www .insider.com/thai-soccer-team-boy-describes-first-contact-with-cave-rescuer-2018-7.

Perper, Rosie. "Divers Who Rescued the Thai Soccer Team from a Cave Practiced Their Techniques on Local Children in a Swimming Pool," Business Insider, July 12, 2018, https://www.businessinsider.com/thailand-cave-rescue-divers-practiced-on-local-kids-in-swimming-pool-2018-7.

Scholet, Nicole. "Honoring the US Coast Guard Cutter Alexander Hamilton WPG-34," Alexander Hamilton Awareness Society, August 23, 2013, https://the-aha-society.com/index.php/publications/articles/87-aha-society-articles/147-alexander-hamilton-cutter.

Team Blue Immersion. "Expedition Alexander Hamilton by OceanReef," July 30, 2013, https://scubadiverlife.com/expedition-alexander-hamilton-by-oceanreef/.

"Thai Cave Rescue: How the Boys Were Saved," BBC News, July 18, 2018, https://www.bbc.com/news/world-asia-44695232.

"'You Can't See Your Hands in Front of Your Face': Canadian Diver on Thailand Cave Rescue," Global News, July 13, 2018, https://globalnews.ca/news/4329504/erik-brown-thailand-cave-rescue/.

Bill Ayotte: Battle with a Bear

Canadian Press. "Manitoba Honours Man Who Saved Woman Attacked by Polar Bear in Churchill," CTV News, October 3, 2014, https://winnipeg.ctvnews.ca/manitoba-honours-man-who-saved-woman-attacked-by-polar-bear-in-churchill-1.2038530.

Chura, Peter. "Manitoba Man Who Fought Off Polar Bear to Receive Star of Courage," Global News, April 29, 2015, https://globalnews.ca/news/1968579/manitoba-man-who-fought-off-polar-to-receive-star-of-courage/.

"Churchill Man Who Rescued Woman from Polar Bear Attack Honoured," CBC News, October 3, 2014, https://www.cbc.ca/news/canada/manitoba/churchill-man-who-rescued-woman-from-polar-bear-attack-honoured-1.2787343.

Greenslade, Brittany. "Exclusive: Polar Bear Attack Victim on the Mend and Heading Home," Global News, November 13, 2013, https://globalnews .ca/news/964766polar-bear-attack-victim-on-the-mend-and-heading-home/.

Hunter, Paul. "He Saved a Woman from a Polar Bear. 'Then the Mauling Was on for Me,'" *Toronto Star*, May 20, 2017, https://www.thestar.com/news/ insight/2017/05/20/he-saved-a-woman-from-a-polar-bear-then-the-mauling-was-on-for-me.html.

"Manitoban Receives Star of Courage for Saving Woman from Polar Bear," CBC News, April 29, 2015, https://www.cbc.ca/news/canada/manitoba/ manitoban-receives-star-of-courage-for-saving-woman-from-polar-bear-1.3054425.

Mulvaney, Kieran. "'If It Gets Me, It Gets Me': The Town Where Residents Live Alongside Polar Bears," *The Guardian*, February 13, 2019, https://www. theguardian.com/world/2019/feb/13/churchill-canada-polar-bear-capital.

Proudfoot, Shannon. "'I Don't Want to Die on the Ground Like an Animal,'" *Maclean's*, June 26, 2014, https://www.macleans.ca/news/canada/saving-life-surviving-polar-bear-mauling-manitoba/.

Schroeder, Lara. "Two Mauled in Churchill Polar Bear Attack," Global News, November 1, 2013, https://globalnews.ca/news/939840/polar-bear-attack-injures-two-in-churchill-man/.

Selden, Steve. "Polar Bear Attack Hero Receives Award," Churchill News, May 2, 2015, https://churchillpolarbears.org/2015/05/polar-bear-attack-hero-receives-award/.

"Woman Recounts Harrowing Attack by Churchill Polar Bear," CBC News, December 19, 2013, https://www.cbc.ca/news/canada/manitoba/ woman-recounts-harrowing-attack-by-churchill-polar-bear-1.2469766.

Mona Parsons: The Role of a Lifetime

"An Excerpt of the Letter Mona Wrote to Her Father and Stepmother between May 3 and 5, 1945," MonaParsons.ca, n.d., http://www.monaparsons.ca/ letters.htm.

Berry, Steve. "Statue Honouring Nova Scotia Woman, Who Hid Allied Airman from Nazis, Unveiled," CBC News, May 6, 2017, https://www.cbc.ca/news/ canada/nova-scotia/mona-parsons-statue-unveiled-1.4102941.

"From Privilege to Prison," Veterans Affairs Canada, February 14, 2019, https://
        www.veterans.gc.ca/eng/remembrance/information-for/educators/
        learning-modules/netherlands/resisting-bullying/privilege-to-prison.

Hill, Andria. "Remembering Mona Parsons," Canada's History, March 14, 2017,
        https://www.canadashistory.ca/explore/women/remembering-mona-parsons.

Watson, Patrick. "The Remarkable Courage of Mona Parsons," *Canadian Encyclopedia*,
        March 22, 2013, https://www.thecanadianencyclopedia.ca/en/article/mona-
        parsons-acting-was-a-matter-of-life-and-death-feature.

James Kitchen and William Ward: On Thin Ice

"Frobisher Bay Helicopter Rescuers to Receive Medals," CBC News, April 24,
        2014, https://www.cbc.ca/news/canada/north/frobisher-bay-helicopter-
        rescuers-to-receive-medals-1.2620247.

"Iqaluit Hunter, David Alexander, Rescued from Sea Ice," CBC News, March 14,
        2011, https://www.cbc.ca/news/canada/north/iqaluit-hunter-david-alexander-
        rescued-from-sea-ice-1.993570.

Kitchen, James. Email correspondence with author, February 16, 2020.

Lypka, Ben. "Squamish Man Involved in Heroic Rescue," *Squamish Chief*, March 19,
        2015, https://www.squamishchief.com/news/local-news/squamish-man-
        involved-in-heroic-rescue-1.1797896.

"Pilot Recognized by Governor General for Nunavut Rescue," CBC News, March 23,
        2015, https://www.cbc.ca/news/canada/north/pilot-recognized-by-governor-
        general-for-nunavut-rescue-1.3004973.

Ward, William. Phone interview with author, February 27, 2020.

Clark Whitecalf: Into the Flames

Adam, Betty Ann. "Here's the Story of How Clark Whitecalf Saved 18-Year-Old
        Jolie Fineday from a Fire," *Saskatoon StarPhoenix*, October 18, 2016,
        https://thestarphoenix.com/news/local-news/bravery-award-recipient-kept-
        cool-head-in-emergency.

Bridges, Alicia. "Sask. Man Receives Carnegie Medal for 'Extraordinary Risk'
        Dragging Woman from Burning House," CBC News, December 21, 2016,
        https://www.cbc.ca/news/canada/saskatoon/clark-whitecalf-receives-
        carnegie-medal-1.3906443.

"Clark Whitecalf," Carnegie Hero Fund Commission, n.d., https://www.carnegiehero
    .org/clark-whitecalf/.

"Heroes Honoured for Saving Lives, Awarded Certificates of Bravery in Regina," CBC
    News, October 11, 2017, https://www.cbc.ca/news/canada/saskatchewan/
    bravery-awards-oct-10-1.4349001.

Hune-Brown, Nicholas. "Rescued from a House Fire," *Reader's Digest* (Canada),
    August 1, 2018, https://www.pressreader.com/canada/readers-digest-canada/
    20180801/282913796184443.

Erick Marciano: A Crash Course in Courage

Canadian Press. "City of Montreal Honours 'Hero' Driver Who Used His SUV
    to Shield Pedestrians," CTV News, November 18, 2019, https://montreal
    .ctvnews.ca/city-of-montreal-honours-hero-driver-who-used-his-suv-to-
    shield-pedestrians-1.4691021.

Deschamps, Richard. "I'm Not a Hero, Says Quick-Thinking Motorist Who Used
    SUV to Save Pedestrians' Lives," iHeartRadio.ca, November 13, 2019,
    https://www.iheartradio.ca/cjad/news/i-m-not-a-hero-says-quick-thinking-
    motorist-who-used-suv-to-save-pedestrians-lives-1.10215227.

"'I Didn't Want Him to Hurt Anybody,' Says Montrealer Who Used
    SUV to Protect Pedestrians from Speeding Car," CBC News,
    November 13, 2019, https://www.cbc.ca/news/canada/montreal/
    montreal-hero-driver-suv-daybreak-1.5357526.

Lau, Rachel. "'I Don't Think I'm a Hero,' SUV Driver Who Used His Car
    to Save Pedestrians Humbled by Experience," CTV News, November 13,
    2019, https://montreal.ctvnews.ca/i-don-t-think-i-m-a-hero-suv-
    driver-who-used-his-car-to-save-pedestrians-humbled-by-experience-
    1.4683595.

"Motorist Uses SUV to Shield Pedestrians from Teen Driver Fleeing Montreal
    Police," CBC News, November 12, 2019, https://www.cbc.ca/news/canada/
    montreal/motorist-blocks-runaway-suspect-1.5357193.

Staff. "Mercedes SUV Driver Risks Safety to Save Pedestrians: Montreal Police,"
    Montreal Gazette, November 13, 2019, https://montrealgazette.com/news/
    local-news/mercedes-suv-driver-risked-his-safety-to-save-pedestrians-
    montreal-police.

Sophia LeBlanc: Small But Mighty

Burke, David. "6-Year-Old Honoured for Helping Rescue Family from Car Crash in Nova Scotia," CBC News, January 17, 2019, https://www.cbc.ca/news/canada/nova-scotia/child-6-year-old-heroism-rescue-car-crash-1.4981468.

Campbell, Francis. "Bravery Medals: Little Girl Who Helped Save Her Family, Young Fisherman Who Tried to Save His Dad," Saltwire Network, December 4, 2019, https://www.saltwire.com/news/local/bravery-medals-little-girl-who-helped-save-her-family-young-fisherman-who-tried-to-save-his-dad-384314/.

Canadian Press. "N.S. Girl Earns Bravery Award for Saving Family from Van That Plunged into River," CTV News, December 4, 2019, https://atlantic.ctvnews.ca/n-s-girl-earns-bravery-award-for-saving-family-from-van-that-plunged-into-river-1.4714907.

Cole, Darrell. "Eight-Year-Old Amherst Girl Youngest to Earn Nova Scotia Medal Of Bravery," *Chronicle Herald*, December 4, 2019, https://www.thechronicleherald.ca/news/provincial/eight-year-old-amherst-girl-youngest-to-earn-nova-scotia-medal-of-bravery-384383/.

Quon, Alexander. "8-Year-Old Sophia LeBlanc the Youngest to Earn Nova Scotia Medal of Bravery," Global News, December 4, 2019, https://globalnews.ca/news/6253489/8-year-old-sophia-leblanc-the-youngest-to-earn-nova-scotia-medal-of-bravery/.

Trevor Smith: Swept Away

"Avalanche," National Geographic, n.d. https://www.nationalgeographic.org/encyclopedia/avalanche/.

Croft, David. "Yukon Avalanche Rescuer Honoured for Bravery," CBC News, August 8, 2011, https://www.cbc.ca/news/canada/north/yukon-avalanche-rescuer-honoured-for-bravery-1.1025202.

Joannou, Ashley. "'He Didn't Look Good,' Hero Says of Victim," *Whitehorse Daily Star*, August 5, 2011, https://www.whitehorsestar.com/News/he-didnt-look-good-hero-says-of-victim.

Beachcomber: The Wings of War

"Battle Log: 'Very Heavy Casualties in Men and Ships,'" *Windsor Star*, August 17, 2012, https://windsorstar.com/life/from-the-vault/battle-log-very-heavy-casualties-in-men-and-ships.

Granatstein, Jack. "Dieppe: A Colossal Blunder," Canada's History, May 29, 2014,
    https://www.canadashistory.ca/explore/military-war/dieppe-a-colossal-blunder.

Hawthorne, Peter. *The Animal Victorian Cross: The Dickin Medal*. Barnsley, UK:
    Pen & Sword Books, 2012.

Jackman, Philip. "The Homing Front," *Globe and Mail*, January 8, 2018, updated
    April 26, 2018, https://www.theglobeandmail.com/news/world/
    the-homing-front/article1049820/.

Long, David. *Animal Heroes: Inspiring Stories of Courageous Animals*. New York:
    Random House, 2012.

O'Connor, Bernard. *Bletchley Park and the Pigeon Spies*, self-published, 2018.

Ryan Barnett and Josh McSweeney: In the Nick of Time

Fanfair, Ron. "Lifesavers Named Officers of Year," TPSNews, May 8, 2019, http://
    tpsnews.ca/stories/2019/05/lifesavers-named-officers-year/.

Ferreira, Victor. "'There Was Panic, There Was Praying'": How Two Toronto Men
    Narrowly Escaped Drowning in a Flooded Elevator," *London Free Press*,
    August 9, 2018, https://lfpress.com/news/toronto/there-was-panic-there-
    was-praying-how-two-toronto-men-narrowly-escaped-drowning-
    in-a-flooded-elevator/.

Fox, Chris, and Chris Herhalt. "Men Rescued from Flooded Elevator Say They
    Were Minutes Away from Being Submerged," CP24, August 9, 2018,
    https://www.cp24.com/news/men-rescued-from-flooded-elevator-say-they-
    were-minutes-away-from-being-submerged-1.4044936.

Hayes, Molly. "Just Inches of Air Left for Two Men Rescued from Flooded
    Elevator," *Globe and Mail*, August 8, 2019, https://www.theglobeandmail
    .com/canada/toronto/article-just-inches-of-air-left-for-two-men-rescued-
    from-flooded-elevator/.

Miller, Jason. "Two Officers Who Rescued Stranded Men from Submerged Elevator
    Named Toronto's Police Officer of the Year," *Toronto Star*, May 7, 2019,
    https://www.thestar.com/news/gta/2019/05/07/two-officers-who-rescued-
    two-men-from-a-submerbed-elevator-named-torontos-police-officer-of-
    the-year.html.

Riete, John. "Men Trapped in Flooded Elevator Punched through Ceiling to Make
    Lifesaving 911 Call," CBC News, August 8, 2018, https://www.cbc.ca/
    news/canada/toronto/toronto-elevator-rescue-1.4777629.

"Toronto Police Officers Describe Extraordinary Coincidences Leading to
      Last-Minute Elevator Rescue," Global News YouTube video, August 8,
      2018, 18:58, https://www.youtube.com/watch?v=a1q3vPoiqAE.

Rebecka Blackburn: Right Place, Right Time

Blackburn, Rebecka. Email correspondence with author, April 24–May 11, 2020.
"Local Teen Performs River Rescue," *Devon Dispatch*, July 5, 2018, https://www.
      devondispatch.ca/2018/07/05/local-teen-performs-river-rescue/.
Makrugin, Shelly. "Leduc Teen Received Canadian Red Cross Rescuer Award,"
      Canadian Red Cross blog, December 20, 2018, https://www.redcross.ca/
      blog/2018/12/leduc-teen-receives-canadian-red-cross-rescuer-award.
Wong, Julia. "Teen Lifeguard Saves Man from North Saskatchewan River near
      Devon," Global News, June 21, 2018, https://globalnews.ca/news/4289781/
      alberta-teen-lifeguard-north-saskatchewan-river-rescue/.

Les Lehmann: Shots in the Dark

Canadian Press, "Canadian Les Lehmann Shot Defending School Group in
      Dominican Republic," O.Canada.com, February 10, 2014, https://o.canada.
      com/news/canadian-les-lehmann-shot-defending-school-group-in-
      dominican-republic.
"Dominican Republic Attacks Could Happen Anywhere, Says Manitoban Shot
      10 Times," CBC News, April 12, 2016, https://www.cbc.ca/news/canada/
      manitoba/lehmann-dominican-republic-robbery-1.3531014.
Hopper, Tristan. "Manitoba Man Survives Being Shot Nine Times While
      Fighting Off Dominican Robbers," *National Post*, February 7, 2014,
      https://nationalpost.com/news/manitoba-man-survives-being-shot-nine-
      times-while-driving-off-dominican-robbers.
Hunter, Paul. "Canadian with One Bat Takes on Two Robbers with Pistols:
      'It Never Did Scare Me,'" *Toronto Star*, May 20, 2017, https://www.thestar.
      com/news/insight/2017/05/20/canadian-with-one-bat-takes-on-two-
      robbers-with-pistols-it-never-did-scare-me.html.
Karstens-Smith, Gemma. "Canadian Man a Hero in Dominican Republic," *Guelph
      Mercury Tribune*, February 9, 2014, https://www.guelphmercury.com/
      news-story/4359141-canadian-man-a-hero-in-dominican-republic/.

"Man Injured in Confrontation on Student Trip Recovering in Hospital,"
Winnipeg Free Press, February 6, 2014, https://www.winnipegfreepress.com/
breakingnews/Man-injured-in-confrontation-on-student-trip-recovering-
in-hopsital-244008201.html.

"Manitoba Students Witness Shooting on a Humanitarian Trip," CBC
News, January 31, 2014, https://www.cbc.ca/news/canada/manitoba/
manitoba-students-witness-shooting-on-humanitarian-trip-1.2519208.

Russell, Andrew, and Mike Le Couteur. "Winnipeg Man Shot 10 Times
Protecting Manitoba Students in D.R. Given Star of Courage," Global
News, October 28, 2016, https://globalnews.ca/news/3032115/
winnipeg-man-shot-10-times-protecting-manitoba-students-in-d-r-
given-star-of-courage/.

Ralph Joyce: Out on the Edge

Bradshaw, Don. "Inspiring NL: Life-Saving Moment by Lark Harbour Neighbour,"
NTV, July 30, 2020, http://ntv.ca/inspiring-n-l-life-saving-moment-by-
lark-harbour-neighbour/.

Crocker, Diane. "Lark Harbour Man Recognized for His Bravery and Quick
Thinking in Saving Life of Another Man," *The Telegram*, August 7, 2020,
https://www.thetelegram.com/news/provincial/lark-harbour-man-
recognized-for-his-bravery-and-quick-thinking-in-saving-life-of-another-
man-482630/.

Turner, Troy. "Lark Harbour Man Honoured with Bravery Award for Icy, Cliffside
Rescue," CBC News, July 31, 2020, https://www.cbc.ca/news/canada/
newfoundland-labrador/ralph-joyce-bravery-1.5669409.

Liam Bernard and Shane Bernard: Playing with Fire

"Cape Breton Man Recognized for Act of Heroism," *Cape Breton Post*, September 20,
2018, https://www.capebretonpost.com/news/local/
cape-breton-man-recognized-for-act-of-heroism-243136/.

Doucette, Keith. "'I Just Knew I Had to Do Something': Nova Scotia Honours
Four for Bravery," 680 News, November 8, 2017, https://www.680news
.com/2017/11/08/i-just-knew-i-had-to-do-something-nova-scotia-honours-
four-for-bravery/.

Googoo, Maureen. "Two Mi'kmaw Men from Waycobah Receive NS Medal of
        Bravery," *Ku'Ku'Wes News*, November 8, 2017, http://kukukwes.com/
        2017/11/08/two-mikmaw-men-from-waycobah-receive-ns-medal-
        of-bravery/.

"Liam Bernard," Carnegie Hero Fund Commission, n.d., https://www
        .carnegiehero.org/liam-bernard/.

Pace, Natasha. "'I Don't Really Consider Myself a Hero': Four Nova Scotians
        Honoured for Their Bravery," Global News, November 8, 2017,
        https://globalnews.ca/news/3850274/i-dont-really-consider-myself-a-
        hero-four-nova-scotians-honoured-for-their-bravery/.

SaltWire Network. "Rescuer Recalls What Happened during Tragic
        Accident," *Cape Breton Post*, September 17, 2016, https://www.saltwire
        .com/news/provincial/rescuer-recalls-what-happened-during-tragic-
        accident-12627/.

SaltWire Network. "Waycobah Men Pull Crash Survivors from Burning
        Vehicle," *Cape Breton Post*, September 16, 2016, http://www.capebretonpost
        .com/News/Local/2016-09-16/article-4643119/Waycobah-men-pull-
        crash-survivors-from-burning-vehicle/12632/.

Sullivan, Nikki. "Waycobah Men to Receive Provincial Award for Bravery on
        Wednesday," *Cape Breton Post*, November 7, 2017, https://www
        .capebretonpost.com/news/local/waycobah-men-to-receive-governor-
        generals-award-for-bravery-on-wednesday-159665/.

Colleen O'Reilly: Everything for a Reason

Bird, Lindsay. "First Aid Training Helps Woman Save Choking Child at St. John's
        GEO Centre," CBC News, July 19, 2016, https://www.cbc.ca/news/canada/
        newfoundland-labrador/first-aid-training-helps-woman-save-choking-
        child-1.3685159.

O'Reilly, Colleen. Telephone interview with author, September 1, 2020.

Whiffen, Glen. "Life-Saving Bravery of Newfoundlanders and Labradorians
        Recognized," *The Telegram*, May 24, 2018, https://www.thetelegram.com/
        news/local/life-saving-bravery-of-newfoundlanders-and-labradorians-
        recognized-212919/.

Russell Fee: Keeping the Wolf from the Door

Asmelash, Leah. "A Family of Four Was on a Camping Trip in Canada. Then a Wolf Attacked While They Were Sleeping," CNN, August 16, 2019, https://www.cnn.com/2019/08/14/us/wolf-attack-canada-trnd/index.html.

Babych, Stephanie. "'Like Something out of a Horror Movie': Wolf Dragged Man from Tent as Wife Held His Legs," *Calgary Herald*, August 13, 2019, https://calgaryherald.com/news/local-news/family-recalls-unusual-wolf-attack-at-banff-campground-on-social-media-campground-reopens.

Babych, Stephanie. "Man Who Stopped Banff Wolf Attack Receives Medal of Bravery," *Calgary Herald*, July 1, 2020, https://calgaryherald.com/news/local-news/man-who-stopped-banff-wolf-attack-receives-medal-of-bravery.

Mark, Michelle. "A Canadian Man Saved a Family of 4 from a Wolf That Ripped Their Tent Apart and Tried to Drag the Father Away," Insider, August 14, 2019, https://www.insider.com/canada-wolf-attack-banff-campsite-rescue-2019-8.

Payette, Julie. Facebook page, August 13, 2020, https://www.facebook.com/GGJuliePayette.

Rispoli, Elisa. Facebook page, August 9, 2019, https://www.facebook.com/erispoli.

"Survivors of Rare Wolf Attack in Banff Recount How Animal Tried to Drag Man from Tent in Middle of the Night," CBC News, August 13, 2019, https://www.cbc.ca/news/canada/calgary/wolf-attack-rampart-creek-banff-1.5245105.

Shaun De Grandpré: Double Trouble

De Grandpré, Shaun. Email correspondence with author, April 22–May 4, 2020.

"Mountie Honoured for Beaufort Sea Rescue," CBC News, November 2, 2010, https://www.cbc.ca/news/canada/north/mountie-honoured-for-beaufort-sea-rescue-1.889571.

"Mountie Rescues Pair from Beaufort Sea," CBC News, June 30, 2010, https://www.cbc.ca/news/canada/north/mountie-rescues-pair-from-beaufort-sea-1.889573.

Peacock, Emelie. "Medals of Bravery for Yellowknife Rescues—from Burning Buildings, Dog Attack," MyYellowknifeNow, April 3, 2019, https://www.myyellowknifenow.com/38427/medals-of-bravery-for-yellowknife-rescues-from-burning-buildings-dog-attacks/.

Aymen Derbali: In the Line of Fire

Derbali, Aymen. Telephone interview with author, January 18, 2021.

Hinkson, Kamila. "Shot 7 Times in Quebec City Mosque Attack, Survivor Fights to Reclaim His Life," CBC News, January 25, 2018, https://www.cbc.ca/news/canada/montreal/quebec-mosque-shooting-injured-aymen-derbali-1.4503703.

Kassam, Ashifa. "Quebec Community Rallies for Mosque Attack Hero: 'He Sacrificed His Legs for Us,'" *The Guardian*, January 26, 2018, https://www.theguardian.com/world/2018/jan/26/quebec-mosque-attack-survivor-one-year-later-aymen-derbali.

Marandola, Sabrina. "'This Is a Canadian Hero': Group Launches Campaign to Help Buy New Home for Mosque Shooting Victim," CBC News, December 20, 2017, https://www.cbc.ca/news/canada/montreal/aymen-derbali-crowdfunding-campaign-1.4457487.

Page, Julia. "Survivor of Quebec City Mosque Shooting Sets Out to Combat Hate," CBC News, January 29, 2019, https://www.cbc.ca/news/canada/montreal/quebec-city-mosque-shooting-aymen-derbali-1.4995802.

Peritz, Ingrid. "'I've Come a Long Way': Aymen Derbali and His Family Find a New Life after Quebec's Mosque Tragedy," *Globe and Mail*, January 9, 2019, https://www.theglobeandmail.com/canada/article-ive-come-a-long-way-aymen-derbali-and-his-family-find-a-new-life/.

Peritz, Ingrid. "At the Quebec Mosque Shooting, This Man Risked His Life to Save Others. Who Will Save Him Now?" *Globe and Mail*, December 14, 2017, https://www.theglobeandmail.com/news/national/quebec-mosque-shooting-survivor-paralyzed/article37301950/.

Riga, Andy. "Quebec Mosque Shooting: Survivor Aymen Derbali Says Bissonnette Is Insincere," *Montreal Gazette*, April 17, 2018, https://montrealgazette.com/news/local-news/quebec-mosque-shooting-survivor-aymen-derbali-says-bissonnette-is-insincere.

"United with Aymen Derbali," LaunchGood, n.d., https://www.launchgood.com/project/united_with_aymen_derbali__tous_unis_pour_aymen/.

Liane and Daniel Wood: River Rescue

Guthrie Insurance. "Ontario Insurance Broker Saves Life of a Teen in
    Rescue Attempt," InsurePlus, February 22, 2013, https://www
    .guthrieinsurance.com/blog/ontario-insurance-broker-saves-
    life-teen-rescue-attempt/.

Hunter, Paul. "They Braved a Raging River to Save a Girl in an SUV:
    'Every Second Felt Like Five Minutes,'" *Toronto Star*, May 20, 2017,
    https://www.thestar.com/news/insight/2017/05/20/they-braved-a-
    raging-river-to-save-a-girl-in-an-suv-every-second-felt-like-five-
    minutes.html.

Lessard, Jerome. "Couple Decorated for Saving Girl's Life," *Kingston Whig-Standard*,
    May 5, 2015, https://www.thewhig.com/2015/05/05/couple-decorated-
    for-saving-girls-life/wcm/ce342aa6-def7-a80a-2175-8a126898bfb0.

Statistics Canada. "Census Profile, 2016 Census. Frankford, Ontario."
    https://www.statcan.gc.ca.

Sergeant Gander: A True Pal

"Gander the Dog, a Canadian War Hero," History Bits, March 3, 2015,
    https://cdnhistorybits.wordpress.com/2015/03/03/gander-the-dog-
    a-canadian-war-hero/.

Moore, Brenda. "Beyond the Call of Duty," Cricket, January 2011,
    http://www.cricketmagkids.com/library/extras/beyond-call-duty-
    brenda-moore.

"'Much Loved' Newfoundland Dog Sergeant Gander Honoured with Statue,"
    CBC News, July 24, 2015, https://www.cbc.ca/news/canada/
    newfoundland-labrador/much-loved-newfoundland-dog-sergeant-
    gander-honoured-with-statue-1.3166092.

Walker, Robin. *Sergeant Gander: A Canadian Hero*. Toronto: Dundurn Press, 2009.

Ward, Bruce. "Heroic Warrior Canine's Name Put on Memorial," *Winnipeg
    Free Press*, August 15, 2009, https://www.winnipegfreepress.com/arts-
    and-life/life/heroic-warrior-canines-name-put-on-memorial-53287192.
    html.

PART 3: COURAGE IN THE FACE OF INJUSTICE

Leesee Papatsie: Fighting for Food

Bell, Jim. "Nunavut Demonstrators Gather to Protest Food Prices, Poverty," *Nunatsiaq News*, June 9, 2012, https://nunatsiaq.com/stories/article/65674nunavut_demonstrators_gather_to_protest_food_prices_poverty/.

Canadian Press. "Inuit Officials to Discuss Solutions to Hunger in Arctic," CTV News, June 24, 2012, https://www.ctvnews.ca/canada/inuit-officials-to-discuss-solutions-to-hunger-in-arctic-1.851028.

Chatelaine editorial team. "When $500 Isn't Enough to Buy Groceries for a Week," *Chatelaine*, June 8, 2015, https://www.chatelaine.com/living/when-500-isnt-enough-to-buy-groceries-for-a-week/.

Devine, Carol. "WonderActivist—Leesee Papatsie," WonderWoman.com., n.d., http://wonderwomenglobal.com/wonderactivist-leesee-papatsie/.

"Facebook Group Plans Food Price Protests," CBC News, June 9, 2012, https://www.cbc.ca/news/canada/north/facebook-group-plans-food-price-protests-1.1143378.

"Feeding My Family—A Story of Grassroots Organizing in Northern Canada," Food Secure Canada, https://foodsecurecanada.org/resources-news/webinars-podcasts/feeding-my-family-story-grassroots-organizing-northern-canada.

Feeding My Family, Facebook, May 21, 2013 post by Leesee Papatsie, https://www.facebook.com/groups/239422122837039/.

"Fighting for Food in Canada's North," CBC Radio, February 25, 2016, https://www.cbc.ca/radio/dnto/putting-food-on-the-table-canadians-cope-with-rising-food-prices-1.3460214/fighting-for-food-in-canada-s-north-1.3462909.

Gladstone, Joshua. "Nutrition North: Feeding My Family: An Interview with Leesee Papatsie," Northern Public Affairs, n.d., http://www.northernpublicaffairs.ca/index/archives-volume-1-issue-2/nutrition-north-feeding-my-family-an-interview-with-leesee-papatsie/.

Murphy, David. " 'Feeding My Family' Goes Viral After June 9 Protest," Nunatsiaq News, June 12, 2012, https://nunatsiaq.com/stories/article/65674feeding_my_family_goes_viral_after_june_9_protest/.

Papatsie, Leesee. Email correspondence with author, January 21, 2021.

QMI Agency, "Nunavut Rallies Against Extreme Food Prices," *Toronto Sun*, June 9, 2012, https://torontosun.com/2012/06/08/nunavut-rallies-against-extreme-food-prices/wcm/011759f7-7866-432e-a6ed-6fb982c5d189.

"Transcsript: Leesee Papatsie: Feeding the North,"TVO, December 1, 2014, https://www.tvo.org/transcript/2267441/leesee-papatsie-feeding-the-north.

"'Way North Foods' Fake Ads Take Aim at Nunavut's High Food Prices," CBC News, January 8, 2016, https://www.cbc.ca/news/canada/north/nunavut-food-prices-fake-ad-1.3394396.

Vishal Vijay: Never Too Young to Make a Difference

Blackburn, Angela. "Oakville Brothers Receive Junior Citizen Awards from Ontario Lt. Governor in Toronto," InsideHalton.com, March 7, 2016, https://www.insidehalton.com/news-story/6380024-oakville-brothers-receive-junior-citizen-awards-from-ontario-lt-governor-in-toronto/.

Ostroff, Joshua. "Vishal Vijay Is Changing the World (After He's Done His Homework," HuffPost, February 8, 2017, https://www.huffingtonpost.ca/2017/02/08/vishal-vijay-every-child-now_n_14501216.html.

Vijay, Vishal. Email correspondence with author, January 11–March 3, 2020.

Kristen Worley: An Olympic Moment

Blackwell, Tom. "Transgender Canadian Cyclist Wins Key Battle in Human Rights Complaint over Policing of Athlete Gender," *National Post*, August 1, 2016, https://nationalpost.com/news/canada/canadian-cyclist-who-became-woman-challenges-world-sports-bodies-gender-rules.

Cutler, Teddy. "Meet the Canadian Athlete Changing Sports' Attitude to Gender," *Newsweek*, May 2, 2016, https://www.newsweek.com/meet-canadian-athlete-changing-sports-attitudes-gender-423405.

Ewing, Lori. "Canadian Cyclist Worley Blazes Own Trail as Voice for Gender Diversity in Sport," *Globe and Mail*, April 19, 2020, https://www.theglobeandmail.com/sports/article-canadian-cyclist-kristen-worley-blazes-own-trail-as-voice-for-gender/.

Maxwell, Steve, and Joe Harris. "Commentary: The Human Rights Case That Could Change Global Cycling," VeloNews, December 21, 2017, https://www.velonews.com/events/commentary-the-human-rights-case-that-could-change-global-cycling/.

O'Brien, Cillian. "Transgender Cyclist's Memoir Details Her Battle with Olympic
        Officials," CTV News, April 2, 2019, https://www.ctvnews.ca/sports/
        transgender-cyclist-s-memoir-details-her-battle-with-olympic-officials-
        1.4362026.
Worley, Kristen, and Johanna Schneller. *Woman Enough: How a Boy Became a
        Woman and Changed the World of Sport*. Toronto: Random House
        Canada, 2019.
Worley, Kristen. Telephone interviews with author, January 17 and May 15, 2020.

David Howard: Supporting Our Soldiers

Dorozio, Jennifer. "Tiny Home Village for Veterans Opens in Calgary This Week,"
        CBC News, October 28, 2018, https://www.cbc.ca/news/canada/
        calgary/tiny-home-village-for-veterans-calgary-1.5337504.
Homes for Heroes Foundation website: https://homesforheroesfoundation.ca/.
Howard, David. Email correspondence with author, April 22 and May 8, 2020.
Jones, Alexandra Mae. "A Village of Tiny Houses Was Built to Provide Homeless
        Veterans with a Fresh Start," CTV News, October 28, 2019, https://www
        .ctvnews.ca/canada/a-village-of-tiny-houses-was-built-to-provide-
        homeless-veterans-with-a-fresh-start-1.4659926.
Pearson, Heide. "11 Veterans Set to Move into Calgary 'Homes for Heroes' Tiny
        Home Village," Global News, October 28, 2019, https://globalnews.ca/
        news/6093176/calgary-homes-for-heroes-veterans-housing-opening/.
Smith, Alanna. "Father of Fallen Soldier Helping to Build Tiny Home Village
        for Homeless Veterans," *Calgary Herald*, August 1, 2019, https://calgaryherald
        .com/news/local-news/tiny-home-village-set-to-welcome-15-homeless-
        veterans-in-october/.

The Women of Idle No More: Choosing Action

Caven, Febna. "Being Idle No More: The Women Behind the Movement," *Cultural
        Survival Quarterly Magazine*, March 2013, https://www.culturalsurvival
        .org/publications/cultural-survival-quarterly/being-idle-no-more-women-
        behind-movement.
Coates, Ken. *#IdleNoMore and the Remaking of Canada*. Regina: University of
        Regina Press, 2015.

Gordon, Jessica. "'Idle No More' Rally to Oppose Budget Implementation Bill C 45," Idle No More Facebook events page, November 2, 2013, www.facebook .com/events/299767020134614/, quoted in Ken Coates, #IdleNoMore and the Remaking of Canada. Regina: University of Regina Press, 2015.

Living History: December 21, 2012, "National Idle No More Protest in Ottawa," http://www.idlenomore.ca/national_idle_no_more_protest_in_ottawa.

MacLellan, Stephanie. "Idle No More, One Year Later," Toronto Star, December 13, 2013, https://www.thestar.com/news/canada/2013/12/13/idle_no_more_ one_year_later.html.

Marshall, Tabitha. "Idle No More," Canadian Encyclopedia, last edited February 4, 2019, https://www.thecanadianencyclopedia.ca/en/article/ idle-no-more.

Monkman, Lenard, and Brandi Morin. "5 Years after Idle No More, Founders Still Speaking Out," CBC News, December 10, 2017, https://www.cbc.ca/news/ indigenous/idle-no-more-five-years-1.4436474.

Van Gelder, Sarah. "Why Canada's Indigenous Uprising Is about All of Us," Yes Magazine, Spring 2013, https://www.yesmagazine.org/issue/issues-how- cooperatives-are-driving-the-new-economy/2013/02/08/why-canada2019s- indigenous-uprising-is-about-all-of-us/.

Julius Kuhl: An Unsung Hero of the Holocaust

"A Canadian Hero—Julius Kuhl," C4i Canada, September 18, 2017, https://www .c4i.ca/blogs/a-canadian-hero-julius-kuhl.

"Introduction to the Holocaust," United States Holocaust Memorial Museum, last edited March 12, 2018, https://encyclopedia.ushmm.org/content/en/ article/introduction-to-the-holocaust.

Levine, Sara. "The Orthodox Jewish 'Schindler' You Never Heard Of," Jew in the City, April 11, 2018, https://jewinthecity.com/2018/04/the-orthodox- jewish-schindler-you-never-heard-of/.

MacKinnon, Mark. "'He Should Be As Well Known as Schindler': Documents Reveal Canadian Citizen Julius Kuhl as Holocaust Hero," Globe and Mail, August 7, 2017, updated November 12, 2017, https://www.theglobeandmail .com/news/world/holocaust-oskar-schindler-julius-kuhl-canadian/ article35896768/.

Ruel, Maxime. "Julius Kuhl Saved Hundreds, Perhaps Thousands, from the Holo-
        caust," Passport 2017, August 8, 2017, https://passport2017.ca/articles/
        julius-kuhl-canadian-hero-world-war-two.

Margaret Butler: Be Strong, Have Courage

Butler, Hilary. "Why We Run for Rwanda," *Bowen Island Undercurrent*, August 6, 2015,
        https://www.bowenislandundercurrent.com/sports/why-we-run-for-
        rwanda-1.2023425.

Butler, Margaret. Email correspondence with author, January 17 and 18, 2021.

Gill, Robin. "Everyday Hero: Margaret Butler Making Sure Rwanda's Girls Aren't Left
        Behind," Global News, January 15, 2016, https://globalnews.ca/news/2456424/
        everyday-hero-margaret-butler-making-sure-rwandas-girls-arent-left-behind/.

Komera.org. https://komera.org/about.

"Margaret Butler Uses Running to Inspire Young Girls in Rwanda,"
        Altrumedia, February 26, 2016, https://herohighlight.com/
        running-to-inspire-girls-in-rwanda/.

Nordin, Kendra. "Margaret Butler Puts Girls on Track to Succeed," *Christian Science Mon-
        itor*, September 19, 2014, https://www.csmonitor.com/World/Making-a-difference/
        Change-Agent/2014/0919/Margaret-Butler-puts-girls-on-track-to-succeed.

Shanley, Peter. "Nonprofit Promotes Girl Power in Rwanda," *Jamaica Plain
        Gazette*, May 23, 2014, http://jamaicaplaingazette.com/2014/05/23/
        nonprofit-promotes-girl-power-in-rwanda/.

Tripletheelle. "Interview with Margaret Butler of Komera," Sometimes coffee
        sometimes tea (blog), March 31, 2014, https://tripletheelle.wordpress.
        com/2014/03/31/interview-with-margaret-butler-of-komera/.

Tomas Jirousek: Graduating with Honours

Banerjee, Sidhartha. "McGill Drops Redmen Name, Citing Pain Caused to
        Indigenous Students," CTV News, April 12, 2019, https://www.ctvnews.ca/
        sports/mcgill-drops-redmen-name-citing-pain-caused-to-indigenous-
        students-1.4377299.

Canadian Press. "McGill Student Who Led Fight to Drop Offensive Team Name
        Chosen as Valedictorian," *Vancouver Courier*, June 23, 2020, https://www
        .vancourier.com/mcgill-student-who-led-fight-to-drop-offensive-team-
        name-chosen-as-valedictorian-1.24158274.

Deer, Ka'nhehsí:io. "First Nations Athlete Says McGill's Redmen Name Needs to
　　　Change," CBC News, October 15, 2018, https://www.cbc.ca/news/indigenous/
　　　mcgill-redmen-indigenous-students-name-change-1.4863218.

Deer, Ka'nhehsí:io. "First Nations Student Honoured as McGill Valedictorian after
　　　Leading Fight Against 'Redmen' Team Name," CBC News, June 22, 2020,
　　　https://www.cbc.ca/news/indigenous/first-nations-valedictorian-mcgill-
　　　1.5619676.

Deer, Ka'nhehsí:io. "'Not Your Redmen': Students Hold Rally to Protest McGill
　　　University Team Name," CBC News, October 31, 2018, https://www
　　　.cbc.ca/news/indigenous/mcgill-redmen-team-name-protest-rally-
　　　1.4885697.

Dunlevy, T'Cha. "McGill Rower Who Campaigned for Redman Name Change Made
　　　Valedictorian," *Montreal Gazette*, June 24, 2020, https://theprovince.com/news/
　　　local-news/mcgill-rower-who-campaigned-for-redmen-name-change-
　　　made-valedictorian/.

McGill Arts. "Virtual Convocation 2020—Valedictorian Addresses," YouTube video,
　　　3:22, June 19, 2020, https://www.youtube.com/watch?v=8k9KJHAmO0A.

Ross, Selena. "Last Year He Forced McGill University to Change Its Racist Team
　　　Name; Now He's Valedictorian," CTV News, June 23, 2020, https://montreal
　　　.ctvnews.ca/last-year-he-forced-mcgill-university-to-change-its-racist-team-
　　　name-now-he-s-valedictorian-1.4995791.

Viola Desmond: Standing Up by Sitting Down

"A Notable Pioneer," *Winnipeg Free Press*, November 24, 2018, https://www
　　　.winnipegfreepress.com/arts-and-life/entertainment/books/a-notable-
　　　pioneer-501130511.html.

Bingham, Russell. "Viola Desmond," *Canadian Encyclopedia*, January 27, 2013,
　　　last edited January 16, 2019, https://www.thecanadianencyclopedia.ca/en/
　　　article/viola-desmond.

Deachman, Bruce. "15 Canadian Stories: Viola Desmond, Reluctant Social Activist,"
　　　Ottawa Citizen, April 10, 2019, https://ottawacitizen.com/news/national/
　　　15-canadian-stories-viola-desmond-reluctant-social-activist.

McLeod, Elizabeth and Mike Deas, ill. *Meet Viola Desmond*. Toronto: Scholastic, 2018.

Reynolds, Graham, with Wanda Robson. *Viola Desmond: Her Life and Times*.
　　　Halifax: Roseway Publishing, 2018.

Vitt, Kaitlin. "New Banknote Features Iconic Canadian Woman," Canada's History, November 20, 2018, https://www.canadashistory.ca/explore/women/new-banknote-features-iconic-canadian-woman.

White, Evelyn C. "Viola Desmond Led Civil Rights Fight," Herizons, n.d., http://www.herizons.ca/node/567.

NOTES

PART 1: COURAGE IN THE FACE OF ADVERSITY

Ryan Straschnitzki: Keeping the Dream Alive

8   "My first instinct": Sammy Hudes, "Bronco Unbroken: From Tragedy to Tenacity, the Straz Strong Journey," *Calgary Herald*, March 27, 2019, https://calgaryherald.com/news/local-news/straz-strong-from-tragedy-comes-tenacity/, accessed April 24, 2020.

9   "I'm going to try out for sledge hockey": Sammy Hudes, "Bronco Unbroken: Another Shot at Life and Hockey," *Calgary Herald*, March 29, 2019, https://calgaryherald.com/news/local-news/bronco-unbroken-another-shot, accessed April 24, 2020.

10   "I'm just hoping one day": Canadian Press, "'I Couldn't Move My Body': Straschnitzki Recalls Humboldt Broncos Bus Crash," *Saskatoon StarPhoenix*, April 25, 2018, https://thestarphoenix.com/news/local-news/humboldt-broncos-bus-crash-ryan-straschnitzki-left-paralyzed-in-deadly-crash-says-survivors-bonding/, accessed April 24, 2020.

10   "I'm just trying to push through": Canadian Press, "'I Couldn't Move My Body.'"

12   "It was good": Zach Laing and Vanessa Hrvatin, "A New Journey: Ryan Straschnitzki Hits the Ice Once Again," *Calgary Herald*, July 22, 2018, https://calgaryherald.com/news/local-news/a-new-journey-ryan-straschnitzki-hits-the-ice-once-again/, accessed April 24, 2020.

12   "I always dreamed of playing for Team Canada": Bill Graveland, "'What a Role Model': Paralyzed Bronco Makes Adidas Ad, Hall of Fame Nominee List," CBC News, September 30, 2019, https://www.cbc.ca/news/canada/saskatoon/ryan-straschnitzki-adidas-humboldt-broncos-1.5302726, accessed April 24, 2020.

13   "When one door closes, another one opens": Hudes, "Bronco Unbroken: Another Shot at Life and Hockey."

13   "It's a great day to be a Bronco": Hudes, "Bronco Unbroken: Another Shot at Life and Hockey."

14   "Obviously, they're watching over us": Hudes, "Bronco Unbroken: Another Shot at Life and Hockey."

Timea Nagy: One Girl at a Time

16   "Young females needed to work in Canada": Timea E. Nagy and Shannon Moroney, *Out of the Shadows: A Memoir* (Toronto: Penguin Random House Canada, 2019), 41.

18   "We were fed one meal a day": "Out of the Shadows: How Timea Nagy Survived International Human Traffickers," CBC News, July 2, 2019, https://www.cbc.ca/news/canada/hamilton/out-of-the-shadows-how-timea-nagy-survived-international-human-traffickers-1.5192342, accessed June 12, 2020.

18   "When you don't speak English": Cillian O'Brien, "She Answered an Ad for Babysitting in Canada, Wound Up a Sex Slave," CTV News, May 28, 2019, https://www.ctvnews.ca/canada/she-answered-an-ad-for-babysitting-in-canada-wound-up-a-sex-slave-1.4440327, accessed June 12, 2020.

20   "I thought that that was enough justice for me": "Timea Nagy, Human Trafficking: Interview," Speak Truth to Power Canada, n.d., https://sttpcanada.ctf-fce.ca/lessons/timea-nagy/interview/, accessed June 12, 2020.

20   "There's nothing you can do to change the past": "Timea Nagy, Human Trafficking: Interview."

21   "When I started": "Timea Nagy, Human Trafficking: Interview."

21   "I can't hide it anymore": "Timea Nagy, Human Trafficking: Interview."

22   "There are so many things going wrong with the world": Nicole Reilly, "Human Trafficking Survivor Timea Nagy Is 'Out of the Shadows' with New Memoir," *Hamilton Spectator*, May 21, 2019, https://www.thespec.com/news/hamilton-region/2019/05/21/human-trafficking-survivor-timea-nagy-is-out-of-the-shadows-with-new-memoir.html, accessed June 12, 2020.

Luca "Lazylegz" Patuelli: No Excuses, No Limits

All quotations not otherwise attributed in this story are taken from the author's email correspondence with Luca Patuelli, January 19, 2021.

24   "You know in movies": News Staff, "Canadian Heroes Fox, Hansen Invoked to Open 2010 Paralympics," CityNews, March 13, 2010, https://toronto. citynews.ca/2010/03/13/canadian-heroes-fox-hansen-invoked-to-open-2010-paralympics/, accessed August 16, 2020.

24   "My father would take me to the hills": Peggy Curran, "Games Were Life-Changing Experience for Breakdancer," *Montreal Gazette*, March 24, 2010, https://www.pressreader.com/canada/montreal-gazette/20100324/283253094087650, accessed August 15, 2020.

25   "After the operations": Curran, "Games Were Life-Changing Experience for Breakdancer."

25   "For me to lift myself up": "B-boy Luca 'Lazylegz' Patuelli Smashes Stereotypes to the Beat," *Abilities*, 2018, https://www.abilities.ca/people/breaking-free/, accessed August 15, 2020.

25   "Dance gave me an opportunity": T'Cha Dunlevy, "For Breakdance Crew ILL-Abilities, Physical Challenges Aren't Crutches," *Montreal Gazette*, November 13, 2018, https://montrealgazette.com/entertainment/local-arts/skys-the-limit-for-ill-abilities-breakdance-crew?, accessed August 15, 2020.

26   "I wanted to start a crew": Marissa Ramnanan, "ILL-Abilities Celebrates Ten Years of Passion and Inspiration," *The Link*, November 20, 2018, https://thelinknewspaper.ca/article/ill-abilities-celebrates-10-years-of-passion-and-inspiration, accessed August 15, 2020.

27   "I told Ellen it was like Christmas": Kathryn Greenaway, "No Excuses, No Limits for Canadian Dance Ambassador Luca 'Lazylegz' Patuelli," *Montreal Gazette*, April 24, 2015, https://montrealgazette.com/entertainment/arts/no-excuses-no-limits-for-canadian-dance-ambassador-luca-lazylegz, accessed August 15, 2020.

27   "It's about making dance inclusive": Greenaway, "No Excuses, No Limits for Canadian Dance Ambassador Luca 'Lazylegz' Patuelli."

28   "Hip-hop . . . was never welcome": Ramnanan, "ILL-Abilities Celebrates Ten Years of Passion and Inspiration."

28   "I remember taking thirty-six airplanes": Greenaway, "No Excuses, No
        Limits for Canadian Dance Ambassador Luca 'Lazylegz' Patuelli."

29   "One of the things I want you guys to know": "B-boy Luca "Lazylegz"
        Patuelli Smashes Stereotypes to the Beat."

29   "Dance has allowed me to accept myself": Dunlevy, "For Breakdance Crew
        ILL-Abilities, Physical Challenges Aren't Crutches."

Terry Fox: Inspiring a Nation to Fight for a Cure

33   "Someday, I'm going to do something like that": "Timeline: Terry Fox,"
        Canadian Encyclopedia, n.d., https://www.thecanadianencyclopedia.ca/en/
        timeline/terry-fox, accessed January 28, 2021.

34   "I could not leave knowing these faces and feelings would still exist": "Terry's
        Story: Terry's Letter Requesting Support," Terry Fox Foundation, n.d.,
        https://terryfox.org/terrys-story/marathon-of-hope/, accessed March 14, 2020.

36   "I had primary cancer in my knee": "Terry Fox's Marathon of Hope: The
        End of the Road," CBC Digital Archives, September 2, 1980 (broadcast
        date), https://www.cbc.ca/archives/entry/reliving-terry-foxs-marathon-of-
        hope-the-end-of-the-road, accessed March 14, 2020.

36   "When I started this run": "Terry's Story: Quotes," Terry Fox Foundation, n.d.,
        https://terryfox.org/terrys-story/marathon-of-hope/, accessed March 14, 2020.

38   "Even if I don't finish": Danielle Milley, "Terry Fox Exhibit on Display at
        Scarborough Civic Centre," Toronto.com, September 23, 2011, https://www
        .toronto.com/news-story/68914-terry-fox-exhibit-on-display-at-scarborough-
        civic-centre/, accessed March 13, 2020.

John Cairns: Making Every Step Count

All quotations not otherwise attributed in this story are taken from the author's
email correspondence with John Cairns, March 6, 2020.

40   "Now I'm standing on top of the world": Sharon Harrison, "John Cairns: Profile,"
        Grapevine Magazine, December 25, 2019, https://grapevinemagazine.ca/
        articles/john-cairns-profile, accessed March 6, 2020.

40   "I boarded the car and put the brake system on": David de la Harpe,
        "Everyday Hero: John Cairns, Wheelchair of Hope Founder," Global News,
        January 13, 2017, https://globalnews.ca/news/3180961/everyday-hero-
        john-cairns-wheelchair-of-hope-founder/, accessed March 6, 2020.

44   "I do what I do from my heart": "Cairns to Be Named to Canada's Walk of
      Fame," Inquinte.ca, September 19, 2016, https://inquinte.ca/story/cairns-to-
      be-named-to-canadas-walk-of-fame, accessed April 17, 2020.

44   "Aspire to inspire": Harrison, "John Cairns."

45   "The ultimate goal was I'm here": Harrison, "John Cairns."

45   "You don't park it": Harrison, "John Cairns."

John Westhaver: Turning Tragedy into Purpose

48   "A regular teenage guy": Sid Tafler, "Burn Victim's Story a Cautionary Tale
      for Students," *Globe and Mail*, May 31, 2007, https://www.theglobeandmail
      .com/news/national/burn-victims-story-a-cautionary-tale-for-students/
      article686328/, accessed June 12, 2020.

48   "We thought we were safe": "Survivor Who Lost 3 Friends in Crash Shares
      Harrowing Story to Save Lives," CBC News, March 14, 2007, https://www
      .cbc.ca/news/canada/british-columbia/survivor-who-lost-3-friends-in-crash-
      shares-harrowing-story-to-save-lives-1.4574934, accessed June 12, 2020.

49   "The next moment": "Courage 2017 Recipient—John Westhaver," YouTube,
      June 15, 2017, 10:59, https://www.youtube.com/watch?v=WOSQTCRZd-
      E, accessed June 12, 2020.

50   "I wanted to crawl in a hole": Tafler, "Burn Victim's Story a Cautionary Tale
      for Students."

50   "Surviving the burns": "Courage 2017 Recipient—John Westhaver."

50   "I was just angry": Michael Kissinger, "Burn Survivor Credits Family in
      Overcoming Accident," *Vancouver Courier*, March 30, 2017, https://www
      .vancourier.com/news/burn-survivor-credits-family-in-overcoming-accident-
      1.13493095, accessed June 12, 2020.

51   "[My dad told me] you can sit around": Kissinger, "Burn Survivor Credits
      Family in Overcoming Accident."

52   "Everyone that cares and loves you": "Survivor Who Lost 3 Friends in
      Crash Shares Harrowing Story to Save Lives."

52   "Heads-up": Tafler, "Burn Victim's Story a Cautionary Tale for Students."

52   "It's simple to make the right choice": Tafler, "Burn Victim's Story a Cautionary
      Tale for Students."

52   "If I can save one person": "Survivor Who Lost 3 Friends in Crash Shares
      Harrowing Story to Save Lives."

53　"One life lost in a car crash": John Westhaver, Zero Fatalities Tour PowerPoint presentation, n.d., https://www.zerofatalities.ca/presentation.html, accessed June 12, 2020.

53　"My hands were badly burnt": Kissinger, "Burn Survivor Credits Family in Overcoming Accident."

Everyday Heroes: Conquering COVID-19

57　"People helped us a lot": All quotations in this story from Ghazala Malik and Sarah Bridge, "Essential Canadians: Meet the People on the Front Lines of the Pandemic," CBC News, July 1, 2020, https://www.cbc.ca/news/canada/front-line-essential-workers-1.5604776, accessed July 3, 2020.

58　"I just couldn't help myself": Malik and Bridge, "Essential Canadians."

59　"I became more of a coach/leader": Kathryn Greenaway, "Nurse Infected with COVID-19 Reflects on Time Working the CHSLD," *Montreal Gazette*, June 23, 2020, https://theprovince.com/diseases-and-conditions/coronavirus/nurse-infected-with-covid-19-reflects-on-time-working-in-chsld/, accessed July 3, 2020.

59　"The next morning, I was sneezing and coughing": Greenaway, "Nurse Infected."

59　"I was devastated": Malik and Bridge, "Essential Canadians."

59　"It's the most rewarding thing I've ever done": Greenaway, "Nurse Infected."

59　"I was just so happy": Malik and Bridge, "Essential Canadians."

60　"I'm sure this is going on in every little community": Dave Croft, "Volunteers Step Forward in Yukon's Klondike to Help During COVID-19 Crisis," CBC News, April 9, 2020, https://www.cbc.ca/news/canada/north/yukon-dawson-city-volunteers-covid-19-1.5528089, accessed July 3, 2020.

61　"We want to help out": Jane Sponagle, "'Our Mission to Help': Whitehorse RV Park Opens Early for Yukoners Self-Isolating," CBC News, April 8, 2020, https://www.cbc.ca/news/canada/north/whitehorse-rv-park-opens-early-1.5525685, accessed July 3, 2020.

61　"Those who are blind": Gilbert Ngabo, "Man Forgoes His 18th Birthday Celebrations to Spread Kindness amid COVID-19," *Toronto Star*, April 27, 2020, https://www.thestar.com/news/gta/2020/04/09/man-foregoes-his-18th-birthday-celebrations-to-spread-kindness-amid-covid-19.html, accessed July 3, 2020.

62   "It just felt like the right thing to do": Joe O'Connor, "Heroes of the
       Pandemic: Teen Celebrates 18th Birthday by Buying (and Delivering)
       Groceries to the Blind," *National Post*, April 23, 2020, https://nationalpost
       .com/news/canada/heroes-of-the-pandemic-teen-celebrates-18th-birthday-
       by-buying-and-delivering-groceries-to-the-blind/, accessed July 3, 2020.

62   "I just wanted to make them feel comfortable": Ngabo, "Man Forgoes
       His 18th Birthday Celebrations."

62   "I still want to go go-karting": O'Connor, "Heroes of the Pandemic."

PART 2: COURAGE IN THE FACE OF DANGER

David Silverberg: On the Wrong Track

All quotations not otherwise attributed in this story are taken from the author's
email correspondence with David Silverberg, March 10–20, 2020.

66   "Just knew what had to be done": "P.E.I. Doctor Rescues Disabled Man
       from D.C. Subway Tracks," CTV News, April 24, 2015, https://www
       .ctvnews.ca/canada/p-e-i-doctor-rescues-disabled-man-from-d-c-subway-
       tracks-1.2343339, accessed March 13, 2020.

70   "It was covered in black [grease] and blood": Canadian Press, "PEI Doctor
       Rescues Man Who Fell onto Subway Tracks in Washington," *Globe and
       Mail*, April 24, 2015, https://www.theglobeandmail.com/news/national/
       pei-doctor-rescues-man-who-fell-onto-subway-tracks-in-washington/
       article24105891/, accessed March 13, 2020.

Erik Brown: Diving in the Dark

73   They weren't planning to be there for long: "The Full Story of
       Thailand's Extraordinary Cave Rescue," BBC News, July 14, 2018,
       https://www.bbc.com/news/world-asia-44791998, accessed
       February 11, 2020.

74   "If they need help": Jon Azpiri, "'9 days, 7 missions and 63 hours Inside':
       B.C. Diver Part of Daring Thai Cave Rescue," Global News, July 10, 2018,
       https://globalnews.ca/news/4324139/b-c-diver-thai-cave-rescue/,
       accessed February 11, 2020.

75   With the ship resting: Team Blue Immersion, "Expedition Alexander Hamilton by OceanReef," July 30, 2013, https://scubadiverlife.com/expedition-alexander-hamilton-by-oceanreef/, accessed February 11, 2020; Nicole Scholet, "Honoring the US Coast Guard Cutter Alexander Hamilton WPG-34," Alexander Hamilton Awareness Society, August 23, 2013, https://the-aha-society.com/index.php/publications/articles/87-aha-society-articles/147-alexander-hamilton-cutter, accessed February 11, 2020.

75   "Ninety per cent of the stuff": Heather Colpitts, "B.C. Diver at Thai Cave Rescue Won't Speculate on Which Actor Should Play Him in Movie," *Vernon Morning Star*, August 9, 2018, https://www.vernonmorningstar.com/home2/langley-diver-at-thai-cave-rescue-wont-speculate-on-which-actor-should-play-him-in-movie/, accessed February 11, 2020.

76   "Every single challenge": "'You Can't See Your Hands in Front of Your Face': Canadian Diver on Thailand Cave Rescue," Global News, July 13, 2018, https://globalnews.ca/news/4329504/erik-brown-thailand-cave-rescue/, accessed February 11, 2020.

77   "[There are] cracks thirty centimetres big": "B.C. Diver Describes Parts of Thai Cave Rescue as 'Zero Visibility—You Can't See Anything,'" CBC News, July 11, 2018, https://www.cbc.ca/news/canada/bc-diver-brown-thai-cave-rescue-1.4742158, accessed February 11, 2020.

77   "Swimming in coffee": Azpiri, "'9 days, 7 Missions and 63 Hours Inside.'"

77   "A shopping bag that sometimes you would hold close to your chest": "Thai Cave Rescue: How the Boys Were Saved," BBC News, July 18, 2018, https://www.bbc.com/news/world-asia-44695232, accessed February 11, 2020.

77   "I got told from the previous divers": "B.C. Diver Describes Parts of Thai Cave Rescue," CBC News.

78   "So you're not really sure how successful it is": Colpitts, "B.C. Diver at Thai Cave Rescue Won't Speculate on Which Actor Should Play Him in Movie."

78   "You had to have your boots on": "B.C. Diver Describes Parts of Thai Cave Rescue," CBC News.

78   Turn his "brain off a little bit": "'You Can't See Your Hands in Front of Your Face,'" Global News.

79   "9 days, 7 missions, and 63 hours inside": Azpiri, "'9 days, 7 Missions and 63 Hours Inside.'"

79   "I find it fairly awkward": Russell Clark, "Erik Brown: Accounts from
        Thailand Cave Rescue, Part 2," Diver, January 30, 2020, https://divermag.
        com/erik-brown-accounts-from-thailands-cave-rescue-part-2/, accessed
        February 11, 2020.

79   "More than happy": Clark, "Erik Brown."

79   "I don't think I'll have a character": Colpitts, "B.C. Diver at Thai Cave
        Rescue Won't Speculate on Which Actor Should Play Him in Movie."

79   "Some of the Thai news": Clark, "Erik Brown."

80   "You literally couldn't write this": "B.C. Diver Describes Parts of Thai
        Cave Rescue," CBC News.

Bill Ayotte: Battle with a Bear

81   A welcome tourist attraction: Kieran Mulvaney, "'If It Gets Me, It Gets
        Me': The Town Where Residents Live Alongside Polar Bears," *The Guardian*,
        February 13, 2019, https://www.theguardian.com/world/2019/feb/13/
        churchill-canada-polar-bear-capital, accessed June 5, 2020.

82   To make sure polar bears don't enter: Lara Schroeder, "Two Mauled in
        Churchill Polar Bear Attack," Global News, November 1, 2013, https://
        globalnews.ca/news/939840/polar-bear-attack-injures-two-in-churchill-
        man/, accessed June 5, 2020.

82   "Guys, watch out, there's a bear": "Woman Recounts Harrowing Attack by
        Churchill Polar Bear," CBC News, December 19, 2013, https://www.cbc
        .ca/news/canada/manitoba/woman-recounts-harrowing-attack-by-
        churchill-polar-bear-1.2469766, accessed June 5, 2020.

83   "I definitely remember it biting my head": Brittany Greenslade,
        "Exclusive: Polar Bear Attack Victim on the Mend and Heading Home,"
        Global News, November 13, 2013, https://globalnews.ca/news/964766/
        polar-bear-attack-victim-on-the-mend-and-heading-home/, accessed
        June 5, 2020.

83   "I just became very weak": Paul Hunter, "He Saved a Woman from a
        Polar Bear. 'Then the Mauling Was on for Me,'" *Toronto Star*, May 20, 2017,
        https://www.thestar.com/news/insight/2017/05/20/he-saved-a-woman-
        from-a-polar-bear-then-the-mauling-was-on-for-me.html, accessed
        June 5, 2020.

83   "Sitting on his haunches was a polar bear": Shannon Proudfoot,
       "'I Don't Want to Die on the Ground Like an Animal,'" *Maclean's*, June 26,
       2014, https://www.macleans.ca/news/canada/saving-life-surviving-polar-
       bear-mauling-manitoba/, accessed June 5, 2020.

83   "She was out there by herself": Proudfoot, "'I Don't Want to Die on the
       Ground Like an Animal.'"

84   "That son-of-a-bitchin' bear has killed me": Proudfoot, "'I Don't Want to
       Die on the Ground Like an Animal.'"

85   "I was on the ground": Hunter, "He Saved a Woman from a Polar Bear."

85   "I wanted to know she was all right": Hunter, "He Saved a Woman from a
       Polar Bear."

85   "Angel in disguise": Hunter, "He Saved a Woman from a Polar Bear."

86   "He risked his own life to save a neighbour": Canadian Press, "Manitoba
       Honours Man Who Saved Woman Attacked by Polar Bear in Churchill,"
       CTV News, October 3, 2014, https://winnipeg.ctvnews.ca/manitoba-
       honours-man-who-saved-woman-attacked-by-polar-bear-in-churchill-
       1.2038530, accessed June 5, 2020.

86   "Heroic intervention": "Churchill Man Who Rescued Woman
       from Polar Bear Attack Honoured," CBC News, October 3, 2014,
       https://www.cbc.ca/news/canada/manitoba/churchill-man-who-rescued-
       woman-from-polar-bear-attack-honoured-1.2787343, accessed
       June 5, 2020.

86   "It was either do something": Proudfoot, "'I Don't Want to Die on the
       Ground Like an Animal.'"

86   "When we think about bravery": Hunter, "He Saved a Woman from a Polar
       Bear."

87   "They don't bother me": Hunter, "He Saved a Woman from a Polar Bear."

87   "Knowing that this community produced someone": Mulvaney, "'If It Gets
       Me, It Gets Me.'"

88   "The greatest grandpa in the world": Proudfoot, "'I Don't Want to Die on
       the Ground Like an Animal.'"

88   "If that bear had a minute more": Hunter, "He Saved a Woman from a Polar
       Bear."

Mona Parsons: The Role of a Lifetime

93   "I knew all eyes were on me": Andria Hill, "Remembering Mona Parsons," *Canada's History*, March 14, 2017, https://www.canadashistory.ca/explore/ women/remembering-mona-parsons, accessed May 2, 2020.

93   "Prison . . . was a hard, nasty, cold, hungry & demoralizing life": "An Excerpt of the Letter Mona Wrote to Her Father and Stepmother between May 3 and 5, 1945," MonaParsons.ca, n.d., http://www.monaparsons.ca/letters. htm, accessed May 1, 2020.

94   "Companion and guardian angel": Hill, "Remembering Mona Parsons."

94   "We were far behind the Nazi lines": Hill, "Remembering Mona Parsons."

James Kitchen and William Ward: On Thin Ice

All quotations not otherwise attributed in this story are taken from the author's email correspondence with James Kitchen, February 16, 2020, and phone conversation with William Ward, February 27, 2020.

101   "I couldn't tell how thick the ice was": "Iqaluit Hunter, David Alexander, Rescued from Sea Ice," CBC News, March 14, 2011, https://www.cbc.ca/ news/canada/north/iqaluit-hunter-david-alexander-rescued-from-sea-ice-1.993570, accessed February 22, 2020.

101   "You got to call for help right away": "Iqaluit Hunter, David Alexander, Rescued from Sea Ice."

102   "All kind of thoughts": "Iqaluit Hunter, David Alexander, Rescued from Sea Ice."

103   "We had to come in backwards to get him": Ben Lypka, "Squamish Man Involved in Heroic Rescue," *Squamish Chief*, March 19, 2015, https://www .squamishchief.com/news/local-news/squamish-man-involved-in-heroic-rescue-1.1797896, accessed February 22, 2020

105   "I don't think I could sit at a desk": Lypka, "Squamish Man Involved in Heroic Rescue."

105   "When you fly in the bush": Lypka, "Squamish Man Involved in Heroic Rescue."

105   "All I really did is go to work": "Pilot Recognized by Governor General for Nunavut Rescue," CBC News, March 23, 2015, https://www.cbc.ca/news/ canada/north/pilot-recognized-by-governor-general-for-nunavut-rescue-1.3004973, accessed February 22, 2020.

106   "While Mr. Kitchen skilfully kept his helicopter hovering": "Pilot Recognized by Governor General for Nunavut Rescue."

Clark Whitecalf: Into the Flames

108   "I think Sonya's house is on fire": Nicholas Hune-Brown, "Rescued from a House Fire," *Reader's Digest* (Canada), August 1, 2018, https://www.pressreader.com/canada/readers-digest-canada/20180801/282913796184443, accessed September 4, 2020.

109   "There's somebody inside": Hune-Brown, "Rescued from a House Fire."

110   "That's when I stood up": Alicia Bridges, "Sask. Man Receives Carnegie Medal for 'Extraordinary Risk' Dragging Woman from Burning House," CBC News, December 21, 2016, https://www.cbc.ca/news/canada/saskatoon/clark-whitecalf-receives-carnegie-medal-1.3906443, accessed September 4, 2020.

110   "I went back in": Bridges, "Sask. Man Receives Carnegie Medal for 'Extraordinary Risk' Dragging Woman from Burning House."

111   "They said if I'd been in there for one or two minutes more": Hune-Brown, "Rescued from a House Fire."

111   "I'm starting to realize": Betty Ann Adam, "Here's the Story of How Clark Whitecalf Saved 18-Year-Old Jolie Fineday from a Fire," *Saskatoon StarPhoenix*, October 18, 2016, https://thestarphoenix.com/news/local-news/bravery-award-recipient-kept-cool-head-in-emergency, accessed September 4, 2020.

111   "But I also felt really good": Hune-Brown, "Rescued from a House Fire."

111   "He has always been responsive": Adam, "Here's the Story of How Clark Whitecalf Saved 18-Year-Old Jolie Fineday from a Fire."

112   "The situation inside the building was a deadly situation": Bridges, "Sask. Man Receives Carnegie Medal for 'Extraordinary Risk' Dragging Woman from Burning House."

112   "I don't take life for granted": "Heroes Honoured for Saving Lives, Awarded Certificates of Bravery in Regina," CBC News, October 11, 2017, https://www.cbc.ca/news/canada/saskatchewan/bravery-awards-oct-10-1.4349001, accessed July 22, 2020.

112   "There's a person that's going to die": Bridges, "Sask. Man Receives Carnegie Medal for 'Extraordinary Risk' Dragging Woman from Burning House."

112   "I didn't even think of the dangers": Hune-Brown, "Rescued from a House Fire."

Erick Marciano: A Crash Course in Courage

114   "Burned a stop sign halfway": Rachel Lau, " 'I Don't Think I'm a Hero,' SUV Driver Who Used His Car to Save Pedestrians Humbled by Experience," CTV News, November 13, 2019, https://montreal.ctvnews.ca/i-don-t-think-i-m-a-hero-suv-driver-who-used-his-car-to-save-pedestrians-humbled-by-experience-1.4683595, accessed July 24, 2020.

114   "The policemen kind of cornered him": Lau, "I Don't Think I'm a Hero.' "

114   "This isn't going to happen here": " 'I Didn't Want Him to Hurt Anybody,' Says Montrealer Who Used SUV to Protect Pedestrians from Speeding Car," CBC News, November 13, 2019, https://www.cbc.ca/news/canada/montreal/montreal-hero-driver-suv-daybreak-1.5357526, accessed July 24, 2020.

114   Honking "like crazy": Richard Deschamps, "I'm Not a Hero, Says Quick-Thinking Motorist Who Used SUV to Save Pedestrians' Lives," iHeartRadio.ca, November 13, 2019, https://www.iheartradio.ca/cjad/news/i-m-not-a-hero-says-quick-thinking-motorist-who-used-suv-to-save-pedestrians-lives-1.10215227, accessed July 24, 2020.

114   "I didn't want him to hurt anybody": " 'I Didn't Want Him to Hurt Anybody,'" CBC News.

115   "It was just a natural thing to do": Canadian Press, "City of Montreal Honours 'Hero' Driver Who Used His SUV to Shield Pedestrians," CTV News, November 18, 2019, https://montreal.ctvnews.ca/city-of-montreal-honours-hero-driver-who-used-his-suv-to-shield-pedestrians-1.4691021, accessed July 24, 2020.

115   "It only takes one gesture to make a difference": Staff, "Mercedes SUV Driver Risks Safety to Save Pedestrians: Montreal Police," Montreal Gazette, November 13, 2019, https://montrealgazette.com/news/local-news/mercedes-suv-driver-risked-his-safety-to-save-pedestrians-montreal-police, accessed July 24, 2020.

115   "Remarkable heroism": Canadian Press, "City of Montreal Honours 'Hero'
       Driver Who Used His SUV to Shield Pedestrians."

116   "Pretty cool": Canadian Press, "City of Montreal Honours 'Hero' Driver
       Who Used His SUV to Shield Pedestrians."

116   "He's always thinking about others": Canadian Press, "City of Montreal
       Honours 'Hero' Driver Who Used His SUV to Shield Pedestrians."

116   "It's just metal": Lau, "'I Don't Think I'm a Hero.'"

116   "What matters is the outcome": "'I Didn't Want Him to Hurt Anybody,'"
       CBC News.

116   "I called my insurance company": Deschamps, "I'm Not a Hero."

116   "I'd omit the word 'hero' for now": Deschamps, "I'm Not a Hero."

116   "I did what I had to do": Lau, "'I Don't Think I'm a Hero.'"

Sophia LeBlanc: Small But Mighty

118   "We hit the guardrail": David Burke, "6-Year-Old Honoured for Helping
       Rescue Family from Car Crash in Nova Scotia," CBC News, January 17,
       2019, https://www.cbc.ca/news/canada/nova-scotia/child-6-year-old-
       heroism-rescue-car-crash-1.4981468, accessed August 27, 2020.

119   "I asked Sophia to climb up and wave down a car": Burke, "6-Year-Old
       Honoured for Helping Rescue Family from Car Crash in Nova Scotia."

119   "There was so much bushes": Burke, "6-Year-Old Honoured for Helping
       Rescue Family from Car Crash in Nova Scotia."

120   "She was by herself with first responders": Alexander Quon, "8-Year-Old
       Sophia LeBlanc the Youngest to Earn Nova Scotia Medal of Bravery,"
       Global News, December 4, 2019, https://globalnews.ca/news/6253489/8-
       year-old-sophia-leblanc-the-youngest-to-earn-nova-scotia-medal-of-
       bravery/, accessed August 27, 2020.

120   "It's important to recognize people when they contribute": Burke, "6-Year-
       Old Honoured for Helping Rescue Family from Car Crash in Nova Scotia."

121   "We're really proud that you're here": Canadian Press, "N.S. Girl Earns Bravery
       Award for Saving Family from Van That Plunged into River," CTV News,
       December 4, 2019, https://atlantic.ctvnews.ca/n-s-girl-earns-bravery-award-
       for-saving-family-from-van-that-plunged-into-river-1.4714907, accessed
       August 27, 2020.

122 "I saved my family": Francis Campbell, "Bravery Medals: Little Girl Who Helped Save Her Family, Young Fisherman Who Tried to Save His Dad," Saltwire Network, December 4, 2019, https://www.saltwire.com/news/local/bravery-medals-little-girl-who-helped-save-her-family-young-fisherman-who-tried-to-save-his-dad-384314/, accessed August 27, 2020.

122 A hero "is someone that respects everyone": Quon, "8-Year-Old Sophia LeBlanc the Youngest to Earn Nova Scotia Medal of Bravery."

122 "I'm going to put it in my room": Canadian Press, "N.S. Girl Earns Bravery Award for Saving Family from Van That Plunged into River."

122 "It was an exciting day": Darrell Cole, "Eight-Year-Old Amherst Girl Youngest to Earn Nova Scotia Medal Of Bravery," *Chronicle Herald*, December 4, 2019, https://www.thechronicleherald.ca/news/provincial/eight-year-old-amherst-girl-youngest-to-earn-nova-scotia-medal-of-bravery-384383/, accessed August 27, 2020.

122 "She said I was screaming like a crazy person": Campbell, "Bravery Medals."

122 "If you see anyone else who has a car accident": Burke, "6-Year-Old Honoured for Helping Rescue Family from Car Crash in Nova Scotia."

Trevor Smith: Swept Away

124 "It didn't seem that steep at the time": Ashley Joannou, "'He Didn't Look Good,' Hero Says of Victim," *Whitehorse Daily Star*, August 5, 2011, https://www.whitehorsestar.com/News/he-didnt-look-good-hero-says-of-victim, accessed August 21, 2020.

124 "I couldn't move": Joannou, "'He Didn't Look Good,' Hero Says of Victim."

125 "The first thing you feel is fear": Joannou, "'He Didn't Look Good,' Hero Says of Victim."

126 "If you can hear me, blink": David Croft, "Yukon Avalanche Rescuer Honoured for Bravery," CBC News, August 8, 2011, https://www.cbc.ca/news/canada/north/yukon-avalanche-rescuer-honoured-for-bravery-1.1025202, accessed August 21, 2020.

126 "I am proud to present this award": Croft, "Yukon Avalanche Rescuer Honoured for Bravery."

126 "Very humbled and grateful": Joannou, "'He Didn't Look Good,' Hero Says of Victim."

126   "The award means a lot": Croft, "Yukon Avalanche Rescuer Honoured for Bravery."

127   "Very quick to respond": Croft, "Yukon Avalanche Rescuer Honoured for Bravery."

127   "He totally deserves this": Joannou, "'He Didn't Look Good,' Hero Says of Victim."

Beachcomber: The Wings of War

130   "Like every other soldier": Jack Granatstein, "Dieppe: A Colossal Blunder," Canada's History, May 29, 2014, https://www.canadashistory.ca/explore/military-war/dieppe-a-colossal-blunder, accessed January 31, 2020.

130   "Continued lack of participation": Granatstein, "Dieppe."

131   "A tragic humiliation": Granatstein, "Dieppe."

131   "Expressed full confidence": Granatstein, "Dieppe."

131   "Pigeon fancier": Philip Jackman, "The Homing Front," *Globe and Mail*, January 8, 2018, updated April 26, 2018, https://www.theglobeandmail.com/news/world/the-homing-front/article1049820/, accessed January 31, 2020.

134   "For bringing the first news": PDSA, "Dickin Medal Pigeons," n.d., https://www.pdsa.org.uk/about-us/animal-bravery-awards/dickin-medal-pigeons, accessed January 21, 2021.

135   "Beachcomber brought the first detailed news": Peter Hawthorne, *The Animal Victoria Cross: The Dickin Medal* (Barnsley, UK: Pen & Sword Books, 2012), 4.

135   "Very heavy casualties": "Battle Log: 'Very Heavy Casualties in Men and Ships,'" *Windsor Star*, August 17, 2012, https://windsorstar.com/life/from-the-vault/battle-log-very-heavy-casualties-in-men-and-ships, accessed January 21, 2021.

135   "The Germans shot a shell": Bernard O'Connor, *Bletchley Park and the Pigeon Spies* (self-published, 2018), 276.

Ryan Barnett and Josh McSweeney: In the Nick of Time

139   "They have a set of [elevator] doors pried open": All quotations from Constables Barnett and McSweeney not otherwise attributed are taken from the press conference held the day after the rescue, posted in its entirety on Global's YouTube channel. "Toronto Police Officers Describe

Extraordinary Coincidences Leading to Last-Minute Elevator Rescue,"
Global News YouTube video, August 8, 2018, 18:58, https://www.youtube.
com/watch?v=a1q3vPoiqAE, accessed March 27, 2020.

140   "Pretty clear": Chris Fox and Chris Herhalt, "Men Rescued from Flooded
Elevator Say They Were Minutes Away from Being Submerged," CP24,
August 9, 2018, https://www.cp24.com/news/men-rescued-from-flooded-
elevator-say-they-were-minutes-away-from-being-submerged-1.4044936,
accessed March 27, 2020.

141   "We were trying to find emergency latches": Fox and Herhalt, "Men Rescued
from Flooded Elevator."

141   "I was using the elevator buttons as a reference": Fox and Herhalt, "Men
Rescued from Flooded Elevator."

142   "Once we knew we'd be OK": Victor Ferreira, "'There Was Panic, There
Was Praying'": How Two Toronto Men Narrowly Escaped Drowning in a
Flooded Elevator," *London Free Press*, August 9, 2018, https://lfpress
.com/news/toronto/there-was-panic-there-was-praying-how-two-toronto-
men-narrowly-escaped-drowning-in-a-flooded-elevator/, accessed
March 27, 2020.

143   "Nothing else comes close": Ron Fanfair, "Lifesavers Named Officers of
Year," TPSNews, May 8, 2019, http://tpsnews.ca/stories/2019/05/lifesavers-
named-officers-year/, accessed March 27, 2020.

144   "As far as I'm concerned": Jason Miller, "Two Officers Who Rescued Stranded
Men from Submerged Elevator Named Toronto's Police Officer of the Year,"
Toronto Star, May 7, 2019, https://www.thestar.com/news/gta/2019/05/07/
two-officers-who-rescued-two-men-from-a-submerbed-elevator-named-
torontos-police-officer-of-the-year.html, accessed March 27, 2020.

Rebecka Blackburn: Right Place, Right Time

All quotations not otherwise attributed in this story are taken from the author's
email correspondence with Rebecka Blackburn, April 24–May 11, 2020.

147   "One of his buddies": Julia Wong, "Teen Lifeguard Saves Man from North
Saskatchewan River near Devon," Global News, June 21, 2018, https://
globalnews.ca/news/4289781/alberta-teen-lifeguard-north-saskatchewan-
river-rescue/, accessed May 8, 2020.

147   "Oh my gosh, here we go": Wong, "Teen Lifeguard."

148   "Very strong and well-trained": Wong, "Teen Lifeguard."

149   "I have never experienced a rescue that was as scary": Shelly Makrugin,
       "Leduc Teen Received Canadian Red Cross Rescuer Award," Canadian Red
       Cross blog, December 20, 2018, https://www.redcross.ca/blog/2018/12/leduc-
       teen-receives-canadian-red-cross-rescuer-award, accessed May 8, 2020.

149   "It just goes to show": Wong, "Teen Lifeguard."

Les Lehmann: Shots in the Dark

155   "I was responsible for these young kids": Paul Hunter, "Canadian with One
       Bat Takes on Two Robbers with Pistols: 'It Never Did Scare Me,'" *Toronto
       Star*, May 20, 2017, https://www.thestar.com/news/insight/2017/05/20/
       canadian-with-one-bat-takes-on-two-robbers-with-pistols-it-never-did-
       scare-me.html, accessed July 31, 2020.

156   "The doctors in the Dominican Republic": "Man Injured in Confrontation
       on Student Trip Recovering in Hospital," *Winnipeg Free Press*, February 6,
       2014, https://www.winnipegfreepress.com/breakingnews/Man-injured-
       in-confrontation-on-student-trip-recovering-in-hopsital-244008201
       .html, accessed July 31, 2020.

156   "The first thought through my mind": Hunter, "Canadian with One Bat
       Takes on Two Robbers with Pistols."

156   "When you get shot from ten feet away": Hunter, "Canadian with One Bat
       Takes on Two Robbers with Pistols."

157   "Even 30 seconds after it happened": "Dominican Republic Attacks Could
       Happen Anywhere, Says Manitoban Shot 10 Times," CBC News, April 12,
       2016, https://www.cbc.ca/news/canada/manitoba/lehmann-dominican-
       republic-robbery-1.3531014, accessed July 31, 2020.

157   "There was two guns pointed at me": Andrew Russell and Mike Le Couteur,
       "Winnipeg Man Shot 10 Times Protecting Manitoba Students in D.R.
       Given Star of Courage," Global News, October 28, 2016, https://globalnews
       .ca/news/3032115/winnipeg-man-shot-10-times-protecting-manitoba-
       students-in-d-r-given-star-of-courage/, accessed July 31, 2020.

157   "Acts of conspicuous courage in circumstances of peril": "Levels and Insignia,"
       The Governor General of Canada, https://www.gg.ca/en/honours/canadian-
       honours/decorations-bravery/levels-and-insignia, accessed January 8, 2021.

157   "He doesn't feel what [he] did was heroic": Andrew Russell and Mike
       Le Couteur, "Winnipeg Man Shot 10 Times Protecting Manitoba
       Students in D.R. Given Star of Courage," Global News, October 28, 2016,
       https://globalnews.ca/news/3032115/winnipeg-man-shot-10-times-
       protecting-manitoba-students-in-d-r-given-star-of-courage/, accessed
       July 31, 2020.

158   "It's something that happened": Russell and Le Couteur, "Winnipeg Man Shot
       10 Times Protecting Manitoba Students in D.R. Given Star of Courage."

158   "I don't live in fear": "Dominican Republic Attacks Could Happen Any-
       where, Says Manitoban Shot 10 Times," CBC News.

Ralph Joyce: Out on the Edge

160   "My feet came out from under me": Troy Turner, "Lark Harbour
       Man Honoured with Bravery Award for Icy, Cliffside Rescue," CBC
       News, July 31, 2020, https://www.cbc.ca/news/canada/newfoundland-
       labrador/ralph-joyce-bravery-1.5669409, accessed September 11,
       2020.

161   "I peeped down to make sure that he was still there": Diane Crocker, "Lark
       Harbour Man Recognized for His Bravery and Quick Thinking in Saving
       Life of Another Man," *The Telegram*, August 7, 2020, https://www.thetelegram
       .com/news/provincial/lark-harbour-man-recognized-for-his-bravery-and-
       quick-thinking-in-saving-life-of-another-man-482630/, accessed
       September 11, 2020.

162   "As he was pulling me up": Turner, "Lark Harbour Man Honoured with
       Bravery Award for Icy, Cliffside Rescue."

163   "The main thing was I got him out of it": Crocker, "Lark Harbour Man Recog-
       nized for His Bravery and Quick Thinking in Saving Life of Another Man."

163   "It's absolutely wonderful": Turner, "Lark Harbour Man Honoured with
       Bravery Award for Icy, Cliffside Rescue."

164   "I could have went on just as well as him": Crocker, "Lark Harbour Man Rec-
       ognized for His Bravery and Quick Thinking in Saving Life of Another Man."

164   "Every time I see Ralph": Don Bradshaw, "Inspiring NL: Life-Saving
       Moment by Lark Harbour Neighbour," NTV, July 30, 2020, http://ntv.ca/
       inspiring-n-l-life-saving-moment-by-lark-harbour-neighbour/, accessed
       September 11, 2020.

164   "We're connected": Turner, "Lark Harbour Man Honoured with Bravery Award for Icy, Cliffside Rescue."

Liam Bernard and Shane Bernard: Playing with Fire

166   "Smoke everywhere": Natasha Pace, "'I Don't Really Consider Myself a Hero': Four Nova Scotians Honoured for Their Bravery," Global News, November 8, 2017, https://globalnews.ca/news/3850274/i-dont-really-consider-myself-a-hero-four-nova-scotians-honoured-for-their-bravery/, accessed July 17, 2020.

166   "He couldn't move": SaltWire Network, "Rescuer Recalls What Happened during Tragic Accident," *Cape Breton Post*, September 17, 2016, https://www.saltwire.com/news/provincial/rescuer-recalls-what-happened-during-tragic-accident-12627/, accessed July 17, 2020.

166   "I was thinking": "Cape Breton Man Recognized for Act of Heroism," *Cape Breton Post*, September 20, 2018, https://www.capebretonpost.com/news/local/cape-breton-man-recognized-for-act-of-heroism-243136/, accessed July 17, 2020.

167   "I went in the truck": SaltWire Network, "Rescuer Recalls What Happened during Tragic Accident."

167   "He noticed I couldn't do it": Nikki Sullivan, "Waycobah Men to Receive Provincial Award for Bravery on Wednesday," *Cape Breton Post*, November 7, 2017, https://www.capebretonpost.com/news/local/waycobah-men-to-receive-governor-generals-award-for-bravery-on-wednesday-159665/, accessed July 17, 2020.

167   "I just gathered enough energy": SaltWire Network, "Rescuer Recalls What Happened during Tragic Accident."

168   "It must have been pretty hot": Maureen Googoo, "Two Mi'kmaw Men from Waycobah Receive NS Medal of Bravery," *Ku'Ku'Wes News*, November 8, 2017, http://kukukwes.com/2017/11/08/two-mikmaw-men-from-waycobah-receive-ns-medal-of-bravery/, accessed July 17, 2020.

168   "A minute or two later": SaltWire Network, "Rescuer Recalls What Happened during Tragic Accident."

168   "If it wasn't for those other men": SaltWire Network, "Rescuer Recalls What Happened during Tragic Accident."

168   "She tells me she had witnessed": SaltWire Network, "Waycobah Men Pull
       Crash Survivors from Burning Vehicle," *Cape Breton Post*, September 16, 2016,
       https://www.capebretonpost.com/news/local/waycobah-men-pull-
       crash-survivors-from-burning-vehicle-12632/, accessed July 17, 2020.

169   "That's just what you do": SaltWire Network, "Waycobah Men Pull Crash
       Survivors from Burning Vehicle."

169   "We are both the type of people": Sullivan, "Waycobah Men to Receive
       Provincial Award for Bravery on Wednesday."

169   "They looked pretty scared": Pace, "'I Don't Really Consider Myself a
       Hero'."

169   "Cuts, scrapes, and bruises": Sullivan, "Waycobah Men to Receive Provincial
       Award for Bravery on Wednesday."

170   "I don't know how to feel": Sullivan, "Waycobah Men to Receive Provincial
       Award for Bravery on Wednesday."

170   "I would have to do it again": Sullivan, "Waycobah Men to Receive Provin-
       cial Award for Bravery on Wednesday."

170   "We showed up at those places": Sullivan, "Waycobah Men to Receive
       Provincial Award for Bravery on Wednesday."

170   "I recognize it was a high-risk situation": Googoo, "Two Mi'kmaw Men
       from Waycobah Receive NS Medal of Bravery."

Colleen O'Reilly: Everything for a Reason

All quotations in this story are taken from the author's telephone interview with
Colleen O'Reilly, September 1, 2020.

Russell Fee: Keeping the Wolf from the Door

182   "The screams were so intense": Leah Asmelash, "A Family of Four Was
       on a Camping Trip in Canada. Then a Wolf Attacked While They Were
       Sleeping," CNN, August 16, 2019, https://www.cnn.com/2019/08/14/us/
       wolf-attack-canada-trnd/index.html, accessed September 10, 2020.

182   "Panic immediately sets in": Michelle Mark, "A Canadian Man Saved a Family
       of 4 from a Wolf That Ripped Their Tent Apart and Tried to Drag the
       Father Away," Insider, August 14, 2019, https://www.insider.com/canada-
       wolf-attack-banff-campsite-rescue-2019-8, accessed September 10, 2020.

182   "Just like he's pulling on a toy": Mark, "A Canadian Man Saved a Family of 4 from a Wolf."

182   "I had a good run going": "Survivors of Rare Wolf Attack in Banff Recount How Animal Tried to Drag Man from Tent in Middle of the Night," CBC News, August 13, 2019, https://www.cbc.ca/news/canada/calgary/wolf-attack-rampart-creek-banff-1.5245105, accessed September 10, 2020.

183   "I felt like I had kind of punched someone": "Survivors of Rare Wolf Attack in Banff Recount How Animal Tried to Drag Man from Tent in Middle of the Night."

183   "He was pretty amped up": "Survivors of Rare Wolf Attack in Banff Recount How Animal Tried to Drag Man from Tent in Middle of the Night."

183   "Like something out of a horror movie": Elisa Rispoli's Facebook page, August 9, 2019, https://www.facebook.com/erispoli, accessed September 10, 2020.

183   "We were screaming for help": Rispoli, Facebook post, August 9, 2019.

183   "It didn't even really seem terribly aggressive": Mark, "A Canadian Man Saved a Family of 4 from a Wolf."

184   "Blur of EMTs, good Samaritans": Rispoli, Facebook post, August 9, 2019.

184   "Guardian angel": Rispoli, Facebook post, August 9, 2019.

185   "My advice would be to prepare for all of life's challenges": Julie Payette's Facebook page, August 13, 2020, https://www.facebook.com/GGJuliePayette, accessed September 10, 2020.

185   "It's never felt right to call it brave": Stephanie Babych, "Man Who Stopped Banff Wolf Attack Receives Medal of Bravery," *Calgary Herald*, July 1, 2020, https://calgaryherald.com/news/local-news/man-who-stopped-banff-wolf-attack-receives-medal-of-bravery, accessed September 10, 2020.

185   "We are forever grateful": Rispoli, Facebook post, August 9, 2019.

185   "The Lakes in Alberta and BC": Stephanie Babych, " 'Like Something out of a Horror Movie': Wolf Dragged Man from Tent as Wife Held His Legs," *Calgary Herald*, August 13, 2019, https://calgaryherald.com/news/local-news/family-recalls-unusual-wolf-attack-at-banff-campground-on-social-media-campground-reopens, accessed September 10, 2020.

Shaun De Grandpré: Double Trouble

All quotations not otherwise attributed in this story are taken from the author's email correspondence with Shaun De Grandpré, April 22–May 4, 2020.

187   "Acts of bravery in hazardous circumstances": "Levels and Insignia,"
       The Governor General of Canada, https://www.gg.ca/en/honours/
       canadian-honours/decorations-bravery/levels-and-insignia,
       accessed January 8, 2021.

Aymen Derbali: In the Line of Fire

196   "I thought if he shoots in my direction": Ashifa Kassam, "Quebec Community
       Rallies for Mosque Attack Hero: 'He Sacrificed His Legs for Us,'"
       The Guardian, January 26, 2018, https://www.theguardian.com/world/2018/
       jan/26/quebec-mosque-attack-survivor-one-year-later-aymen-derbali,
       accessed March 7, 2020.

196   "Determination, determination to kill us all": Ingrid Peritz, "At the Quebec
       Mosque Shooting, This Man Risked His Life to Save Others. Who Will
       Save Him Now?" Globe and Mail, December 14, 2017, https://www
       .theglobeandmail.com/news/national/quebec-mosque-shooting-survivor-
       paralyzed/article37301950/, accessed March 7, 2020.

197   "I tried not to panic or flee": Peritz, "At the Quebec Mosque Shooting."

198   "They said there was no hope": Ingrid Peritz, "'I've Come a Long Way':
       Aymen Derbali and His Family Find a New Life after Quebec's Mosque
       Tragedy," Globe and Mail, January 9, 2019, https://www.theglobeandmail
       .com/canada/article-ive-come-a-long-way-aymen-derbali-and-his-family-
       find-a-new-life/, accessed March 7, 2020.

198   "You'll stay with us": Peritz, "I've Come a Long Way."

199   "This is a Canadian hero": Sabrina Marandola, "'This Is a Canadian Hero': Group
       Launches Campaign to Help Buy New Home for Mosque Shooting Victim,"
       CBC News, December 20, 2017, https://www.cbc.ca/news/canada/montreal/
       aymen-derbali-crowdfunding-campaign-1.4457487, accessed March 6, 2020.

200   "There is much more goodness than evil": Julia Page, "Survivor of Quebec
       City Mosque Shooting Sets Out to Combat Hate," CBC News, January
       29, 2019, https://www.cbc.ca/news/canada/montreal/quebec-city-mosque-
       shooting-aymen-derbali-1.4995802, accessed March 7, 2020.

200   "There are people who would want to run": Kamila Hinkson, "Shot 7 Times in Quebec City Mosque Attack, Survivor Fights to Reclaim His Life," CBC News, January 25, 2018, https://www.cbc.ca/news/canada/montreal/quebec-mosque-shooting-injured-aymen-derbali-1.4503703, accessed March 6, 2020.

200   "Sometimes I have to fight the sorrow": Peritz, "'I've Come a Long Way.'"

201   "I thought of all my brothers": Andy Riga, "Quebec Mosque Shooting: Survivor Aymen Derbali Says Bissonnette Is Insincere," *Montreal Gazette*, April 17, 2018, https://montrealgazette.com/news/local-news/quebec-mosque-shooting-survivor-aymen-derbali-says-bissonnette-is-insincere, accessed March 7, 2020.

201   "Incredible demonstration of courage": Peritz, "'I've Come a Long Way.'"

201   "We should take a lesson from you": Riga, "Quebec Mosque Shooting."

202   "When I think positively": Hinkson, "Shot 7 Times in Quebec City Mosque Attack."

Liane and Daniel Wood: River Rescue

204   "Like somebody had run into the church with a car": Paul Hunter, "They Braved a Raging River to Save a Girl in an SUV: 'Every Second Felt Like Five Minutes,'" *Toronto Star*, May 20, 2017, https://www.thestar.com/news/insight/2017/05/20/they-braved-a-raging-river-to-save-a-girl-in-an-suv-every-second-felt-like-five-minutes.html, accessed July 23, 2020.

204   "Megan is in the river": Hunter, "They Braved a Raging River to Save a Girl in an SUV."

205   "While we were praying": Hunter, "They Braved a Raging River to Save a Girl in an SUV."

205   "The current was so strong there": Hunter, "They Braved a Raging River to Save a Girl in an SUV."

206   "As we were feeling the bumper": Guthrie Insurance, "Ontario Insurance Broker Saves Life of a Teen in Rescue Attempt," InsurePlus, February 22, 2013, https://www.guthrieinsurance.com/blog/ontario-insurance-broker-saves-life-teen-rescue-attempt/, accessed July 23, 2020.

206   "I'm here": Hunter, "They Braved a Raging River to Save a Girl in an SUV."

206 "She was incredible": Jerome Lessard, "Couple Decorated for Saving Girl's Life," *Kingston Whig-Standard,* May 5, 2015, https://www.thewhig .com/2015/05/05/couple-decorated-for-saving-girls-life/wcm/ce342aa6-def7-a80a-2175-8a126898bfb0, accessed July 23, 2020.

206 "In a 2013 Juke": Guthrie Insurance, "Ontario Insurance Broker Saves Life of a Teen in Rescue Attempt."

207 "A big nightmare": Lessard, "Couple Decorated for Saving Girl's Life."

207 "I just remember thinking": Hunter, "They Braved a Raging River to Save a Girl in an SUV."

208 "It was a very good career in insurance": Hunter, "They Braved a Raging River to Save a Girl in an SUV."

208 "It was such an honour": Lessard, "Couple Decorated for Saving Girl's Life."

208 "It was my automatic response": Hunter, "They Braved a Raging River to Save a Girl in an SUV."

Sergeant Gander: A True Pal

209 "And now": "'Much Loved' Newfoundland Dog Sergeant Gander Honoured with Statue," CBC News, July 24, 2015, https://www.cbc.ca/ news/canada/newfoundland-labrador/much-loved-newfoundland-dog-sergeant-gander-honoured-with-statue-1.3166092, accessed January 5, 2020.

210 "He was very playful and gentle": Robin Walker, *Sergeant Gander: A Canadian Hero* (Toronto: Dundurn Press, 2009), 25, accessed via Google Books, January 5, 2020.

212 "No fear of guns or bombs": Bruce Ward, "Heroic Warrior Canine's Name Put on Memorial," *Winnipeg Free Press,* August 15, 2009, https://www.winnipegfreepress.com/arts-and-life/life/heroic-warrior-canines-name-put-on-memorial-53287192.html, accessed January 5, 2020.

212 "Growled and ran at the enemy soldiers": "Gander the Dog, a Canadian War Hero," History Bits, March 3, 2015, https://cdnhistorybits.wordpress .com/2015/03/03/gander-the-dog-a-canadian-war-hero/, accessed January 5, 2020.

212 "Black beast": "Gander the Dog, a Canadian War Hero," History Bits.

213 "Gander must have seen the hand grenades landing": Brenda Moore, "Beyond the Call of Duty," Cricket, January 2011, http://www.cricketmagkids.com/ library/extras/beyond-call-duty-brenda-moore, accessed January 5, 2020.

213 "When the firing eased up": Moore, "Beyond the Call of Duty."

213 "I didn't go near": Moore, "Beyond the Call of Duty."

214 "Conspicuous gallantry or devotion to duty": PDSA, "PDSA Animal Awards Program," n.d., https://www.pdsa.org.uk/what-we-do/animal-awards-programme, accessed January 26, 2021.

214 "For saving the lives of Canadian infantrymen": Walker, *Sergeant Gander*, 101.

215 "It's very emotional": "'Much Loved' Newfoundland Dog," CBC News.

215 "He gave his life defending his soldiers": "'Much Loved' Newfoundland Dog," CBC News.

PART 3: COURAGE IN THE FACE OF INJUSTICE

Leesee Papatsie: Fighting for Food

All quotations not otherwise attributed in this story are taken from the author's email correspondence with Leesee Papatsie, January 21, 2021.

219 "Lower food prices": Carol Devine, "WonderActivist—Leesee Papatsie," WonderWoman.com., n.d., http://wonderwomenglobal.com/ wonderactivist-leesee-papatsie/, accessed January 24, 2020.

220 40 percent of the population: Chatelaine editorial team, "When $500 Isn't Enough to Buy Groceries for a Week," *Chatelaine*, June 8, 2015, https:// www.chatelaine.com/living/when-500-isnt-enough-to-buy-groceries-for-a-week/, accessed January 24, 2020.

221 "2 Many People R Going Hungry": Jim Bell, "Nunavut Demonstrators Gather to Protest Food Prices, Poverty," *Nunatsiaq News*, June 9, 2012, https://nunatsiaq.com/stories/article/65674nunavut_demonstrators_gather_ to_protest_food_prices_poverty/, accessed January 24, 2020.

221   "My main target": "Facebook Group Plans Food Price Protests,"
        CBC News, June 9, 2012, https://www.cbc.ca/news/canada/north/
        facebook-group-plans-food-price-protests-1.1143378, accessed
        January 24, 2020.

222   "I think the reason": Joshua Gladstone, "Nutrition North: Feeding My
        Family: An Interview with Leesee Papatsie," Northern Public Affairs, n.d.,
        http://www.northernpublicaffairs.ca/index/archives-volume-1-issue-2/
        nutrition-north-feeding-my-family-an-interview-with-leesee-papatsie/,
        accessed January 24, 2020.

223   "We were not sure": Feeding My Family, Facebook, May 21, 2013 post by
        Leesee Papatsie, https://www.facebook.com/groups/239422122837039/,
        accessed January 24, 2020.

224   "Nobody offers you less for more": "'Way North Foods' Fake Ads
        Take Aim at Nunavut's High Food Prices," CBC News, January 8, 2016,
        https://www.cbc.ca/news/canada/north/nunavut-food-prices-fake-ad-
        1.3394396, accessed January 24, 2020.

224   "By using the really familiar grocery store ads": "'Way North Foods' Fake
        Ads Take Aim at Nunavut's High Food Prices," CBC News.

225   "[What's surprised me is] people supporting our cause": Devine, "Wonder-
        Activist—Leesee Papatsie."

225   "I didn't expect it to go viral": "Fighting for Food in Canada's North,"
        CBC Radio, February 25, 2016, https://www.cbc.ca/radio/dnto/
        putting-food-on-the-table-canadians-cope-with-rising-food-
        prices-1.3460214/fighting-for-food-in-canada-s-north-1.3462909,
        accessed January 24, 2020.

Vishal Vijay: Never Too Young to Make a Difference

All quotations in this story are taken from the author's email correspondence with Vishal Vijay, January 11–March 3, 2020.

Kristen Worley: An Olympic Moment

All quotations not otherwise attributed in this story are taken from the author's phone interviews with Kristen Worley, January 17 and May 15, 2020.

236 "Gender roles were clearly delineated": Kristen Worley and Johanna Schneller, *Woman Enough: How a Boy Became a Woman and Changed the World of Sport* (Toronto: Random House Canada, 2019), 6.

239 "The process they cooked up was barbaric": Worley and Schneller, *Woman Enough*, 129–30.

241 "I don't 'identify as' that": Worley and Schneller, *Woman Enough*, 187.

David Howard: Supporting Our Soldiers

All quotations not otherwise attributed in this story are taken from the author's email correspondence with David Howard, April 22 and May 8, 2020.

250 "I told them I would push a broom if I needed to": Alanna Smith, "Father of Fallen Soldier Helping to Build Tiny Home Village for Homeless Veterans," *Calgary Herald*, August 1, 2019, https://calgaryherald.com/news/local-news/tiny-home-village-set-to-welcome-15-homeless-veterans-in-october/, accessed May 22, 2020.

The Women of Idle No More: Choosing Action

252 "After I graduated from law school": Sarah Van Gelder, "Why Canada's Indigenous Uprising Is about All of Us," *Yes Magazine*, Spring 2013, https://www.yesmagazine.org/issue/issues-how-cooperatives-are-driving-the-new-economy/2013/02/08/why-canada2019s-indigenous-uprising-is-about-all-of-us/, accessed June 26, 2020.

252 "I told them there's something in law called acquiescence": Van Gelder, "Why Canada's Indigenous Uprising Is about All of Us."

253 "We were all sitting around": Lenard Monkman and Brandi Morin, "5 Years after Idle No More, Founders Still Speaking Out," CBC News, December 10, 2017, https://www.cbc.ca/news/indigenous/idle-no-more-five-years-1.4436474, accessed June 25, 2020.

253 "Our silence is consent": Jessica Gordon, "'Idle No More' Rally to Oppose Budget Implementation Bill C 45," Idle No More Facebook events page, November 2, 2013, www.facebook.com/events/299767020134614/, quoted in Ken Coates, *#IdleNoMore and the Remaking of Canada* (Regina: University of Regina Press, 2015), 4.

254 "I am in this resistance": Van Gelder, "Why Canada's Indigenous Uprising Is about All of Us."

254 "Most amazing day": Living History: December 21, 2012, "National Idle No More Protest in Ottawa," http://www.idlenomore.ca/national_idle_no_more_protest_in_ottawa, accessed June 26, 2020.

255 "We are trying to help people": Febna Caven, "Being Idle No More: The Women Behind the Movement," *Cultural Survival Quarterly Magazine*, March 2013, https://www.culturalsurvival.org/publications/cultural-survival-quarterly/being-idle-no-more-women-behind-movement, accessed June 22, 2020.

255 "I was like wow": Monkman and Morin, "5 Years after Idle No More, Founders Still Speaking Out."

255 "I think we were all completely blown away": Monkman and Morin, "5 Years after Idle No More, Founders Still Speaking Out."

256 "The face of Idle No More": Van Gelder, "Why Canada's Indigenous Uprising Is about All of Us."

256 "Idle No More cannot be extinguished": Stephanie MacLellan, "Idle No More, One Year Later," *Toronto Star*, December 13, 2013, https://www.thestar.com/news/canada/2013/12/13/idle_no_more_one_year_later.html, accessed June 26, 2020.

256 "A lot of people use it": Monkman and Morin, "5 Years after Idle No More, Founders Still Speaking Out."

257 "Both cases highlight": Tabitha Marshall, "Idle No More," Canadian Encyclopedia, last edited February 4, 2019, https://www.thecanadianencyclopedia.ca/en/article/idle-no-more, accessed June 22, 2020.

257 "Indigenous self-determination, sovereignty": Van Gelder, "Why Canada's Indigenous Uprising Is about All of Us."

257 "As more and more people come on board": Van Gelder, "Why Canada's Indigenous Uprising Is about All of Us."

Julius Kuhl: An Unsung Hero of the Holocaust

260 "He was a *ba'al koreh*": Sara Levine, "The Orthodox Jewish 'Schindler' You Never Heard Of," Jew in the City, April 11, 2018, https://jewinthecity.com/2018/04/the-orthodox-jewish-schindler-you-never-heard-of/, accessed February 22, 2020.

261   "He was hired because they needed somebody": Levine, "Orthodox Jewish 'Schindler.'"

262   "He should be as well known as Schindler": Mark MacKinnon, "'He Should Be As Well Known as Schindler': Documents Reveal Canadian Citizen Julius Kuhl as Holocaust Hero," *Globe and Mail*, August 7, 2017, updated November 12, 2017, https://www.theglobeandmail.com/news/world/holocaust-oskar-schindler-julius-kuhl-canadian/article35896768/, accessed February 22, 2020.

263   "Rescuing many hundreds of Polish Jews": MacKinnon, "'He Should Be As Well Known as Schindler.'"

263   "He did this for a certain period in time": MacKinnon, "'He Should Be As Well Known as Schindler.'"

263   "We've bumped into people": Levine, "Orthodox Jewish 'Schindler.'"

264   "My view is that Dr. Kuhl was in the right place at the right time": MacKinnon, "'He Should Be As Well Known as Schindler.'"

Margaret Butler: Be Strong, Have Courage

266   "I was . . . scaring a lot of children": Kendra Nordin, "Margaret Butler Puts Girls on Track to Succeed," *Christian Science Monitor*, September 19, 2014, https://www.csmonitor.com/World/Making-a-difference/Change-Agent/2014/0919/Margaret-Butler-puts-girls-on-track-to-succeed, accessed August 13, 2020.

267   "The boys are seen as a better return": Robin Gill, "Everyday Hero: Margaret Butler Making Sure Rwanda's Girls Aren't Left Behind," Global News, January 15, 2016, https://globalnews.ca/news/2456424/everyday-hero-margaret-butler-making-sure-rwandas-girls-arent-left-behind/, accessed August 13, 2020.

267   "As a young woman in North America": "Margaret Butler Uses Running to Inspire Young Girls in Rwanda," Altrumedia, February 26, 2016, https://herohighlight.com/running-to-inspire-girls-in-rwanda/, accessed August 13, 2020.

267   "One day, this girl said to me": Nordin, "Margaret Butler Puts Girls on Track to Succeed."

268   "It was a great way of starting the conversation": Gill, "Everyday Hero: Margaret Butler Making Sure Rwanda's Girls Aren't Left Behind."

268   "Be strong, have courage": "Mission & Vision," n.d., Komera.org, https://komera.org/about, accessed August 13, 2020.

269   "[It's] everything that an impoverished girl would need": Hilary Butler, "Why We Run for Rwanda," *Bowen Island Undercurrent*, August 6, 2015, https://www.bowenislandundercurrent.com/sports/why-we-run-for-rwanda-1.2023425, accessed August 13, 2020.

269   "During their school holidays": Peter Shanley, "Nonprofit Promotes Girl Power in Rwanda," *Jamaica Plain Gazette*, May 23, 2014, http://jamaicaplaingazette.com/2014/05/23/nonprofit-promotes-girl-power-in-rwanda/, accessed August 13, 2020.

270   "My goal is to work myself out of a job": Gill, "Everyday Hero: Margaret Butler Making Sure Rwanda's Girls Aren't Left Behind." (video, 1:30).

270   "When I met the girls": Gill, "Everyday Hero: Margaret Butler Making Sure Rwanda's Girls Aren't Left Behind."

271   "Fierce female leaders": "Komera Team," n.d., Komera.org, https://komera .org/our-staff, accessed August 13, 2020.

271   "Margaret's dream": Gill, "Everyday Hero: Margaret Butler Making Sure Rwanda's Girls Aren't Left Behind," (video, 1:42).

271   "When you're passionate about something": Tripletheelle, "Interview with Margaret Butler of Komera," Sometimes coffee sometimes tea (blog), March 31, 2014, https://tripletheelle.wordpress.com/2014/03/31/interview-with-margaret-butler-of-komera/, accessed August 13, 2020.

272   "Young women just need an opportunity": Gill, "Everyday Hero: Margaret Butler Making Sure Rwanda's Girls Aren't Left Behind."

272   "My hope for Komera": Gill, "Everyday Hero: Margaret Butler Making Sure Rwanda's Girls Aren't Left Behind."

Tomas Jirousek: Graduating with Honours

273   "I ran into my parents' room": Selena Ross, "Last Year He Forced McGill University to Change Its Racist Team Name; Now He's Valedictorian," CTV News, June 23, 2020, https://montreal.ctvnews.ca/last-year-he-forced-mcgill-university-to-change-its-racist-team-name-now-he-s-valedictorian-1.4995791, accessed July 10, 2020.

274 "Walking through McGill Athletics facilities": Sidhartha Banerjee, "McGill Drops Redmen Name, Citing Pain Caused to Indigenous Students," CTV News, April 12, 2019, https://www.ctvnews.ca/sports/mcgill-drops-redmen-name-citing-pain-caused-to-indigenous-students-1.4377299, accessed July 10, 2020.

275 "Commemoration and renaming": Jessica Deer, "First Nations Athlete Says McGill's Redmen Name Needs to Change," CBC News, October 15, 2018, https://www.cbc.ca/news/indigenous/mcgill-redmen-indigenous-students-name-change-1.4863218, accessed July 10, 2020.

275 "Being Indigenous, being an athlete": Ross, "Last Year He Forced McGill University to Change Its Racist Team Name; Now He's Valedictorian."

275 "Seeing fellow athletes": Deer, "First Nations Athlete Says McGill's Redmen Name Needs to Change."

276 "Listening to the experiences": Deer, "First Nations Athlete Says McGill's Redmen Name Needs to Change."

276 "Just a dumb Indian": Ross, "Last Year He Forced McGill University to Change Its Racist Team Name; Now He's Valedictorian."

276 "It's quite emotionally taxing": Ross, "Last Year He Forced McGill University to Change Its Racist Team Name; Now He's Valedictorian."

276 "Intent Doesn't Erase Impact": Jessica Deer, "First Nations Student Honoured as McGill Valedictorian after Leading Fight Against 'Redmen' Team Name," CBC News, June 22, 2020, https://www.cbc.ca/news/indigenous/first-nations-valedictorian-mcgill-1.5619676, accessed July 10, 2020.

277 "This issue for me": Jessica Deer, "'Not Your Redmen': Students Hold Rally to Protest McGill University Team Name," CBC News, October 31, 2018, https://www.cbc.ca/news/indigenous/mcgill-redmen-team-name-protest-rally-1.4885697, accessed July 10, 2020.

277 "I have learned about the true depths of pain": Banerjee, "McGill Drops Redmen Name, Citing Pain Caused to Indigenous Students."

278 "Reconciliation, I think": Banerjee, "McGill Drops Redmen Name, Citing Pain Caused to Indigenous Students."

278 "We went through this": T'Cha Dunlevy, "McGill Rower Who Campaigned for Redman Name Change Made Valedictorian," *Montreal Gazette*, June 24, 2020, https://theprovince.com/news/local-news/mcgill-rower-who-campaigned-for-redmen-name-change-made-valedictorian/, accessed July 10, 2020.

278 "We've come a long way": Canadian Press, "McGill Student Who Led Fight to Drop Offensive Team Name Chosen as Valedictorian," *Vancouver Courier*, June 23, 2020, https://www.vancourier.com/mcgill-student-who-led-fight-to-drop-offensive-team-name-chosen-as-valedictorian-1.24158274, accessed July 10, 2020.

279 "McGill is about to go into its third century": T'Cha Dunlevy, "McGill Rower Who Campaigned for Redman Name Change Made Valedictorian."

279 "The world needs McGill graduates": McGill arts, YouTube Channel, Virtual Convocation 2020—Valedictorian Addresses, June 19, 2020, 3:22 mins. https://www.youtube.com/watch?v=8k9KJHAmO0A, accessed July 10, 2020.

280 "My passion to help people": T'Cha Dunlevy, "McGill Rower Who Campaigned fro Redman Name Change Made Valedictorian."

280 "As I graduate": Jessica Deer, "First Nations Student Honoured as McGill Valedictorian after Leading Fight Against 'Redmen' Team Name," CBC News, June 22, 2020, https://www.cbc.ca/news/indigenous/first-nations-valedictorian-mcgill-1.5619676, accessed July 10, 2020.

Viola Desmond: Standing Up by Sitting Down

282 "I'm sorry": Russell Bingham, "Viola Desmond," Canadian Encyclopedia, January 27, 2013, last edited January 16, 2019, https://www.thecanadianencyclopedia.ca/en/article/viola-desmond, accessed March 6, 2020.

284 "Objectionable person": Bingham, "Viola Desmond."

284 "Didn't go quietly": "A Notable Pioneer," *Winnipeg Free Press*, November 24, 2018, https://www.winnipegfreepress.com/arts-and-life/entertainment/books/a-notable-pioneer-501130511.html, accessed March 6, 2020.

285 "I took my purse out": "A Notable Pioneer," *Winnpeg Free Press*.

286 "Jim Crow-ism, at its basest": Evelyn C. White, "Viola Desmond Led Civil Rights Fight," Herizons, n.d., http://www.herizons.ca/node/567, accessed March 6, 2020.

286 "One wonders": Bruce Deachman, "15 Canadian Stories: Viola Desmond, Reluctant Social Activist," *Ottawa Citizen*, April 10, 2019, https://ottawacitizen.com/news/national/15-canadian-stories-viola-desmond-reluctant-social-activist, accessed January 28, 2021.

288 "Every individual is equal": Bingham, "Viola Desmond."

288   "Viola Desmond wasn't the first": Kaitlin Vitt, "New Banknote Features
       Iconic Canadian Woman," Canada's History, November 20, 2018,
       https://www.canadashistory.ca/explore/women/new-banknote-features-
       iconic-canadian-woman, accessed March 6, 2020.

288   "It's unbelievable to think": Vitt, "New Banknote Features Iconic Canadian
       Woman."